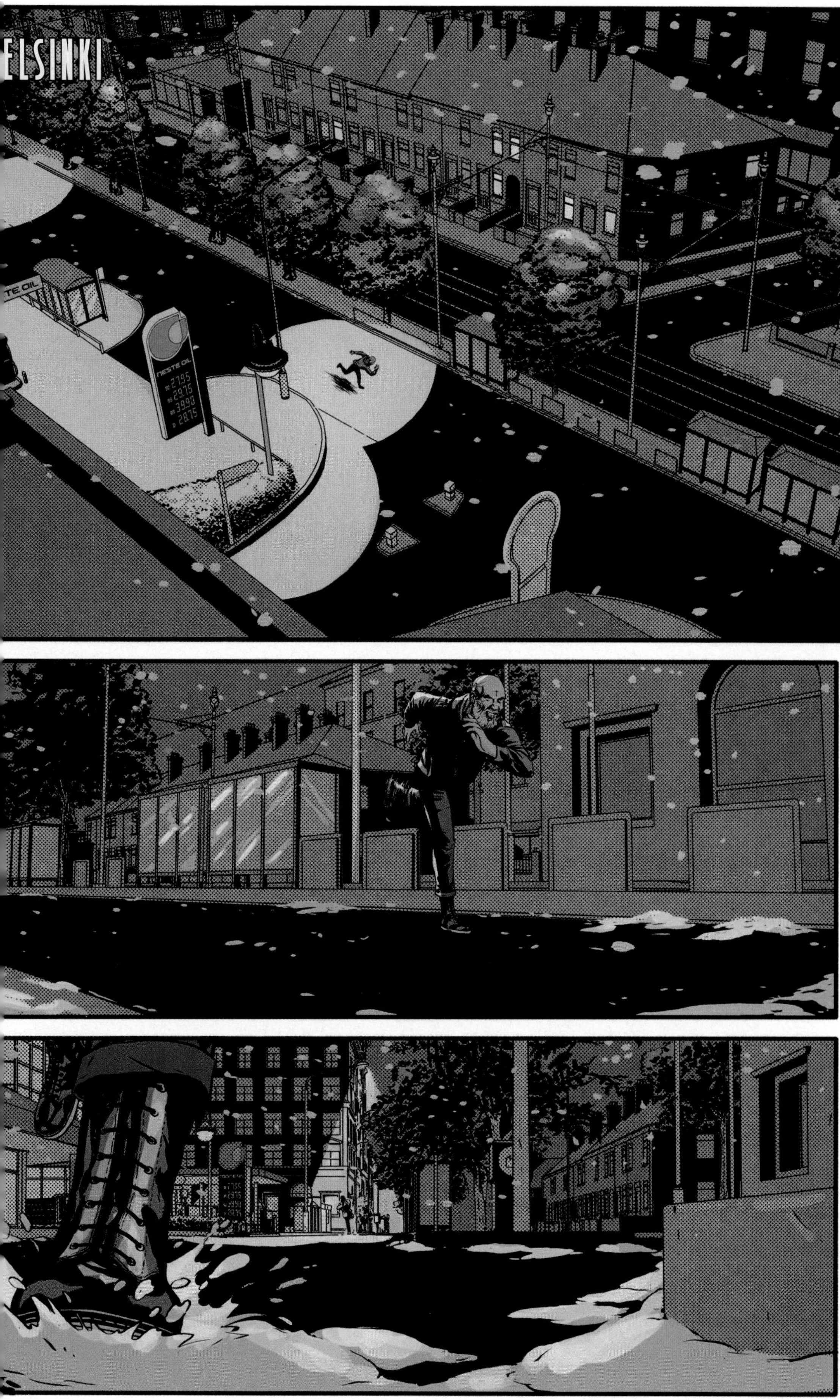
ELSINKI
TE OIL
NESTE OIL
27.95
29.75
39.90
28.75

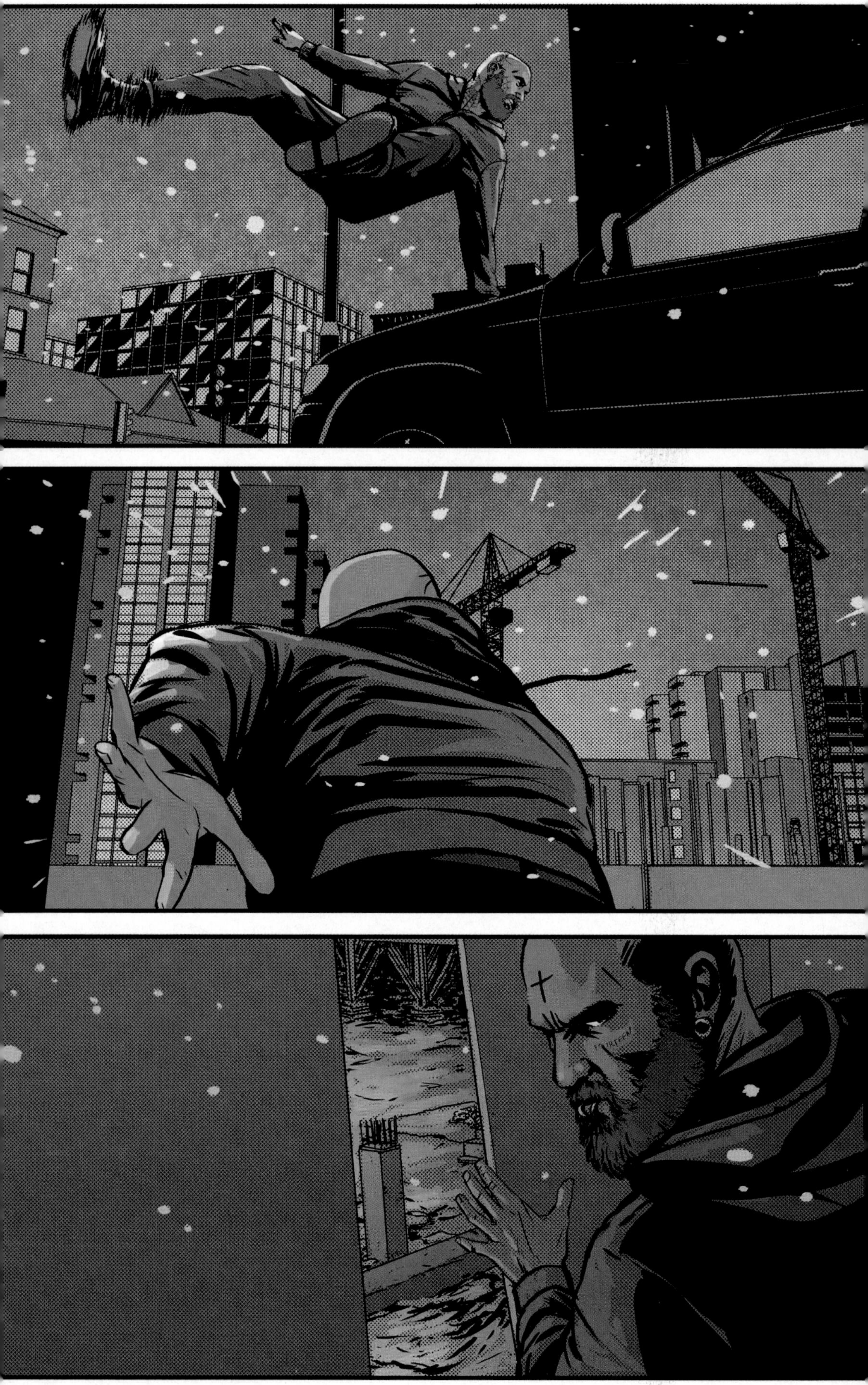

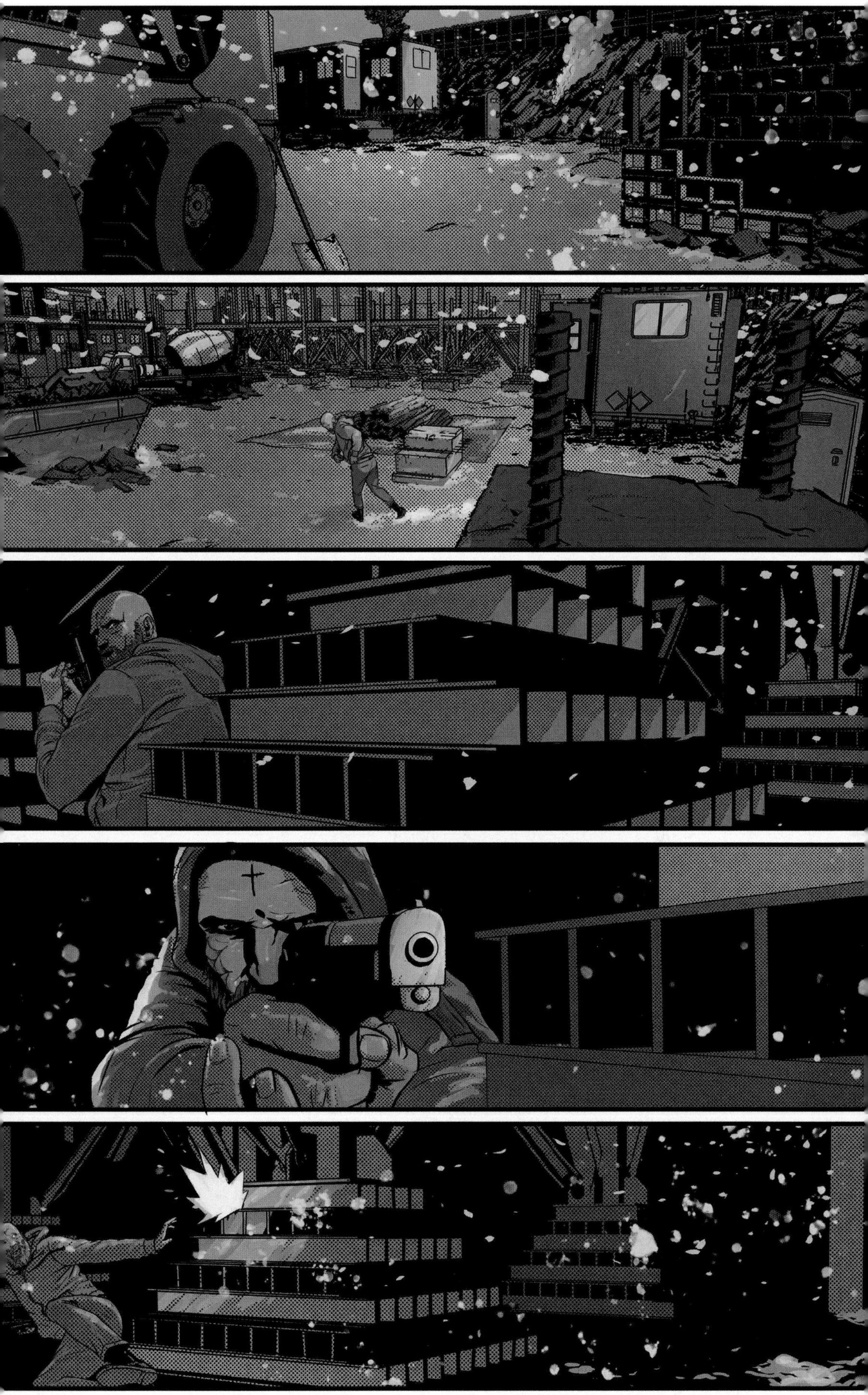

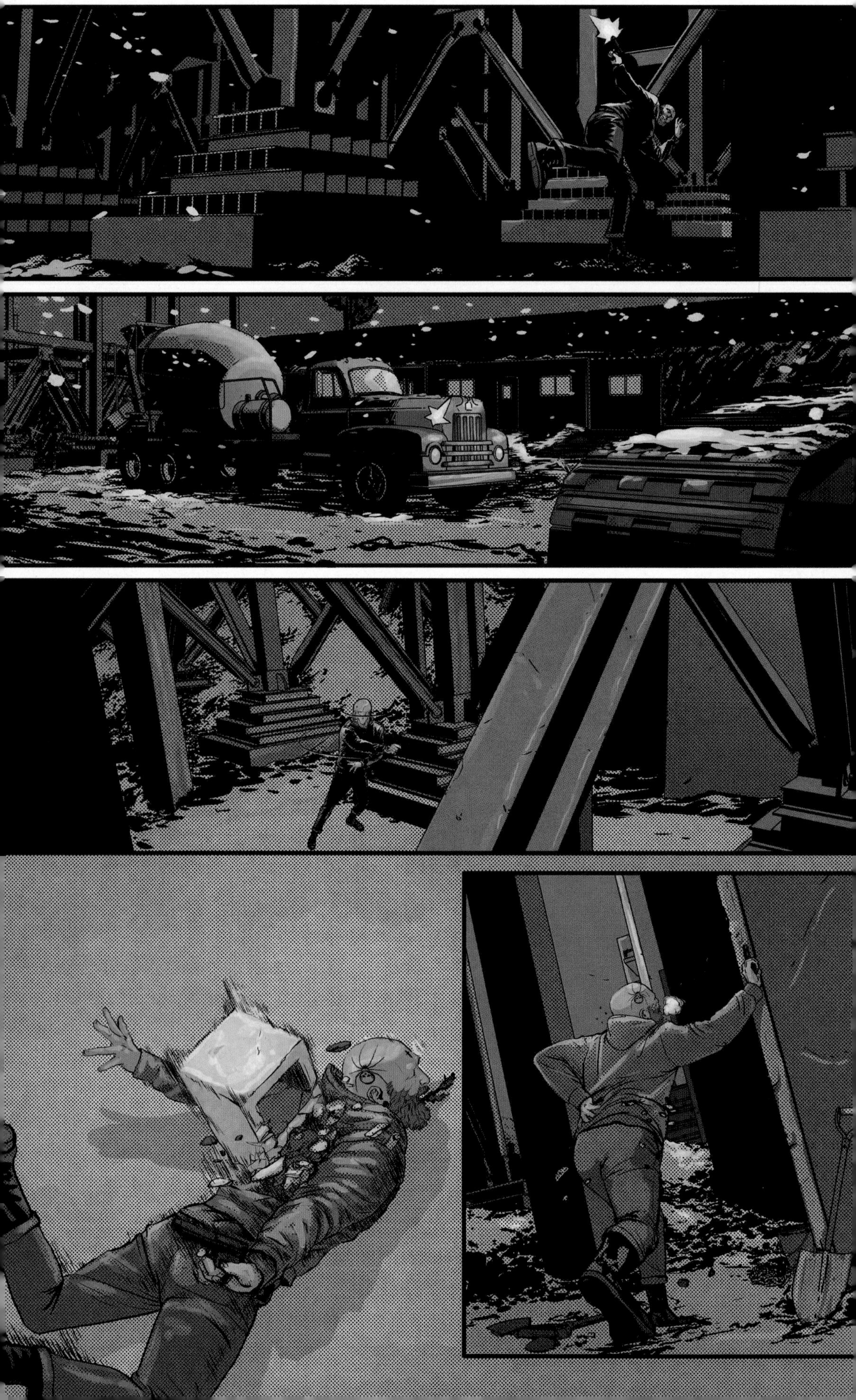

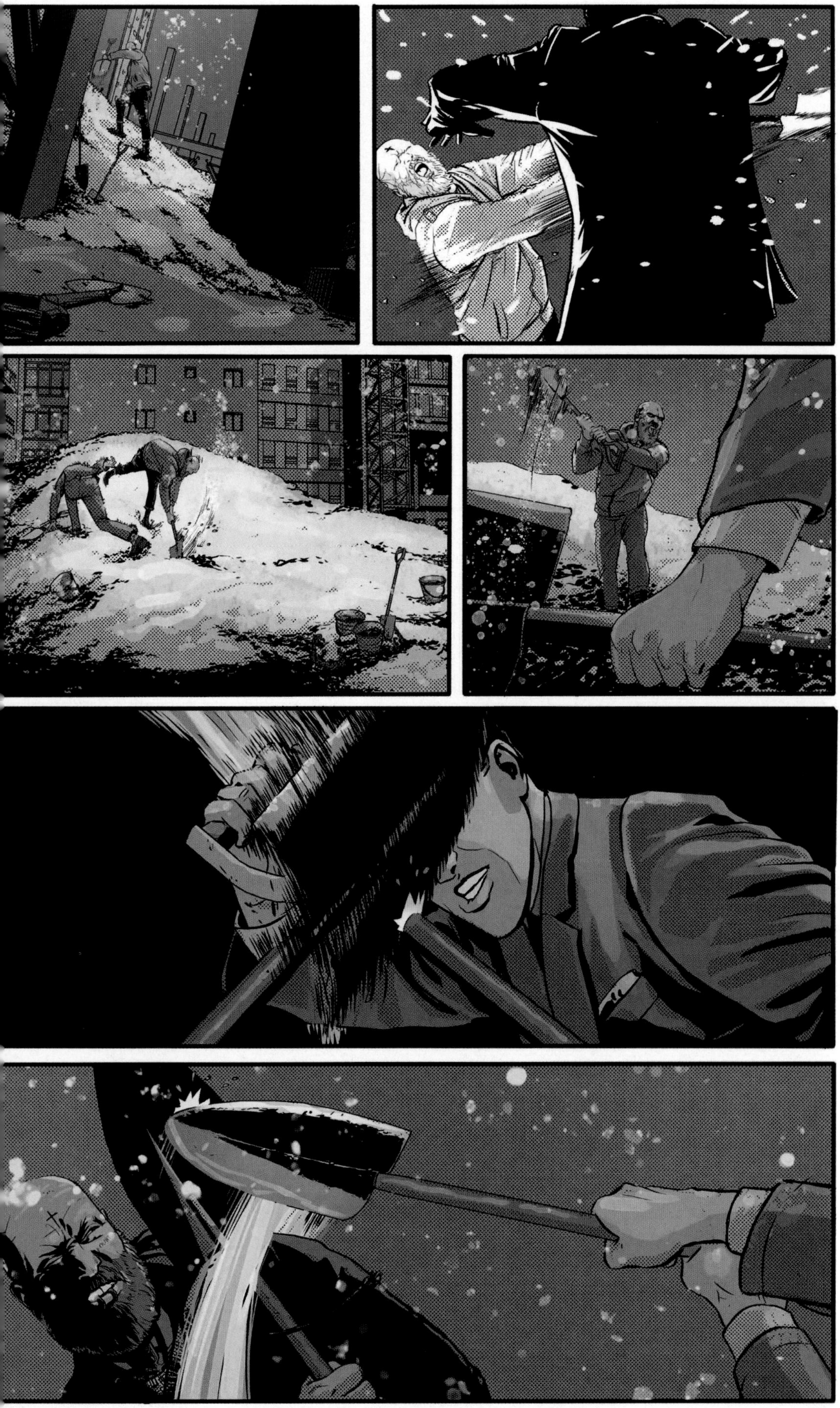

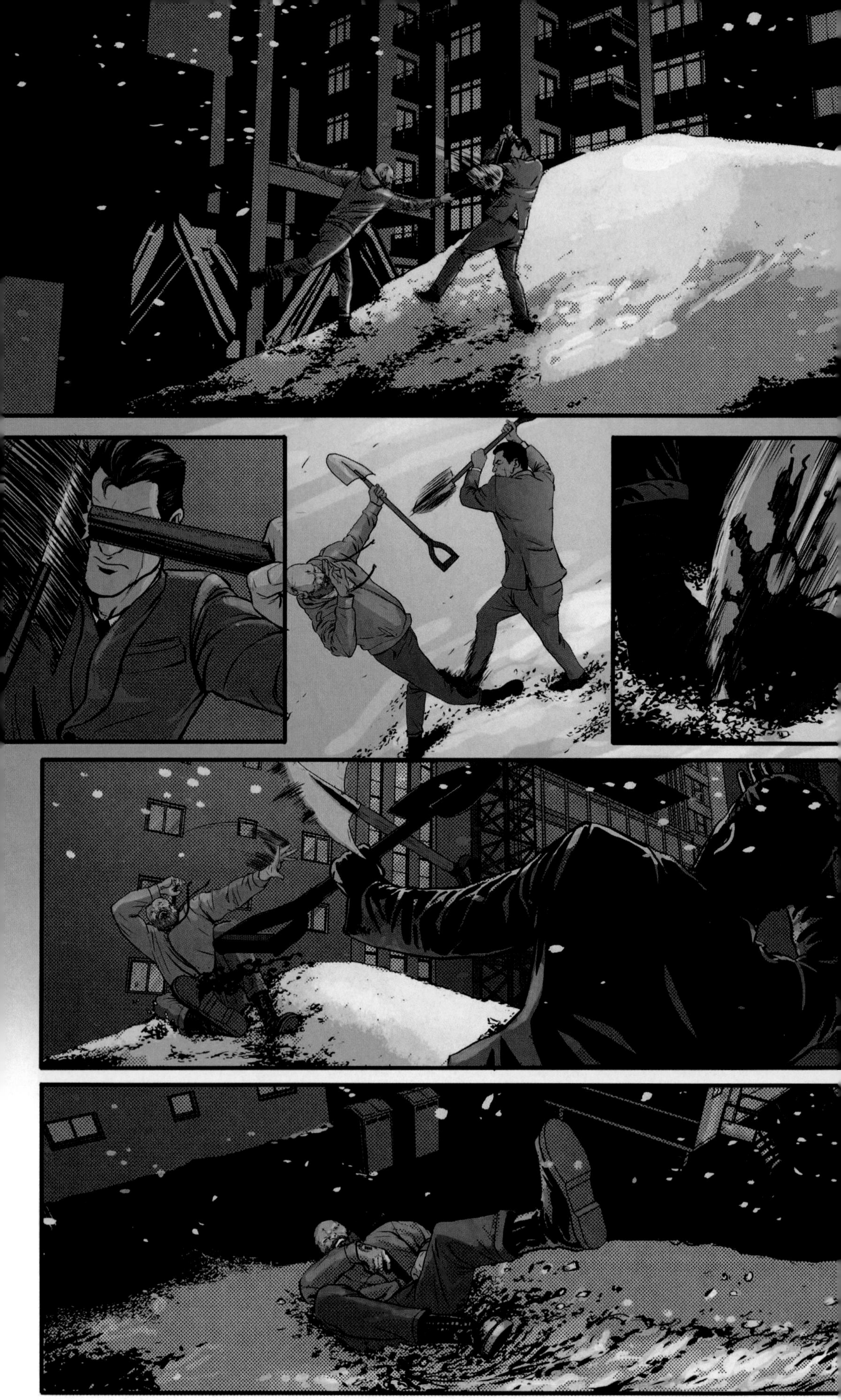

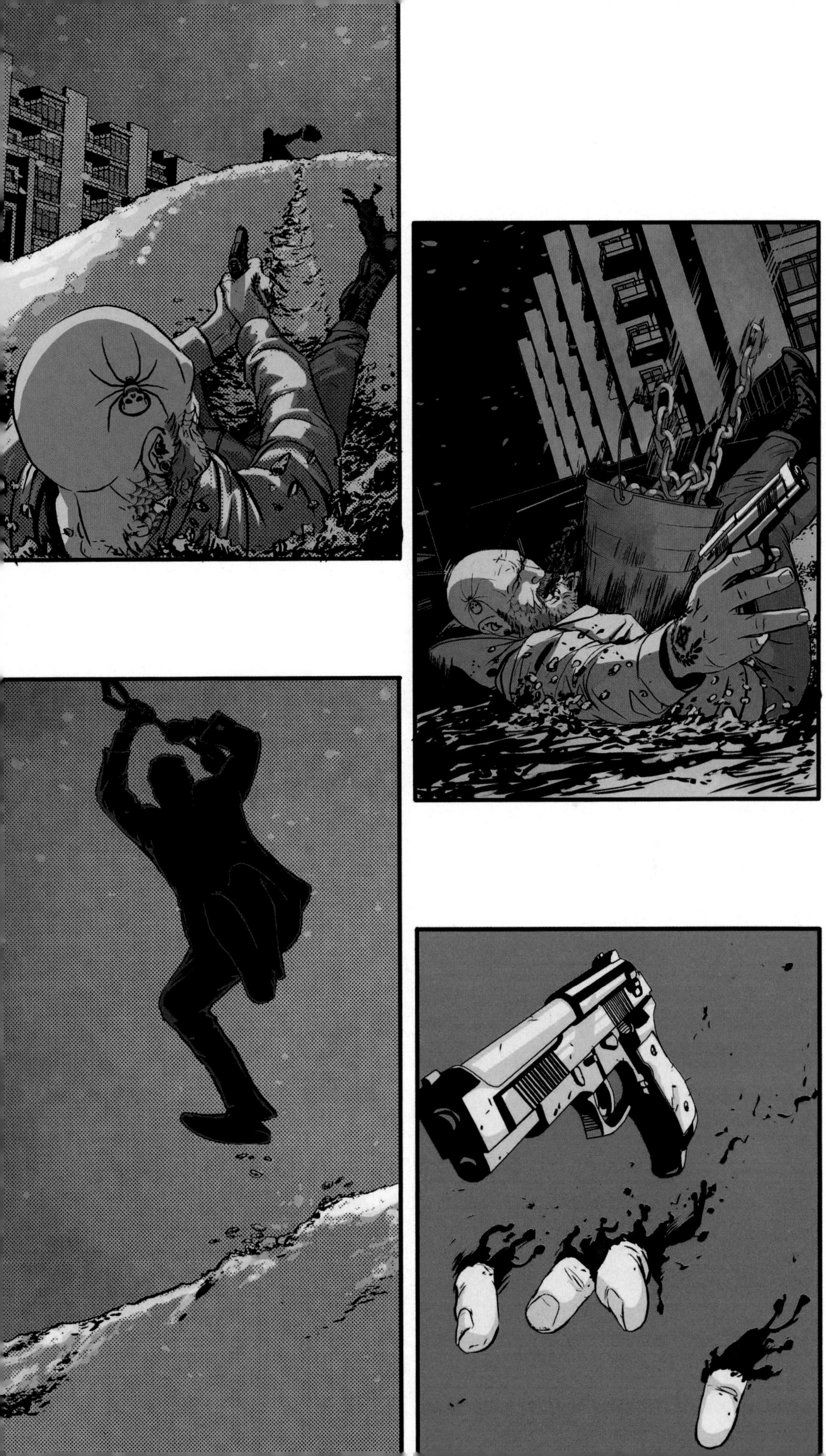

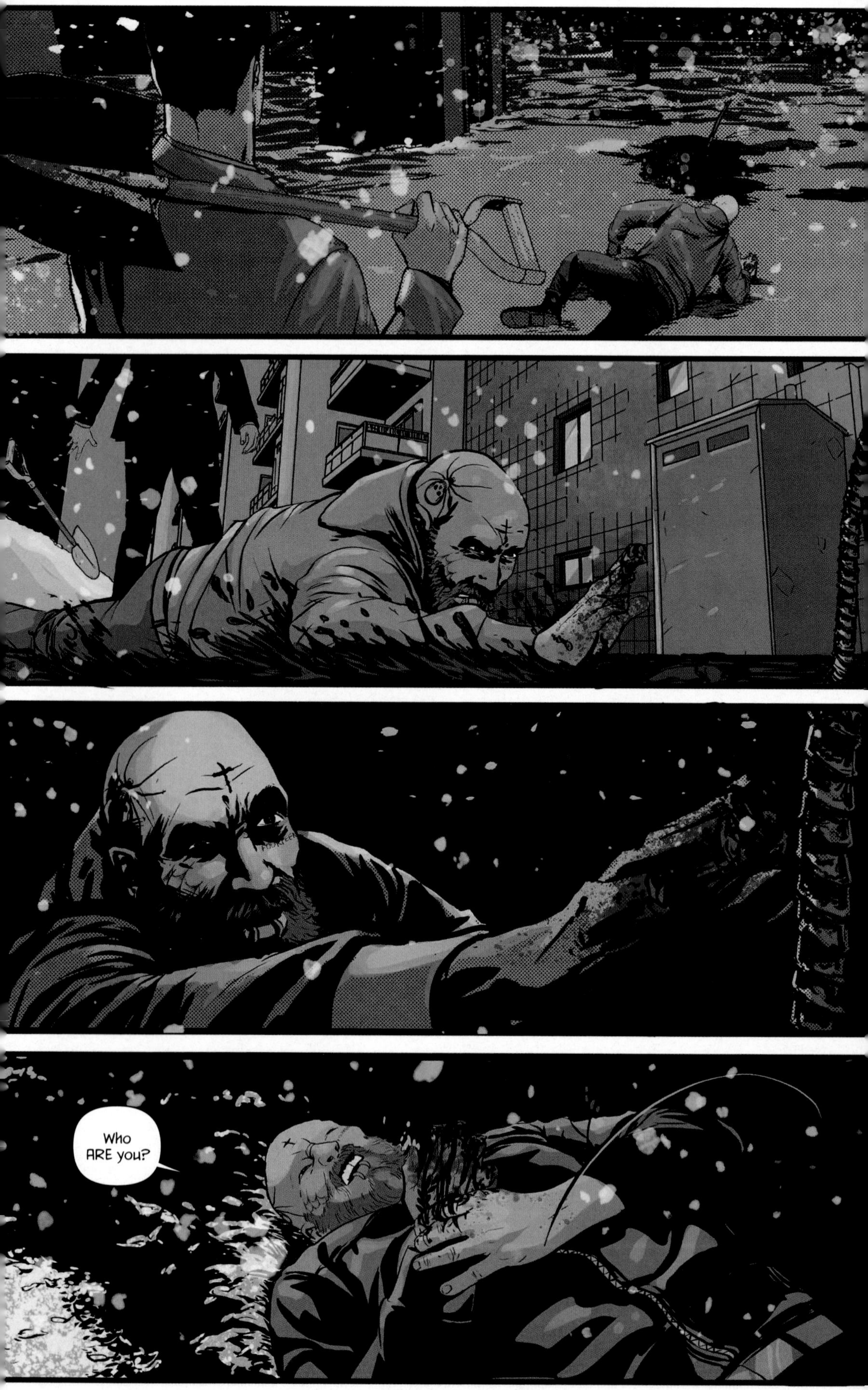
Who ARE you?

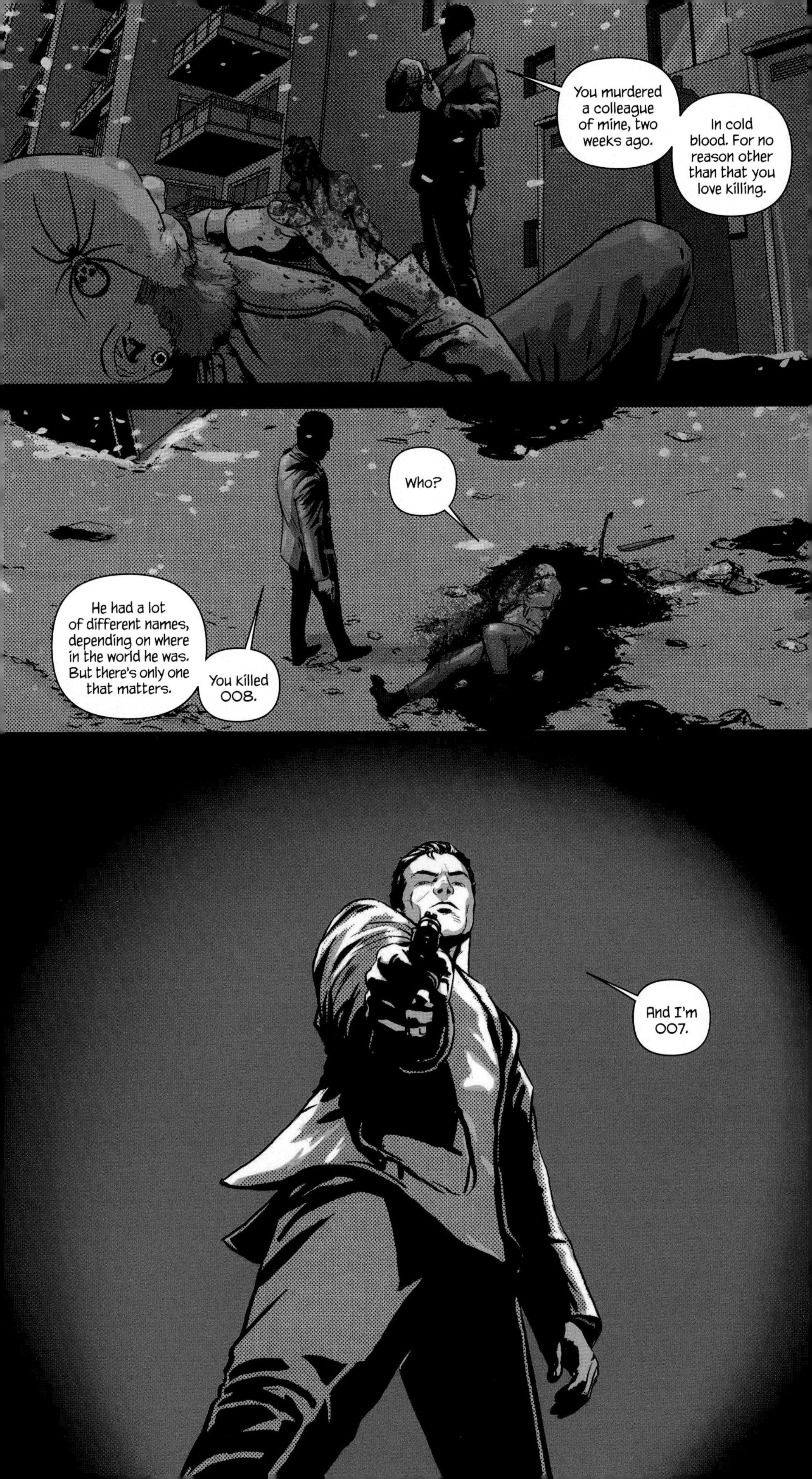
You murdered a colleague of mine, two weeks ago.
In cold blood. For no reason other than that you love killing.
Who?
He had a lot of different names, depending on where in the world he was. But there's only one that matters.
You killed 008.
And I'm 007.

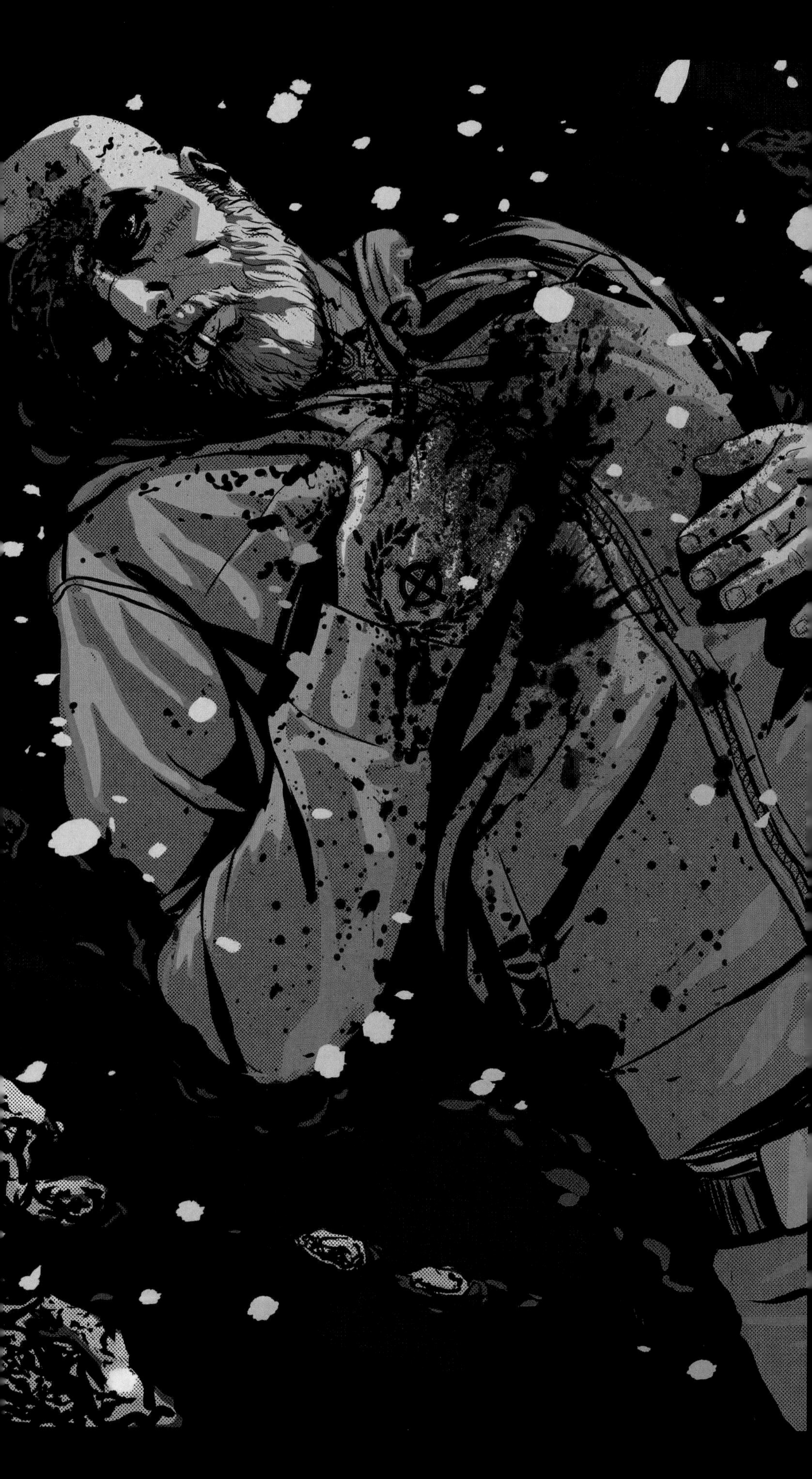

IAN FLEMING'S

JAMES BOND™ 007

IN:

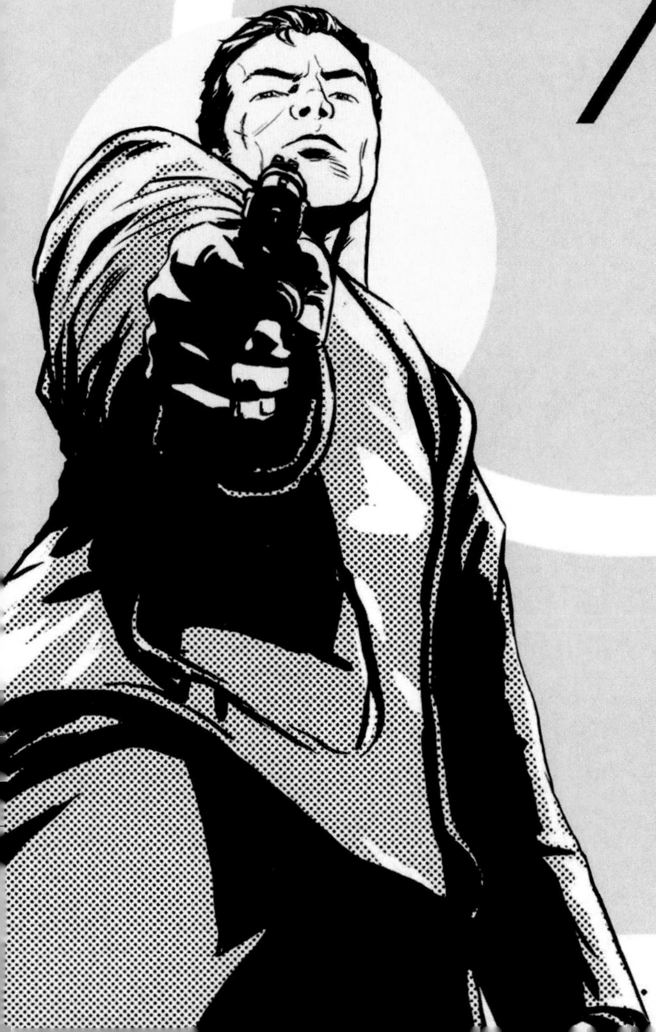

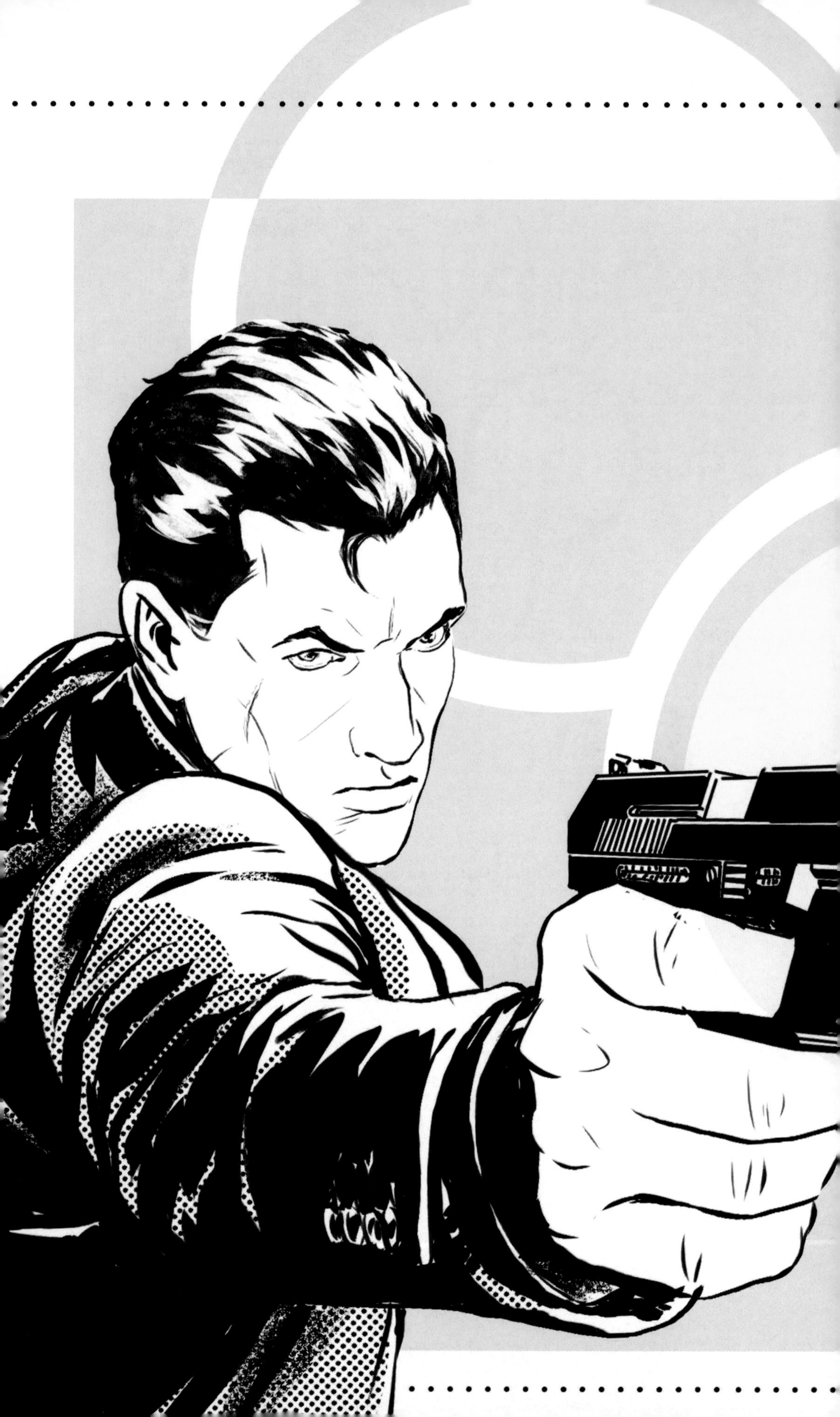

VARGR

JAMES BOND CREATED BY IAN FLEMING

WRITTEN BY:
WARREN ELLIS

ILLUSTRATED BY:
JASON MASTERS

COLORED BY:
GUY MAJOR

LETTERED BY:
SIMON BOWLAND

COLLECTION COVER BY:
JASON MASTERS

EDITOR:
JOSEPH RYBANDT
ASSOCIATE EDITOR:
RACHEL PINNELAS
EDITORIAL CONSULTANT:
MICHAEL LAKE

COLLECTION DESIGN:
JASON ULLMEYER
LOGO AND FRONT COVER DESIGN:
RIAN HUGHES

SPECIAL THANKS TO:
JOSEPHINE LANE, CORINNE TURNER,
AND DIGGORY LAYCOCK AT
IAN FLEMING PUBLICATIONS LTD.
AND JONNY GELLER AT CURTIS BROWN

Online at **www.DYNAMITE.com**
On Facebook **/Dynamitecomics**
On Instagram **/Dynamitecomics**
On Tumblr **dynamitecomics.tumblr.com**
On Twitter **@dynamitecomics**
On YouTube **/Dynamitecomics**

Nick Barrucci, CEO / Publisher
Juan Collado, President / COO

Joe Rybandt, Executive Editor
Matt Idelson, Senior Editor
Rachel Pinnelas, Associate Editor
Anthony Marques, Assistant Editor
Kevin Ketner, Editorial Assistant

Jason Ullmeyer, Art Director
Geoff Harkins, Graphic Designer
Alexis Persson, Production Artist

Chris Caniano, Digital Associate
Rachel Kilbury, Digital Assistant

Brandon Dante Primavera, V.P. of IT and Operatio
Rich Young, Director of Business Development

Alan Payne, V.P. of Sales and Marketing
Keith Davidsen, Marketing Manager
Pat O'Connell, Sales Manager

ISBN10: 1-60690-901-0   ISBN13: 978-1-60690-901-0   First Printing   10 9 8 7 6 5 4 3 2 1

ISSUE 001

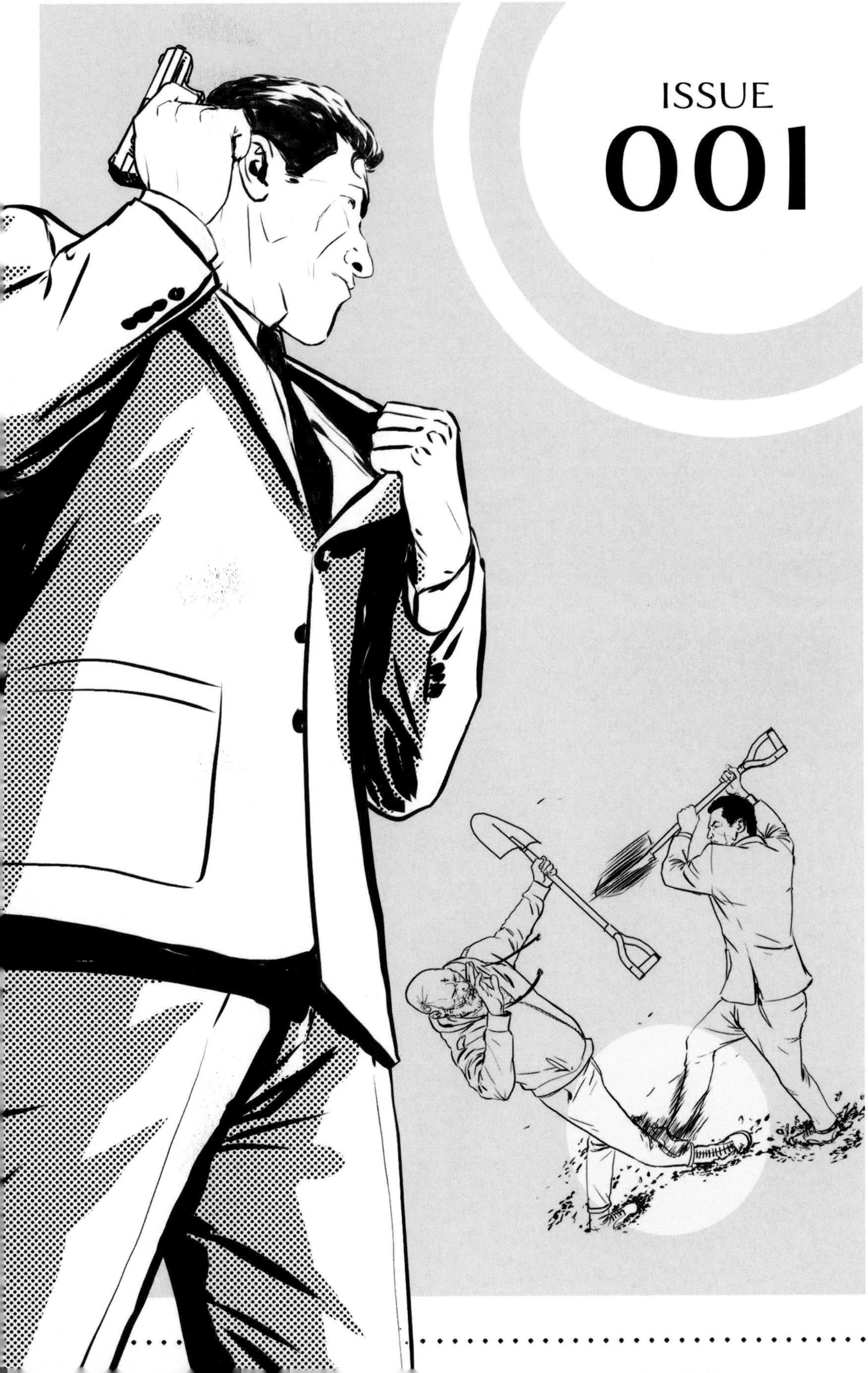

issue #1 main cover by **DOM REARDON**

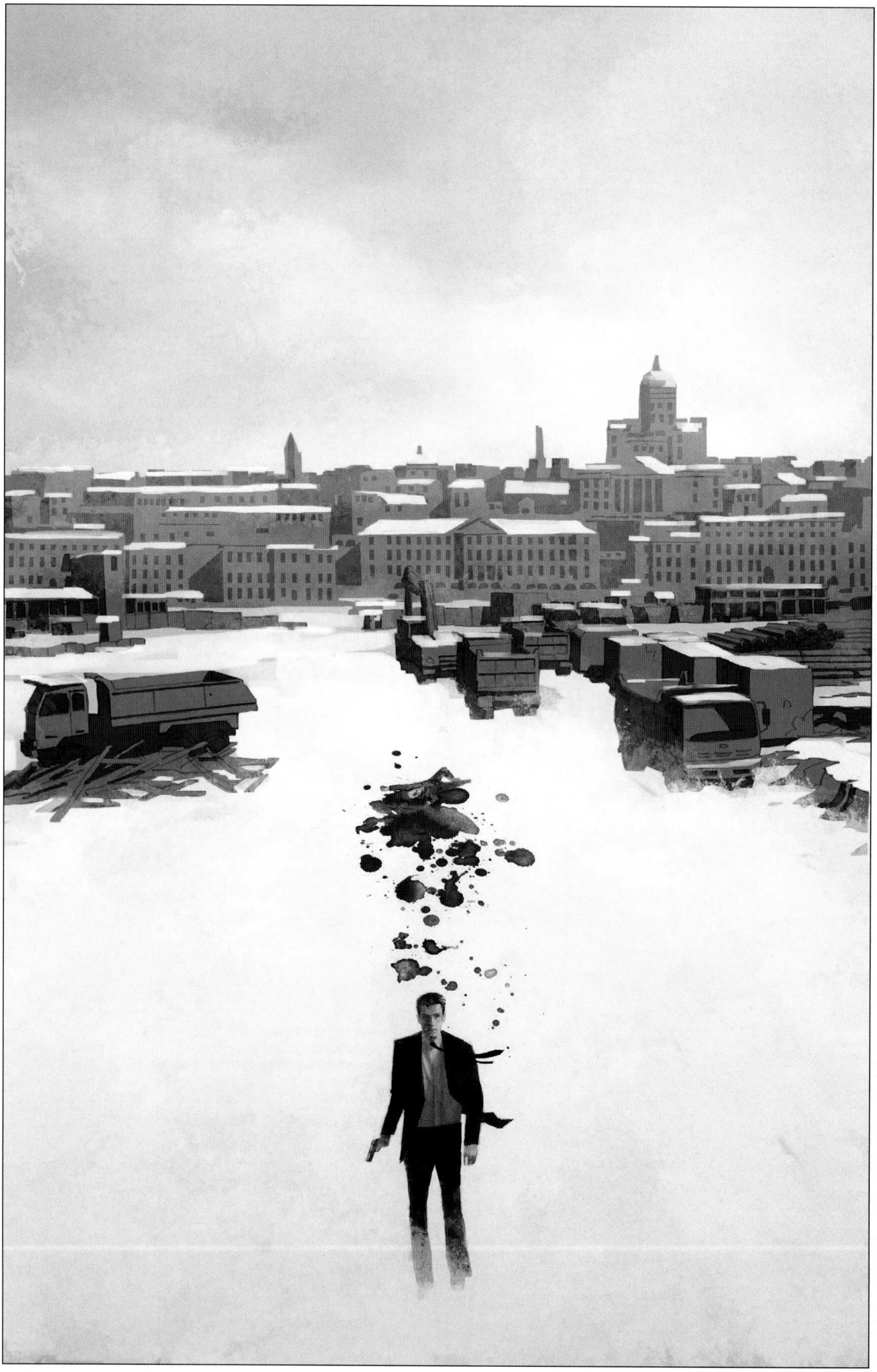

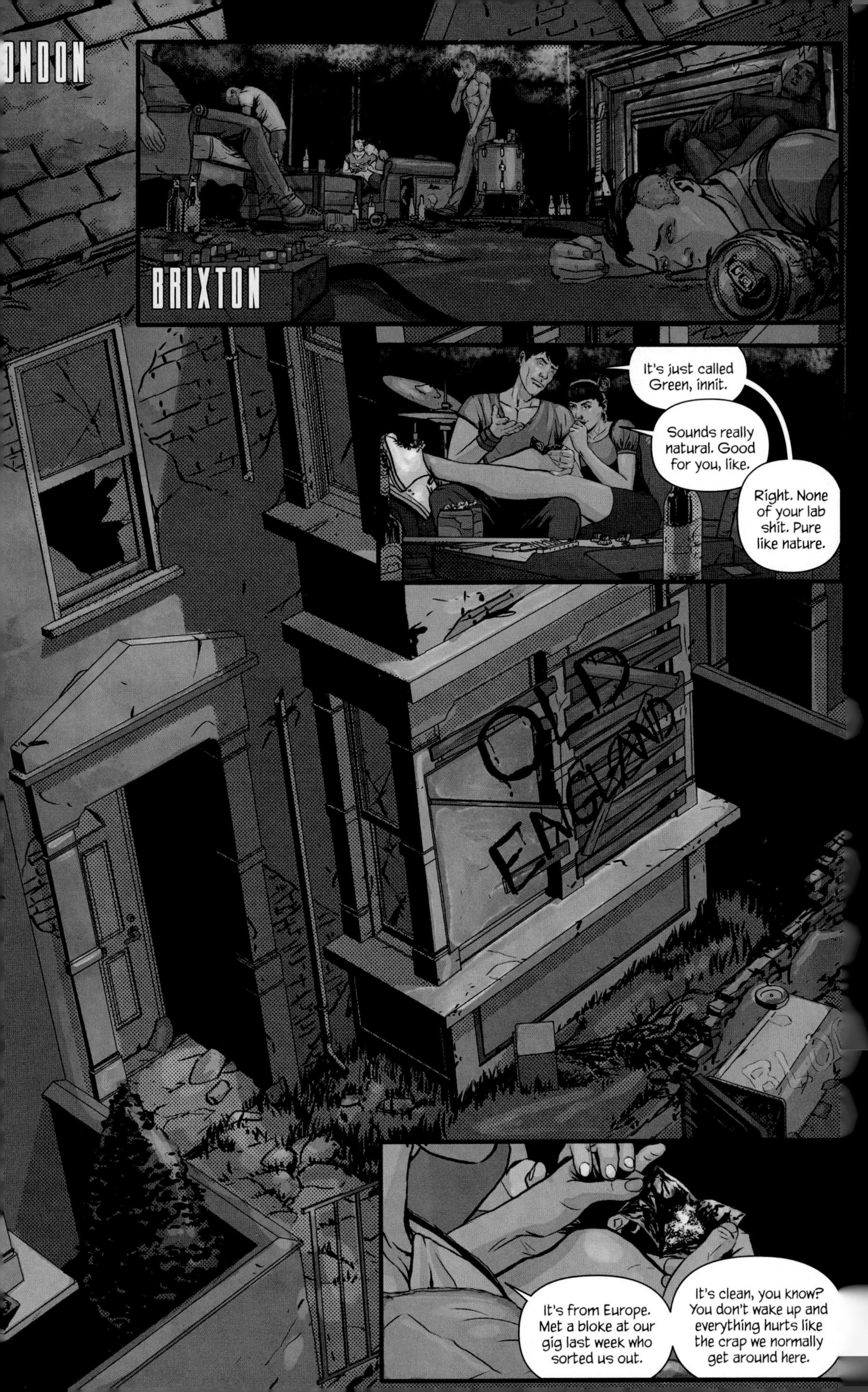

LONDON
BRIXTON
It's just called Green, innit.
Sounds really natural. Good for you, like.
Right. None of your lab shit. Pure like nature.
OLD ENGLAND
It's from Europe. Met a bloke at our gig last week who sorted us out.
It's clean, you know? You don't wake up and everything hurts like the crap we normally get around here.

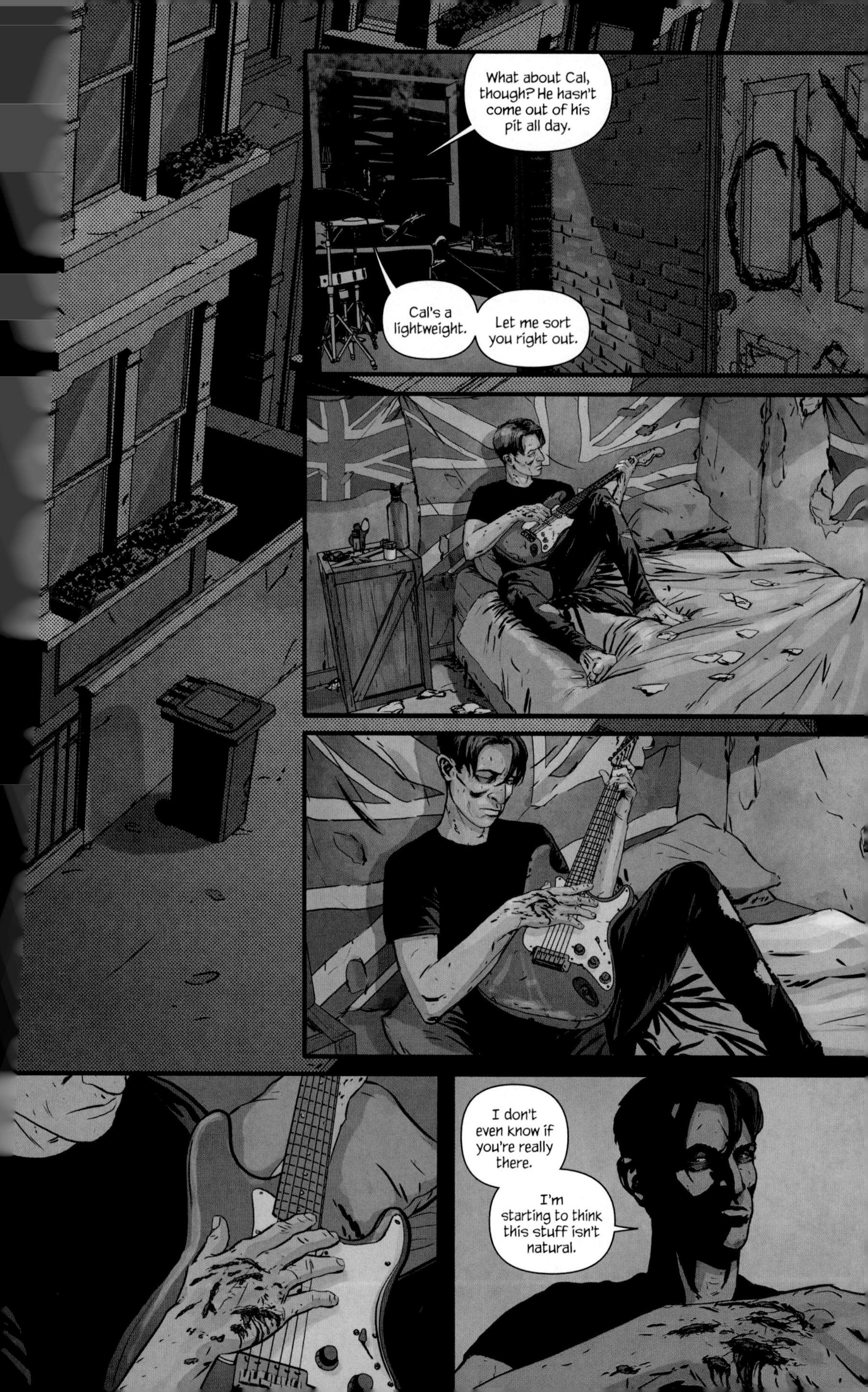
What about Cal, though? He hasn't come out of his pit all day.
Cal's a lightweight.
Let me sort you right out.
I don't even know if you're really there.
I'm starting to think this stuff isn't natural.

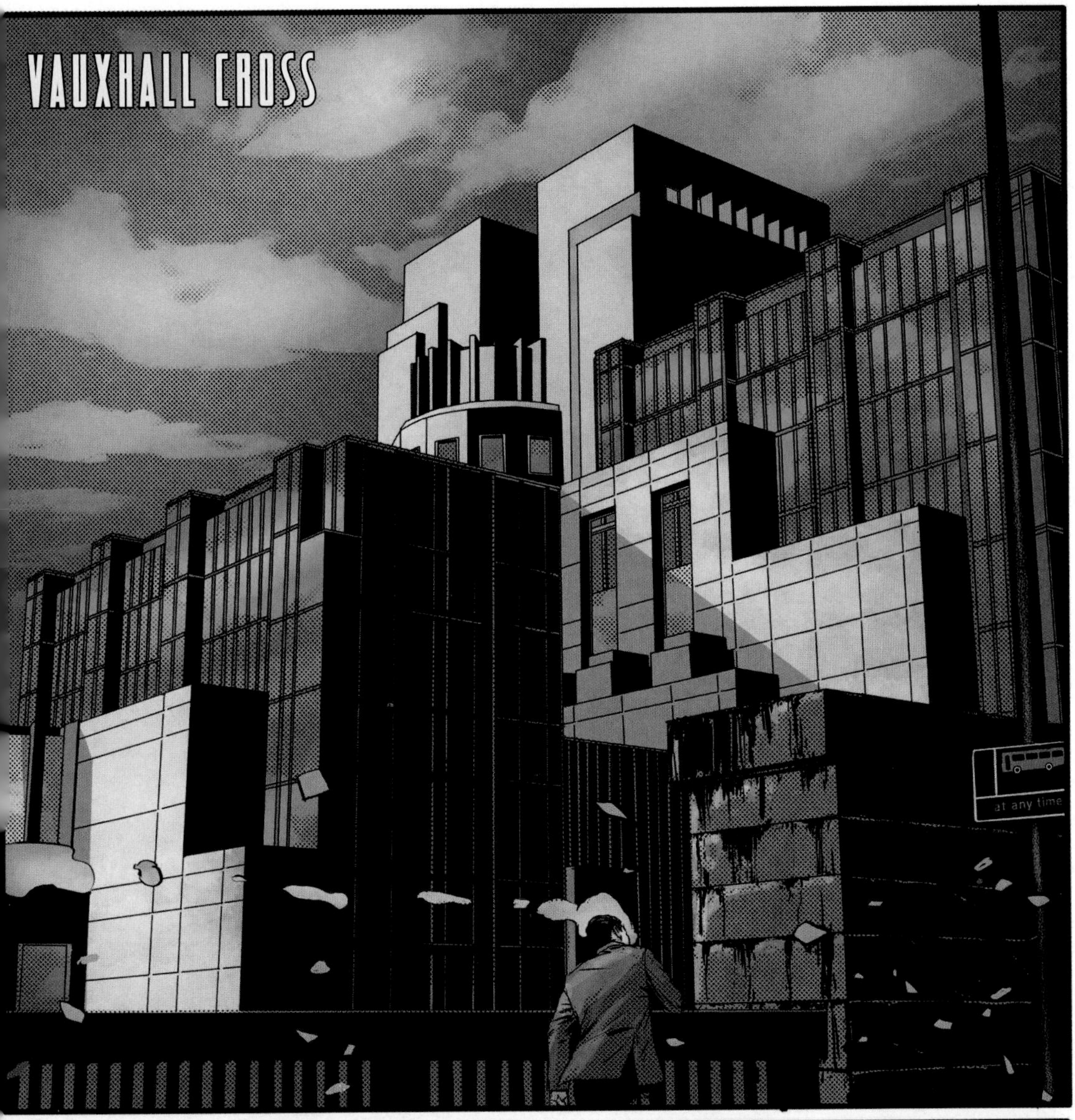
VAUXHALL CROSS
at any time
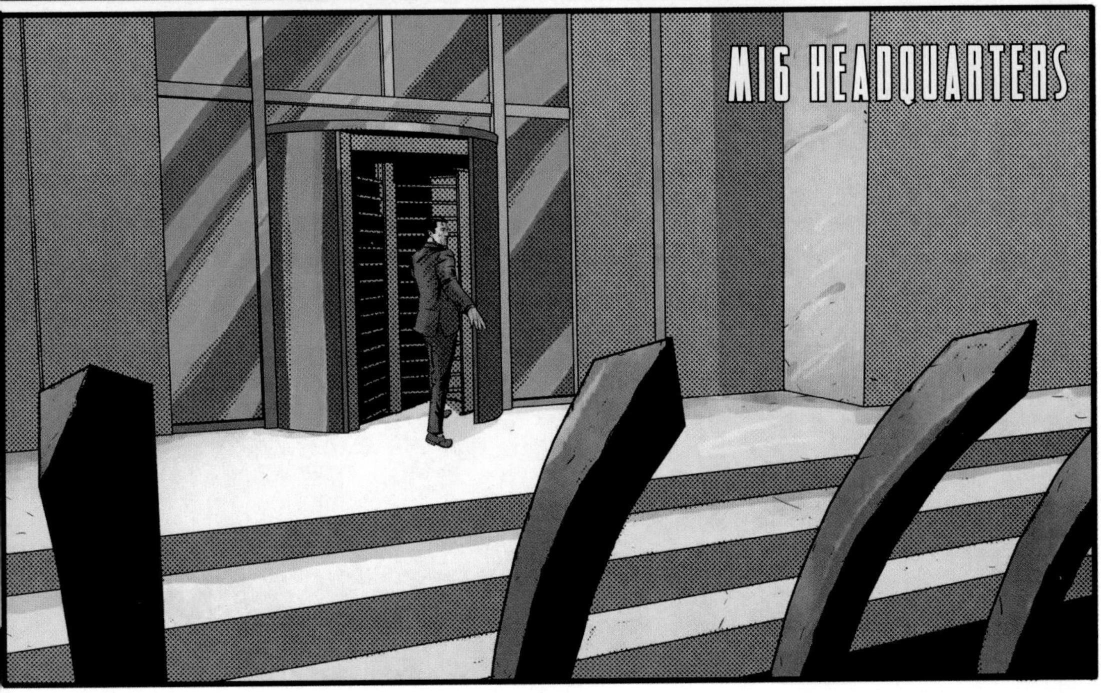
MI6 HEADQUARTERS

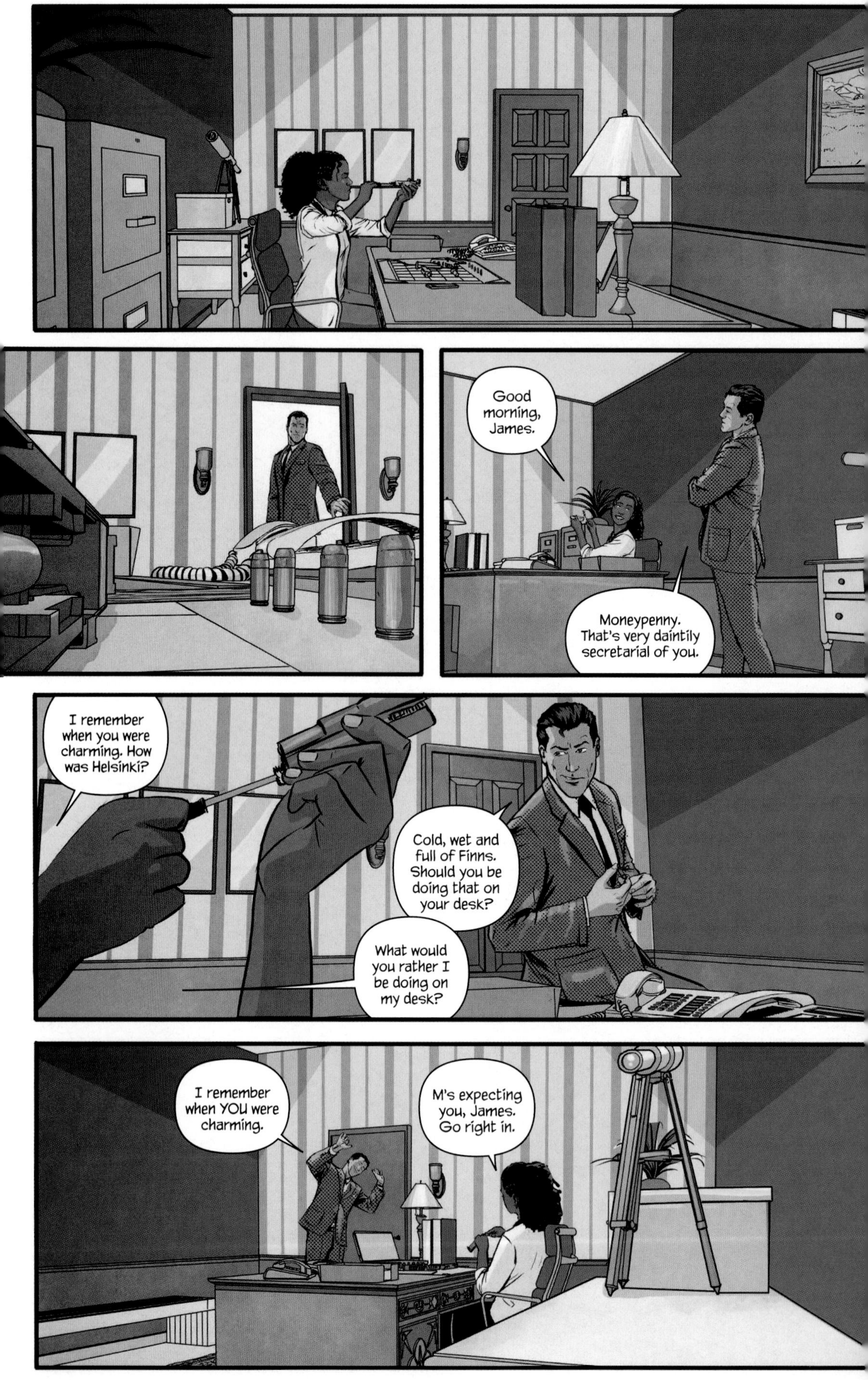
Good morning, James.
Moneypenny. That's very daintily secretarial of you.
I remember when you were charming. How was Helsinki?
Cold, wet and full of Finns. Should you be doing that on your desk?
What would you rather I be doing on my desk?
I remember when YOU were charming.
M's expecting you, James. Go right in.

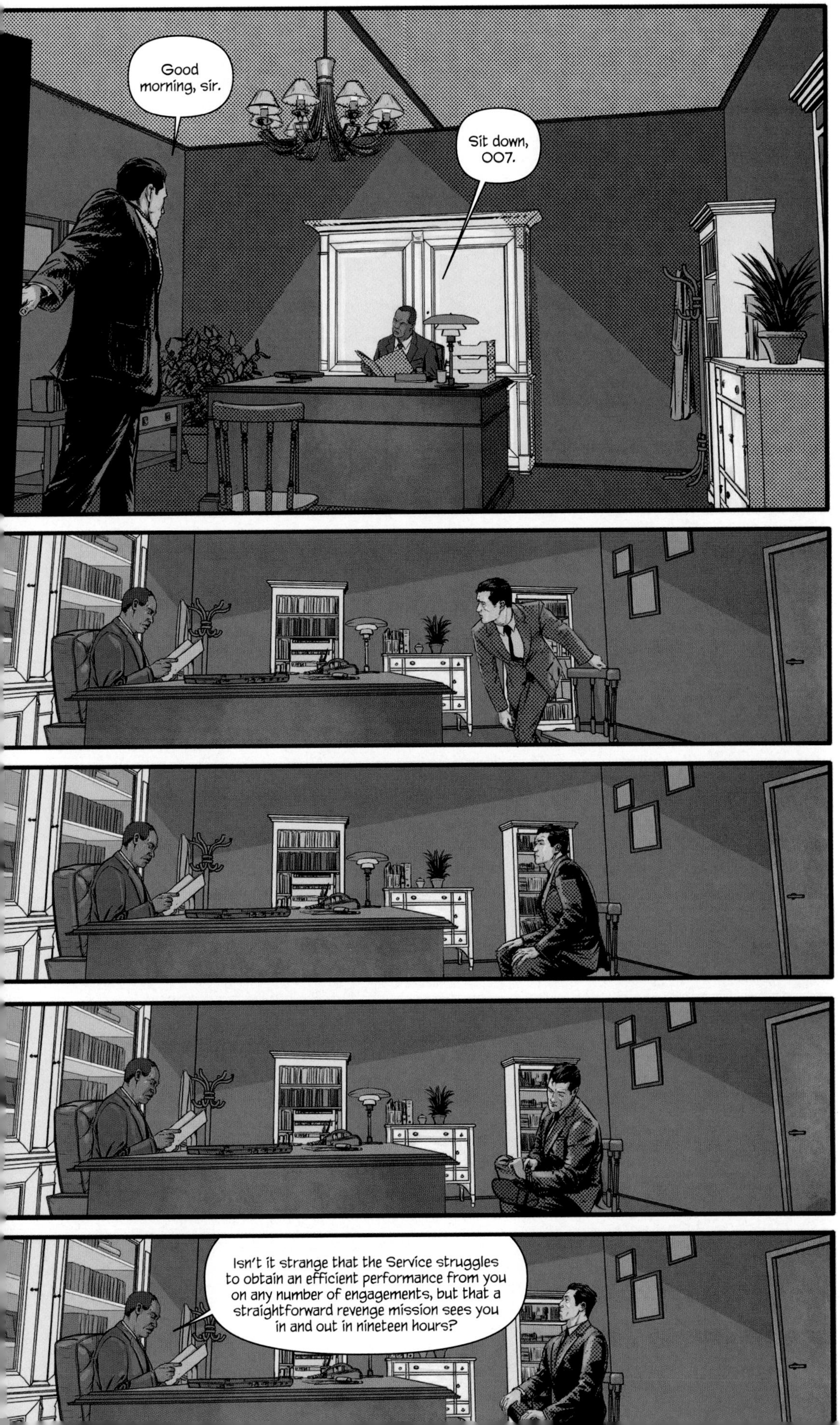
Good morning, sir.
Sit down, 007.
Isn't it strange that the Service struggles to obtain an efficient performance from you on any number of engagements, but that a straightforward revenge mission sees you in and out in nineteen hours?

It was a simple operation, sir.

Killing a man is simple?

Simple as in a lack of complexity. No tradecraft required. All I had to do was locate the actor in question and eliminate him.

Yes. Well. It's not gone unnoticed. People in high places are suggesting I retire the OO Section entirely.

And?

And the conducting of foreign policy still requires access to a small box of blunt instruments. You don't get to retire to a casino quite yet, Bond.

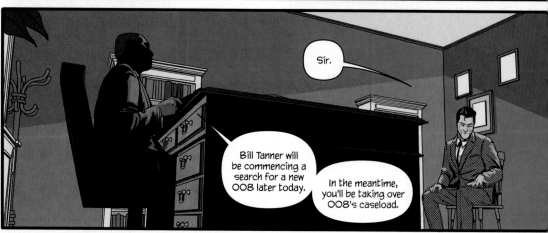

Sir.

Bill Tanner will be commencing a search for a new OO8 later today.

In the meantime, you'll be taking over OO8's caseload.

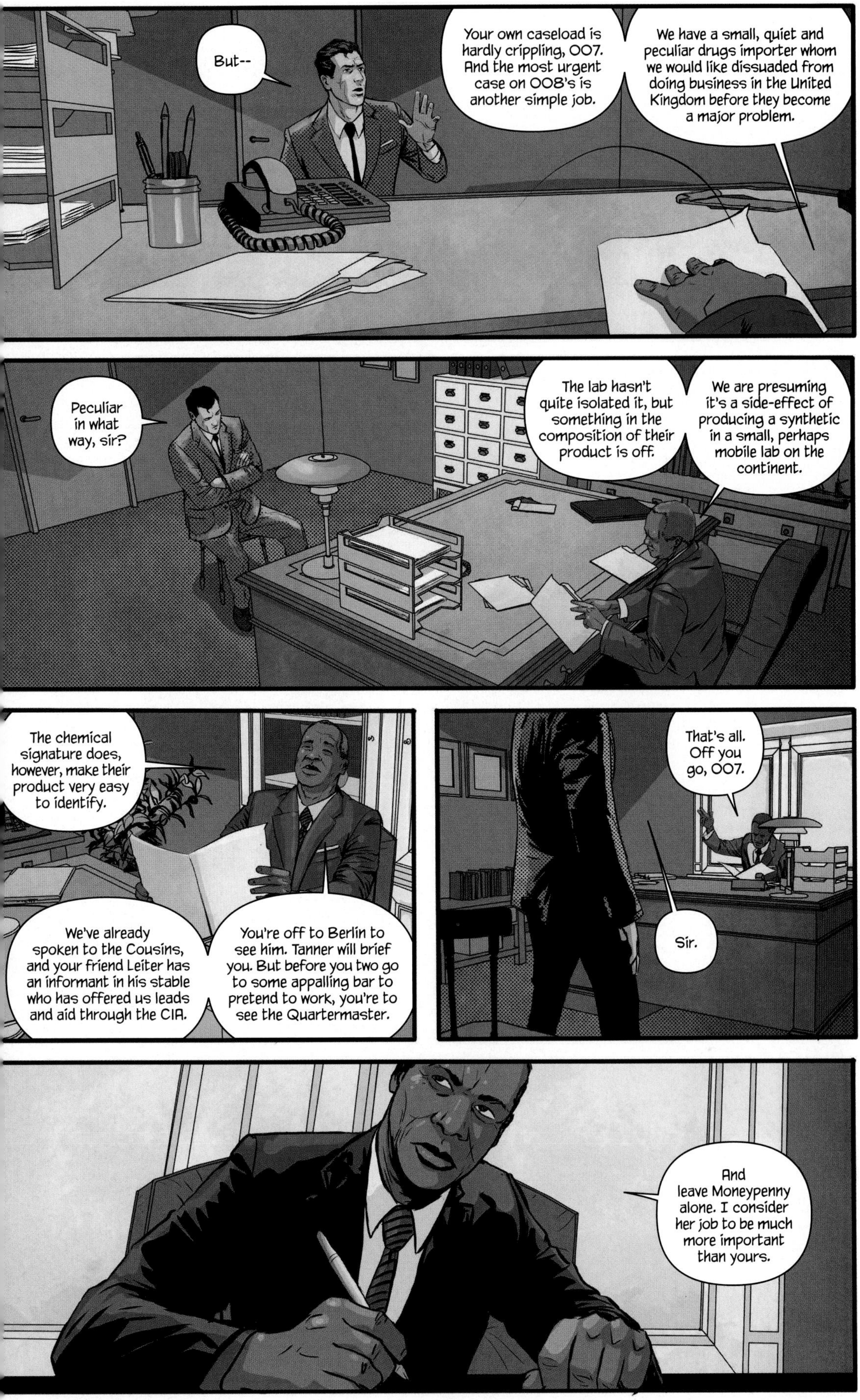
But--
Your own caseload is hardly crippling, 007. And the most urgent case on 008's is another simple job.
We have a small, quiet and peculiar drugs importer whom we would like dissuaded from doing business in the United Kingdom before they become a major problem.
Peculiar in what way, sir?
The lab hasn't quite isolated it, but something in the composition of their product is off.
We are presuming it's a side-effect of producing a synthetic in a small, perhaps mobile lab on the continent.
The chemical signature does, however, make their product very easy to identify.
We've already spoken to the Cousins, and your friend Leiter has an informant in his stable who has offered us leads and aid through the CIA.
You're off to Berlin to see him. Tanner will brief you. But before you two go to some appalling bar to pretend to work, you're to see the Quartermaster.
That's all. Off you go, 007.
Sir.
And leave Moneypenny alone. I consider her job to be much more important than yours.

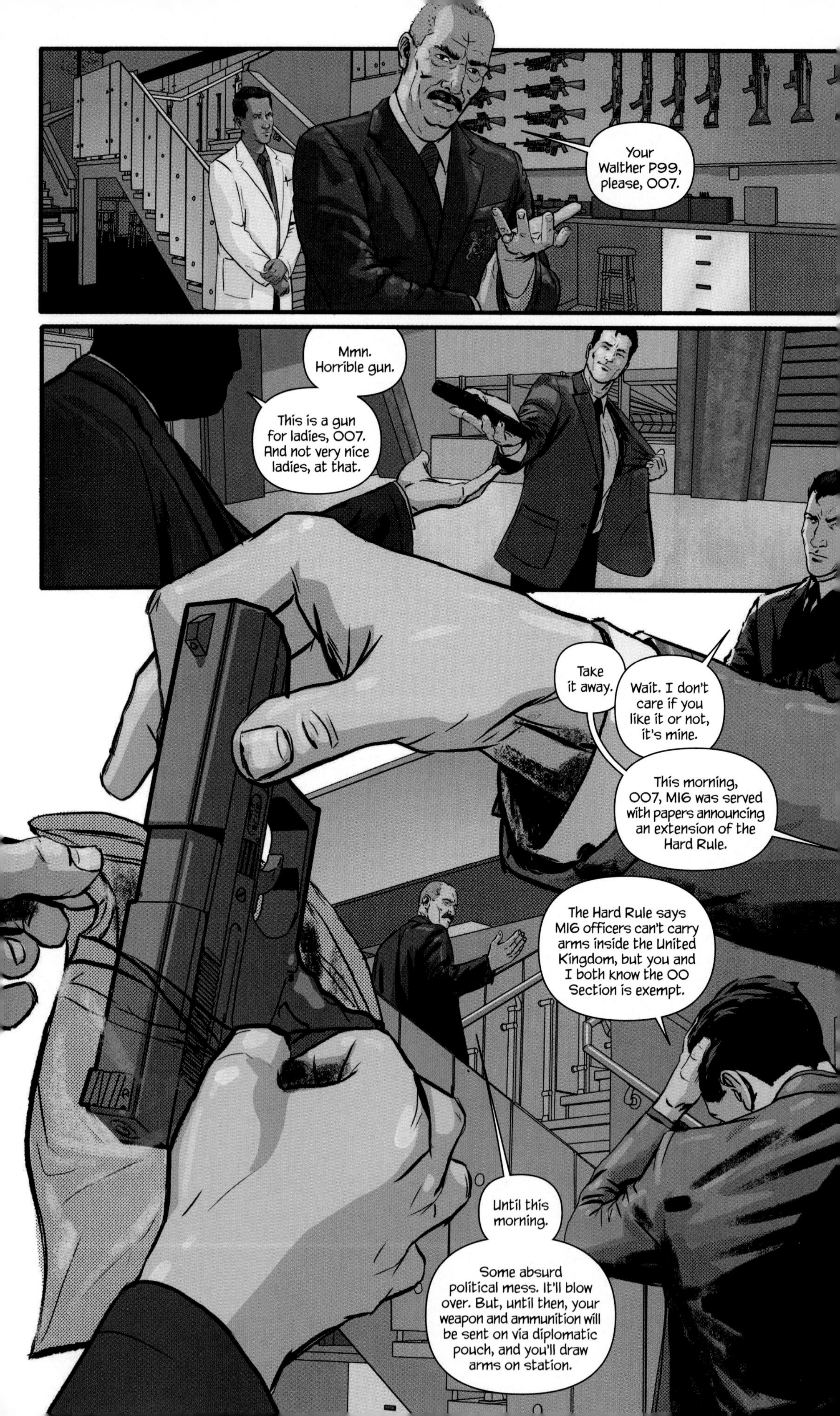
Your Walther P99, please, 007.
Mmn. Horrible gun.
This is a gun for ladies, 007. And not very nice ladies, at that.
Take it away.
Wait. I don't care if you like it or not, it's mine.
This morning, 007, MI6 was served with papers announcing an extension of the Hard Rule.
The Hard Rule says MI6 officers can't carry arms inside the United Kingdom, but you and I both know the 00 Section is exempt.
Until this morning.
Some absurd political mess. It'll blow over. But, until then, your weapon and ammunition will be sent on via diplomatic pouch, and you'll draw arms on station.

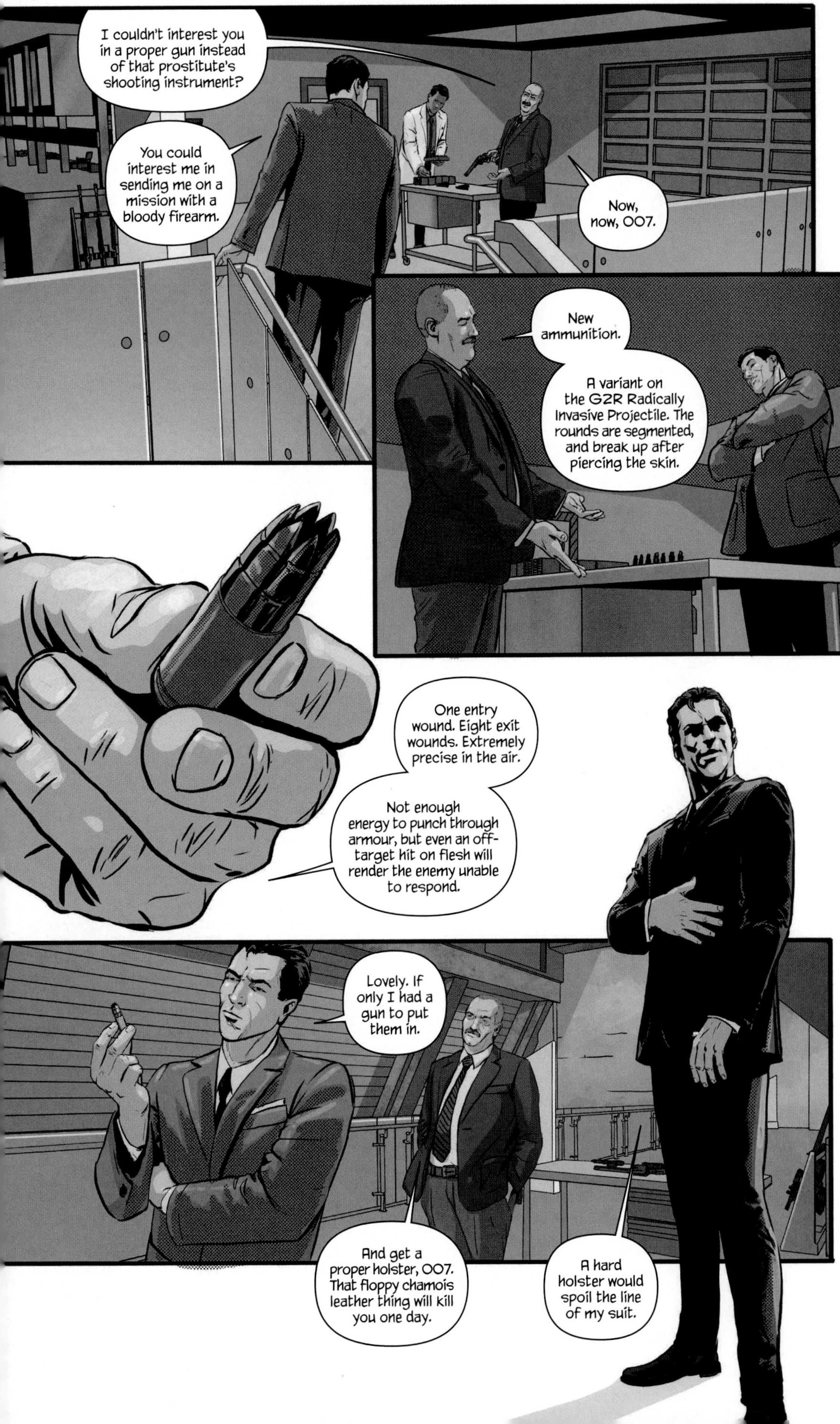
I couldn't interest you in a proper gun instead of that prostitute's shooting instrument?
You could interest me in sending me on a mission with a bloody firearm.
Now, now, 007.
New ammunition.
A variant on the G2R Radically Invasive Projectile. The rounds are segmented, and break up after piercing the skin.
One entry wound. Eight exit wounds. Extremely precise in the air.
Not enough energy to punch through armour, but even an off-target hit on flesh will render the enemy unable to respond.
Lovely. If only I had a gun to put them in.
And get a proper holster, 007. That floppy chamois leather thing will kill you one day.
A hard holster would spoil the line of my suit.

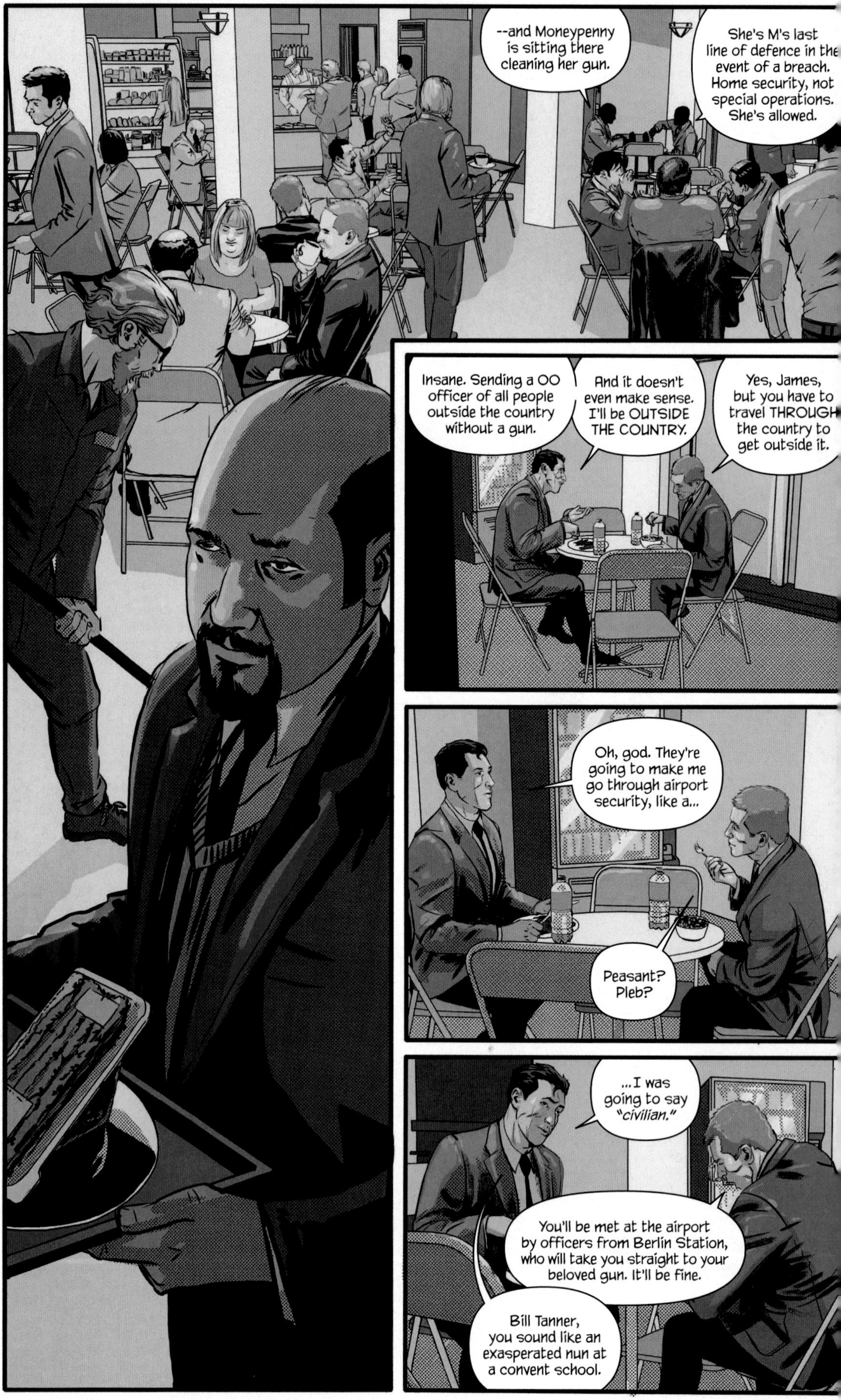
--and Moneypenny is sitting there cleaning her gun.
She's M's last line of defence in the event of a breach. Home security, not special operations. She's allowed.
Insane. Sending a 00 officer of all people outside the country without a gun.
And it doesn't even make sense. I'll be OUTSIDE THE COUNTRY.
Yes, James, but you have to travel THROUGH the country to get outside it.
Oh, god. They're going to make me go through airport security, like a...
Peasant? Pleb?
...I was going to say "civilian."
You'll be met at the airport by officers from Berlin Station, who will take you straight to your beloved gun. It'll be fine.
Bill Tanner, you sound like an exasperated nun at a convent school.

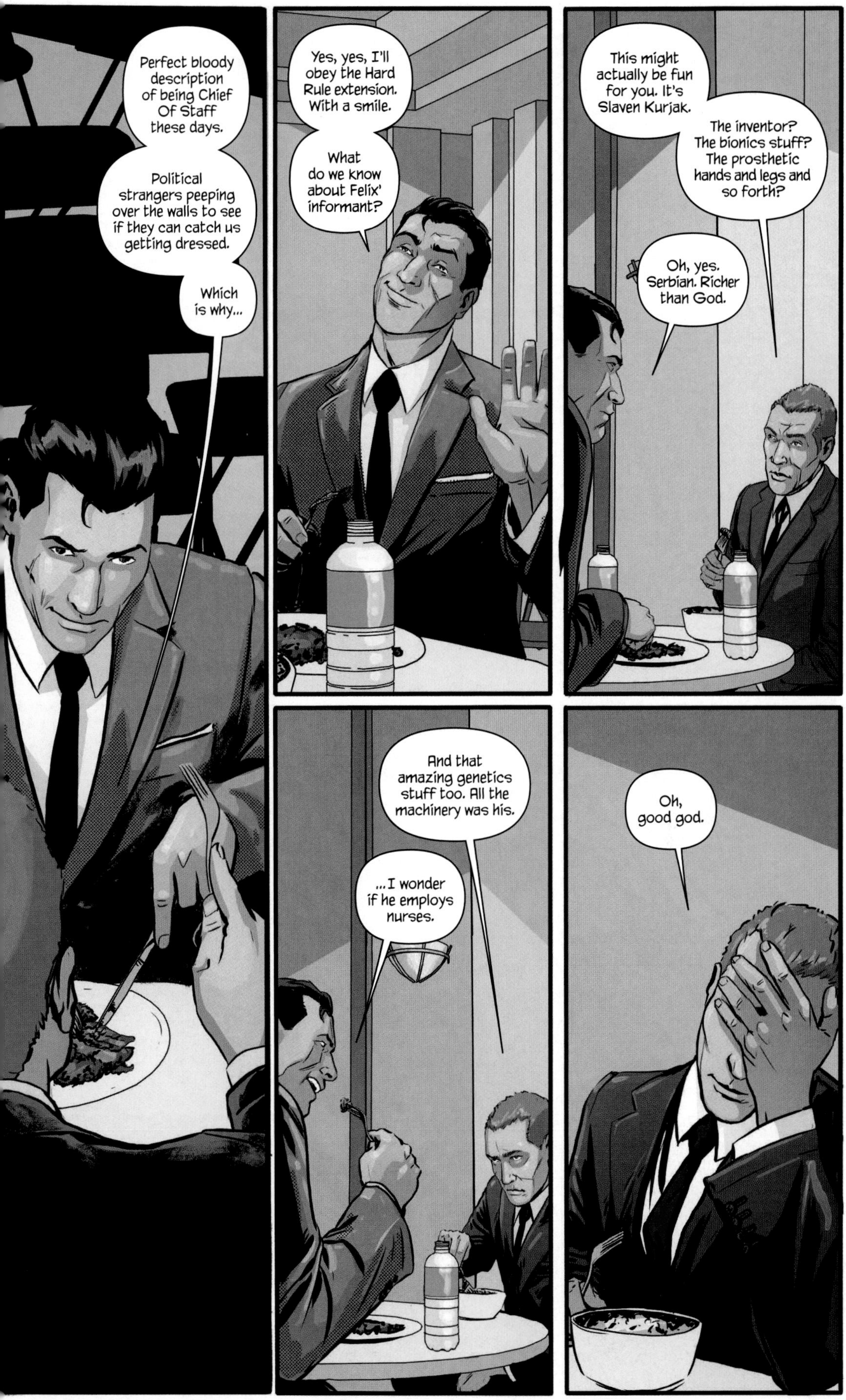
Perfect bloody description of being Chief Of Staff these days.
Political strangers peeping over the walls to see if they can catch us getting dressed.
Which is why...
Yes, yes, I'll obey the Hard Rule extension. With a smile.
What do we know about Felix' informant?
This might actually be fun for you. It's Slaven Kurjak.
The inventor? The bionics stuff? The prosthetic hands and legs and so forth?
Oh, yes. Serbian. Richer than God.
And that amazing genetics stuff too. All the machinery was his.
...I wonder if he employs nurses.
Oh, good god.

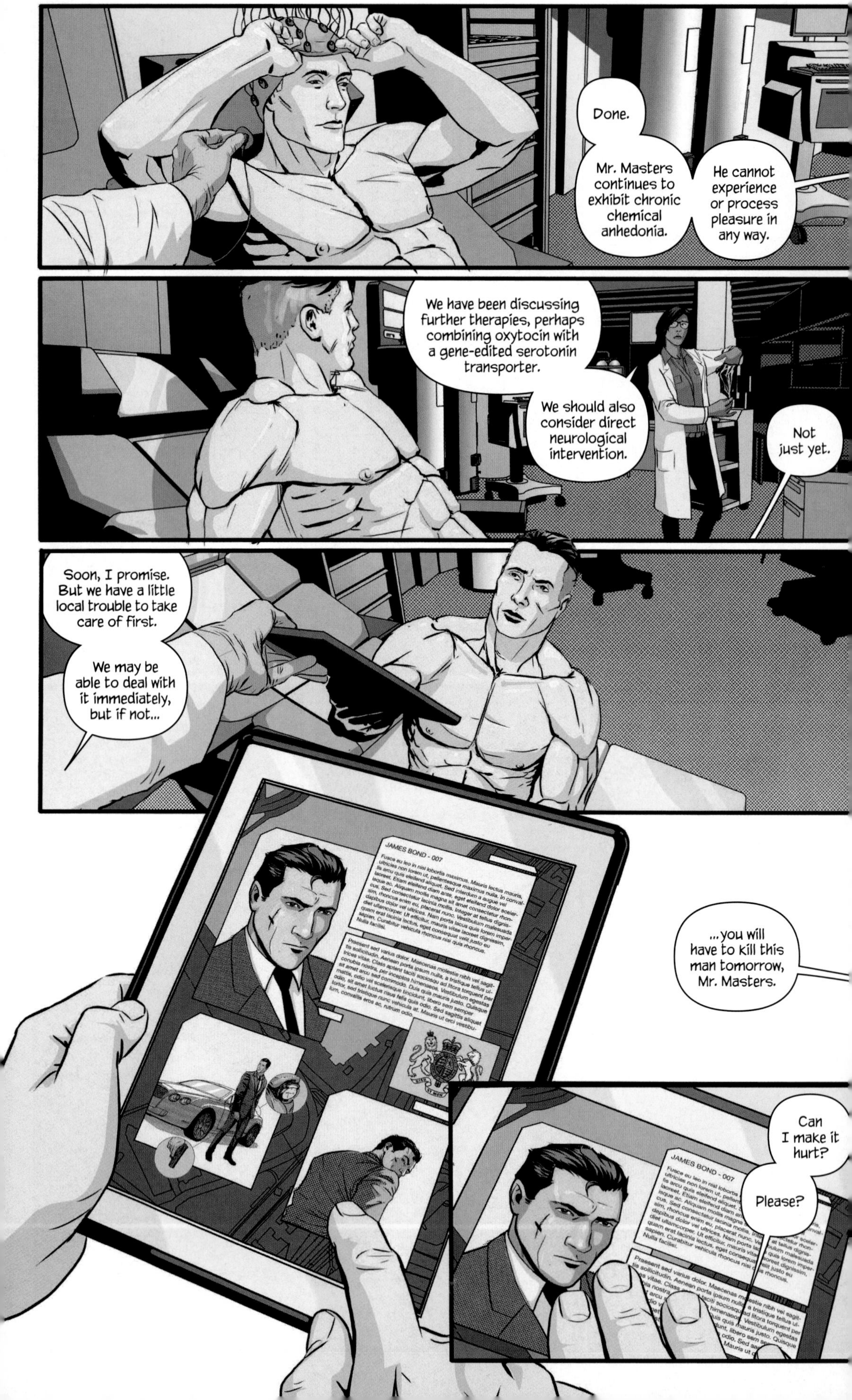
Done.
Mr. Masters continues to exhibit chronic chemical anhedonia.
He cannot experience or process pleasure in any way.
We have been discussing further therapies, perhaps combining oxytocin with a gene-edited serotonin transporter.
We should also consider direct neurological intervention.
Not just yet.
Soon, I promise. But we have a little local trouble to take care of first.
We may be able to deal with it immediately, but if not...
JAMES BOND - 007
...you will have to kill this man tomorrow, Mr. Masters.
Can I make it hurt?
Please?

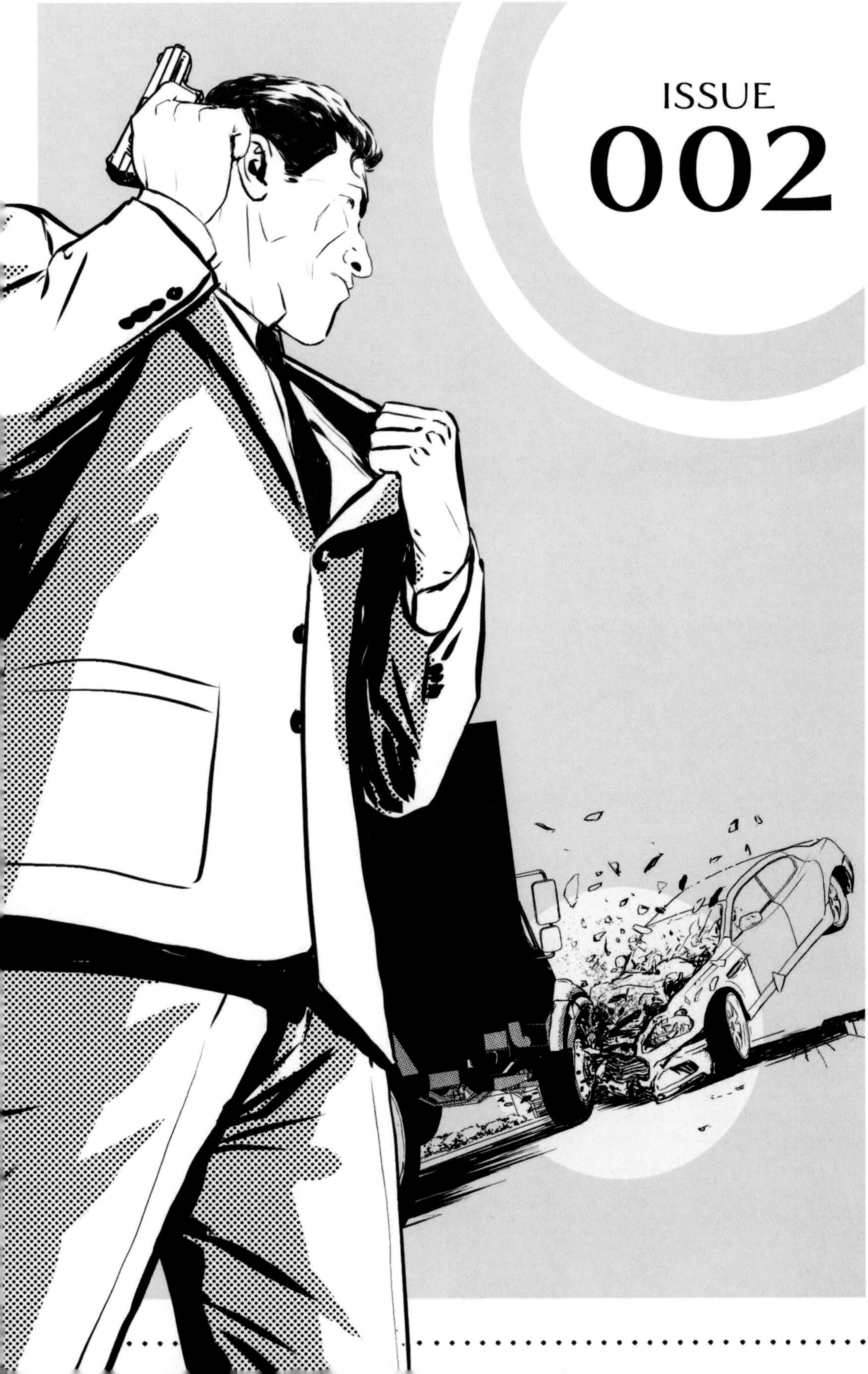
ISSUE
002

issue #2 main cover by **DOM REARDON**

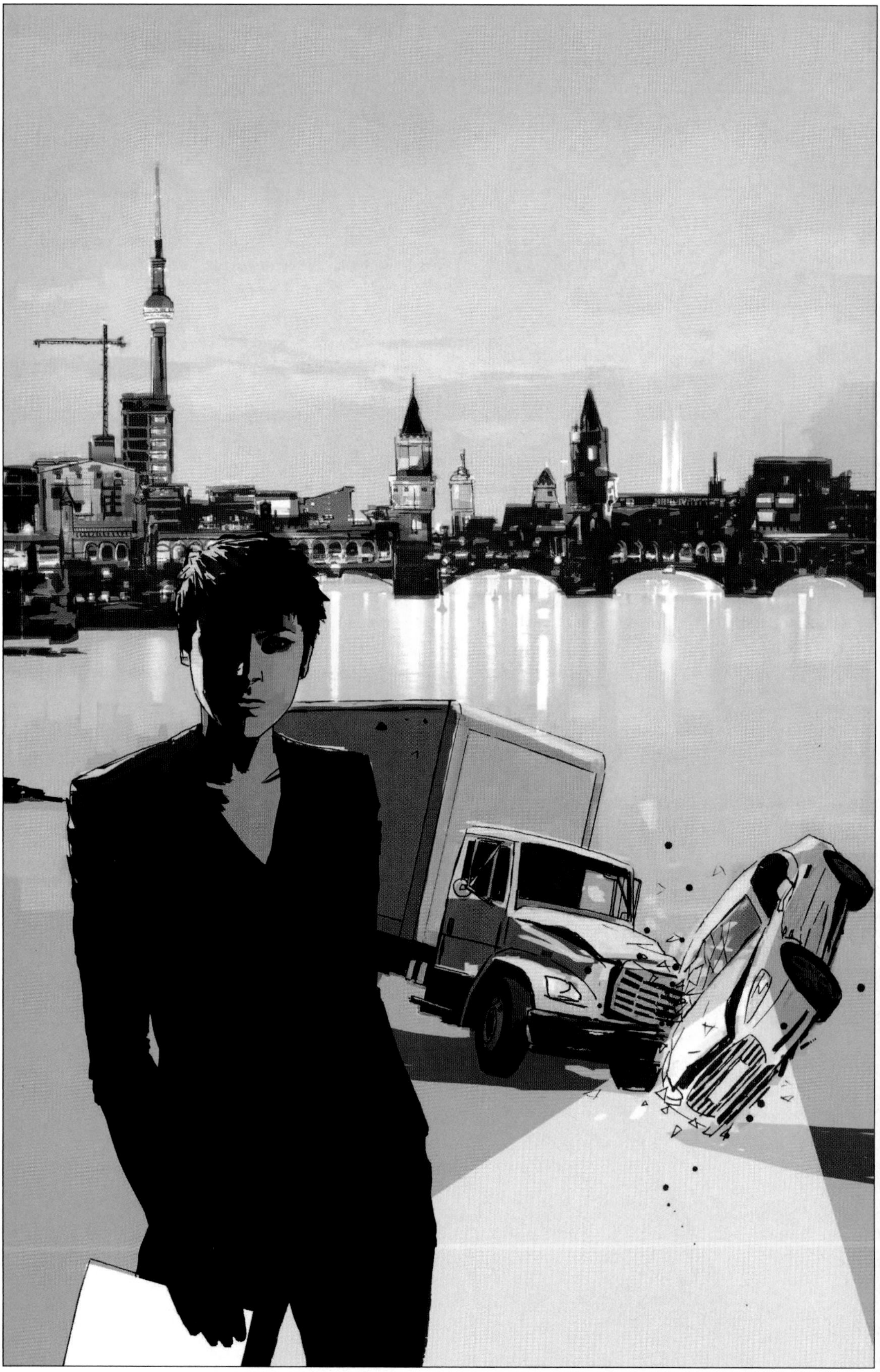

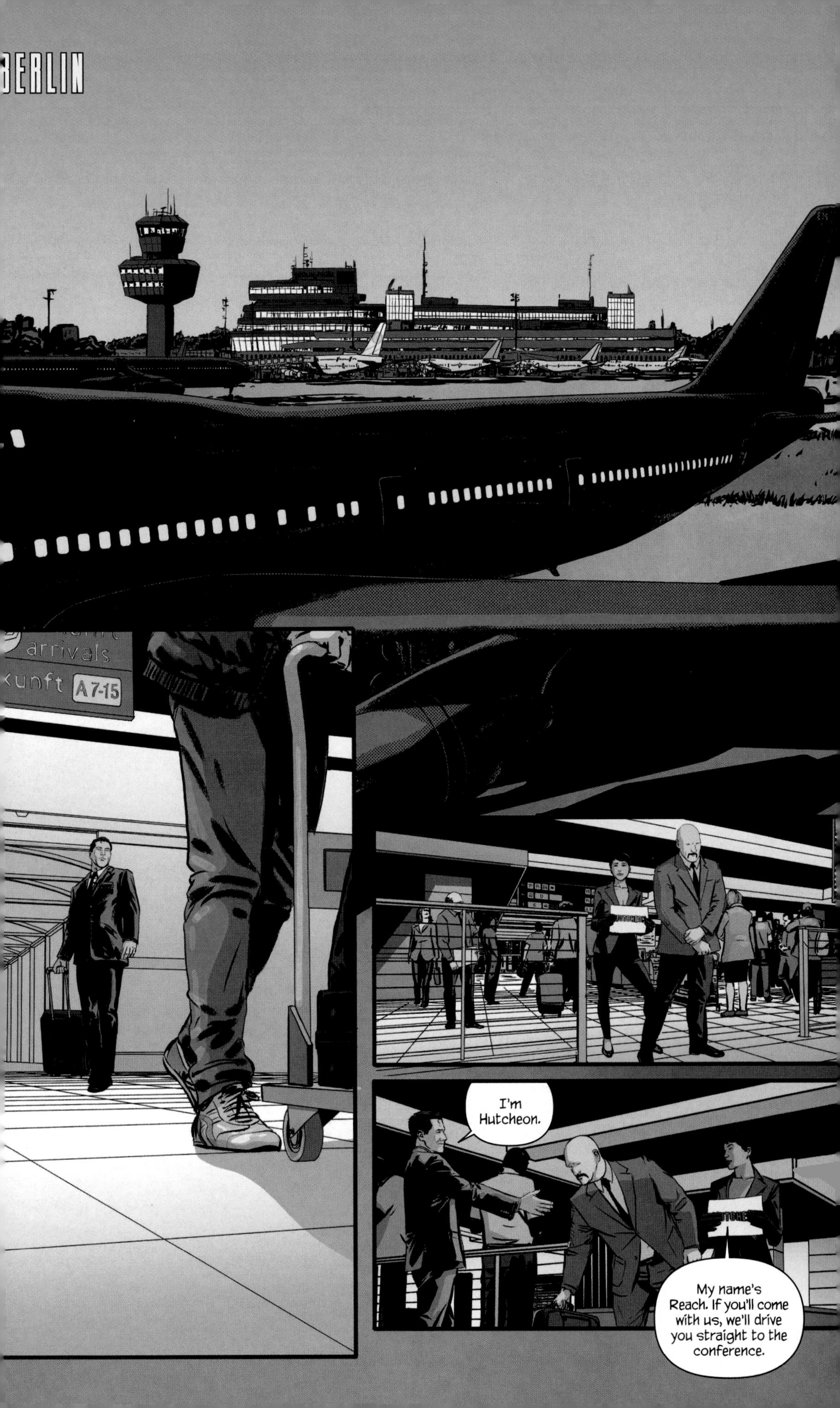
BERLIN
arrivals
kunft A7-15
I'm Hutcheon.
My name's Reach. If you'll come with us, we'll drive you straight to the conference.

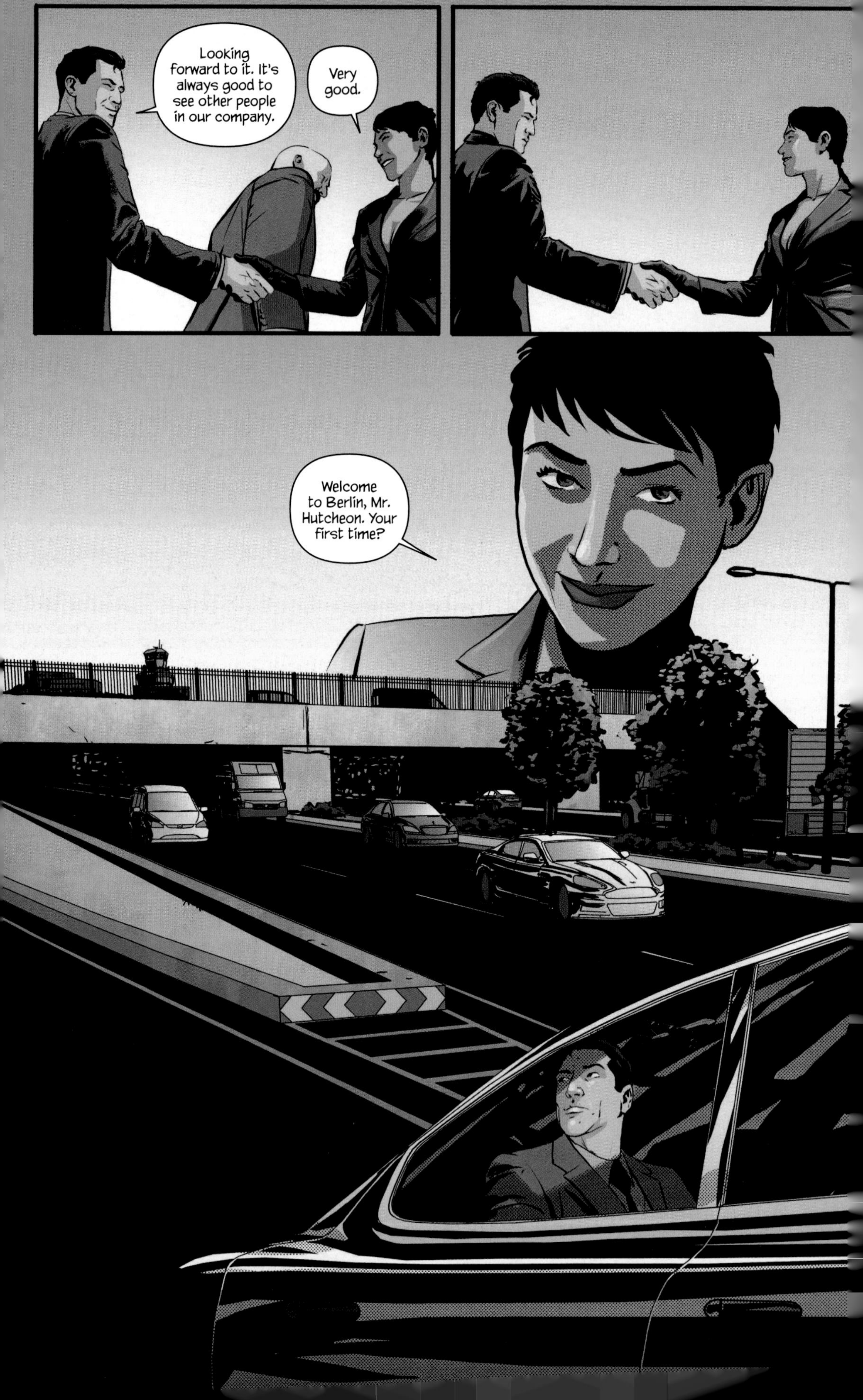
Looking forward to it. It's always good to see other people in our company.
Very good.
Welcome to Berlin, Mr. Hutcheon. Your first time?

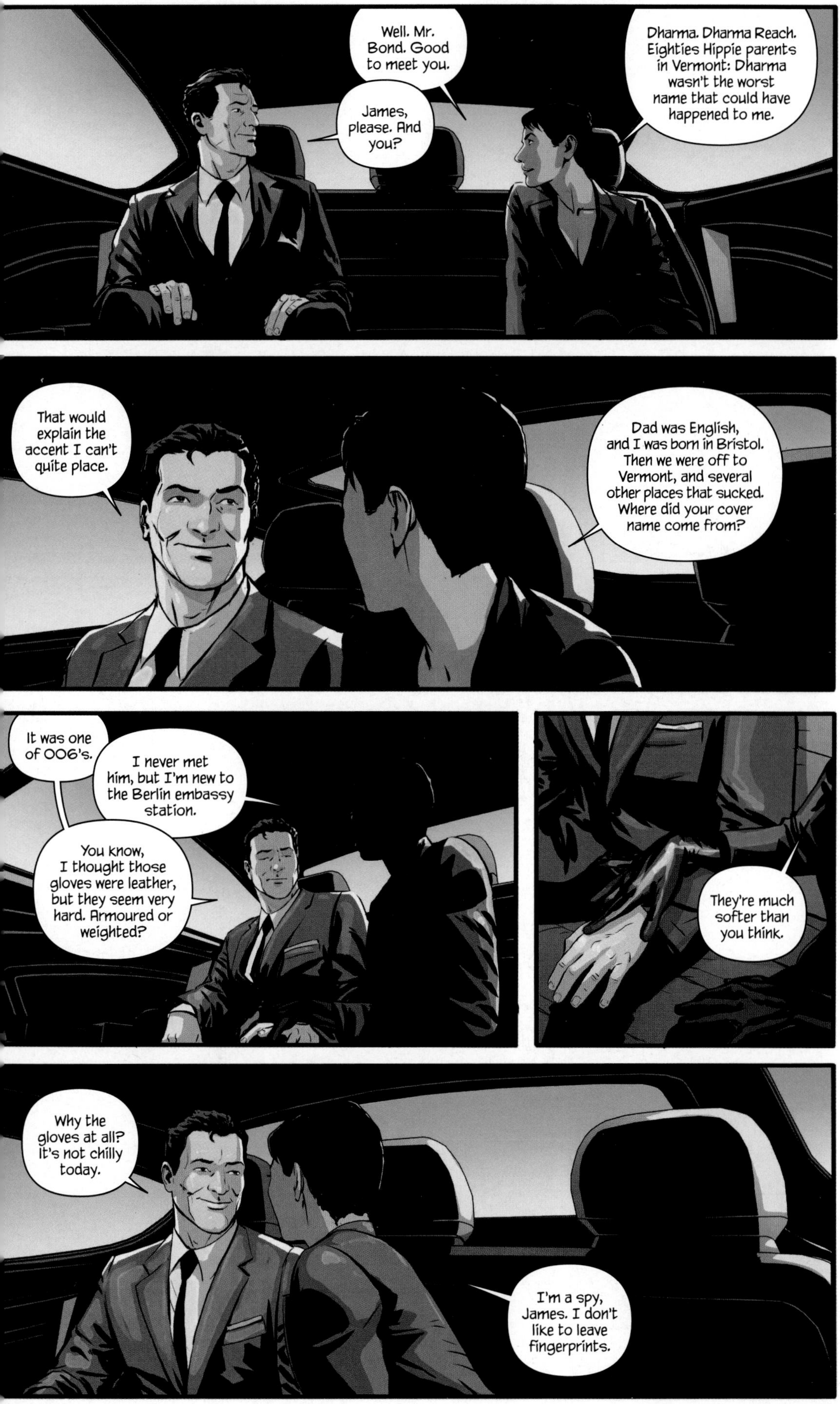
Well. Mr. Bond. Good to meet you.
James, please. And you?
Dharma. Dharma Reach. Eighties Hippie parents in Vermont: Dharma wasn't the worst name that could have happened to me.
That would explain the accent I can't quite place.
Dad was English, and I was born in Bristol. Then we were off to Vermont, and several other places that sucked. Where did your cover name come from?
It was one of 006's.
I never met him, but I'm new to the Berlin embassy station.
You know, I thought those gloves were leather, but they seem very hard. Armoured or weighted?
They're much softer than you think.
Why the gloves at all? It's not chilly today.
I'm a spy, James. I don't like to leave fingerprints.

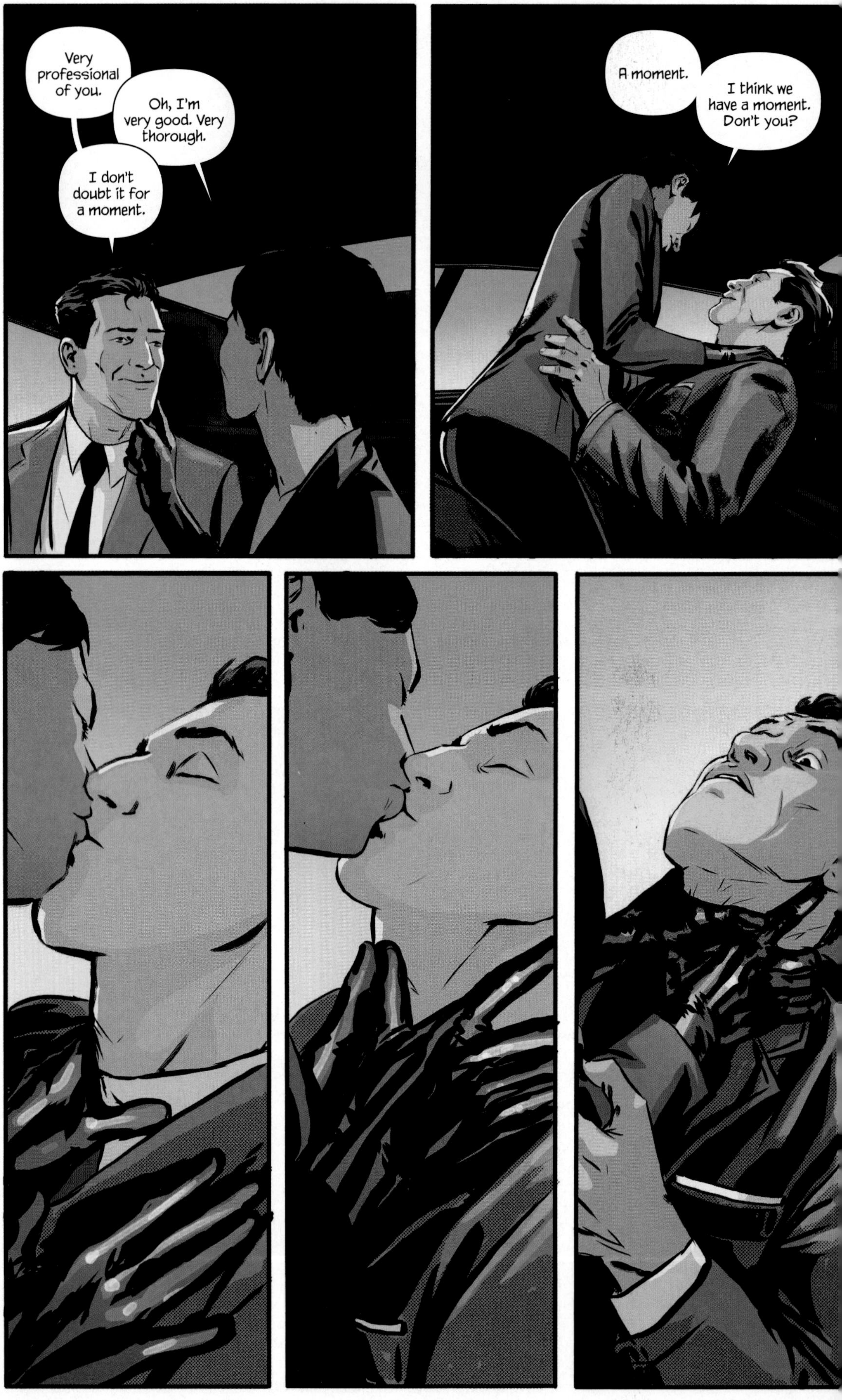
Very professional of you.
Oh, I'm very good. Very thorough.
I don't doubt it for a moment.
A moment.
I think we have a moment. Don't you?

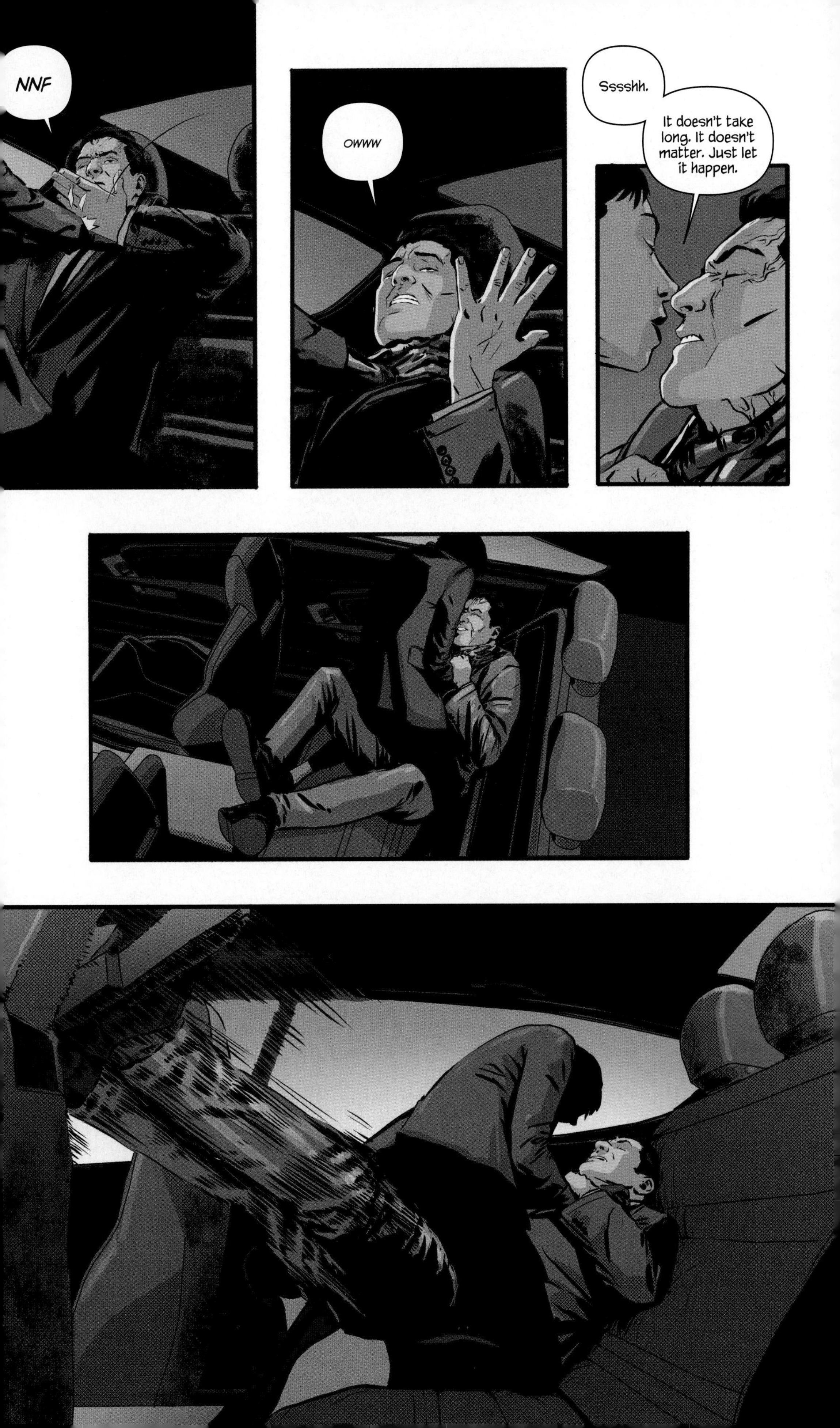
NNF
OWWW
Sssshh.
It doesn't take long. It doesn't matter. Just let it happen.

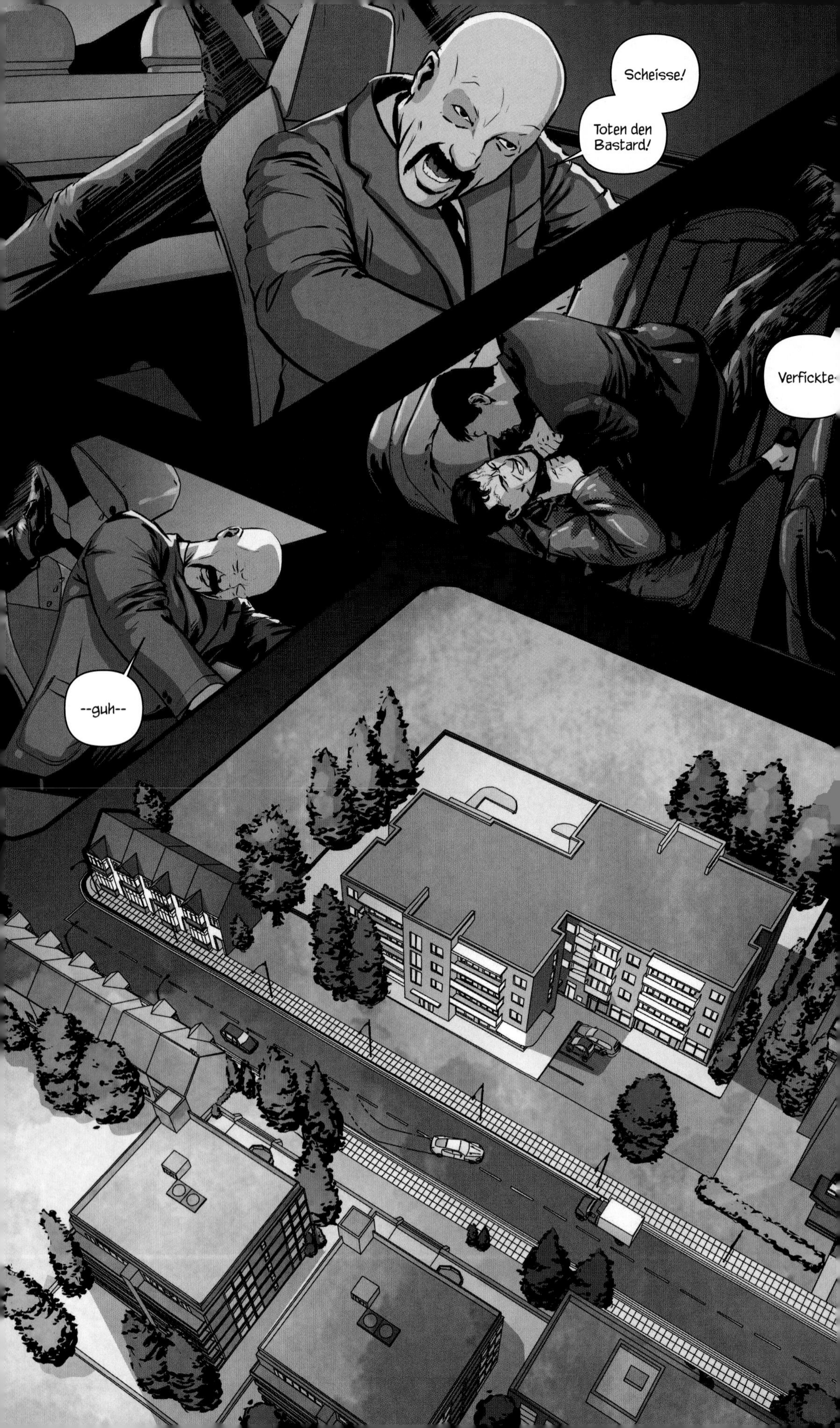
Scheisse!
Toten den Bastard!
Verfickte-
--guh--

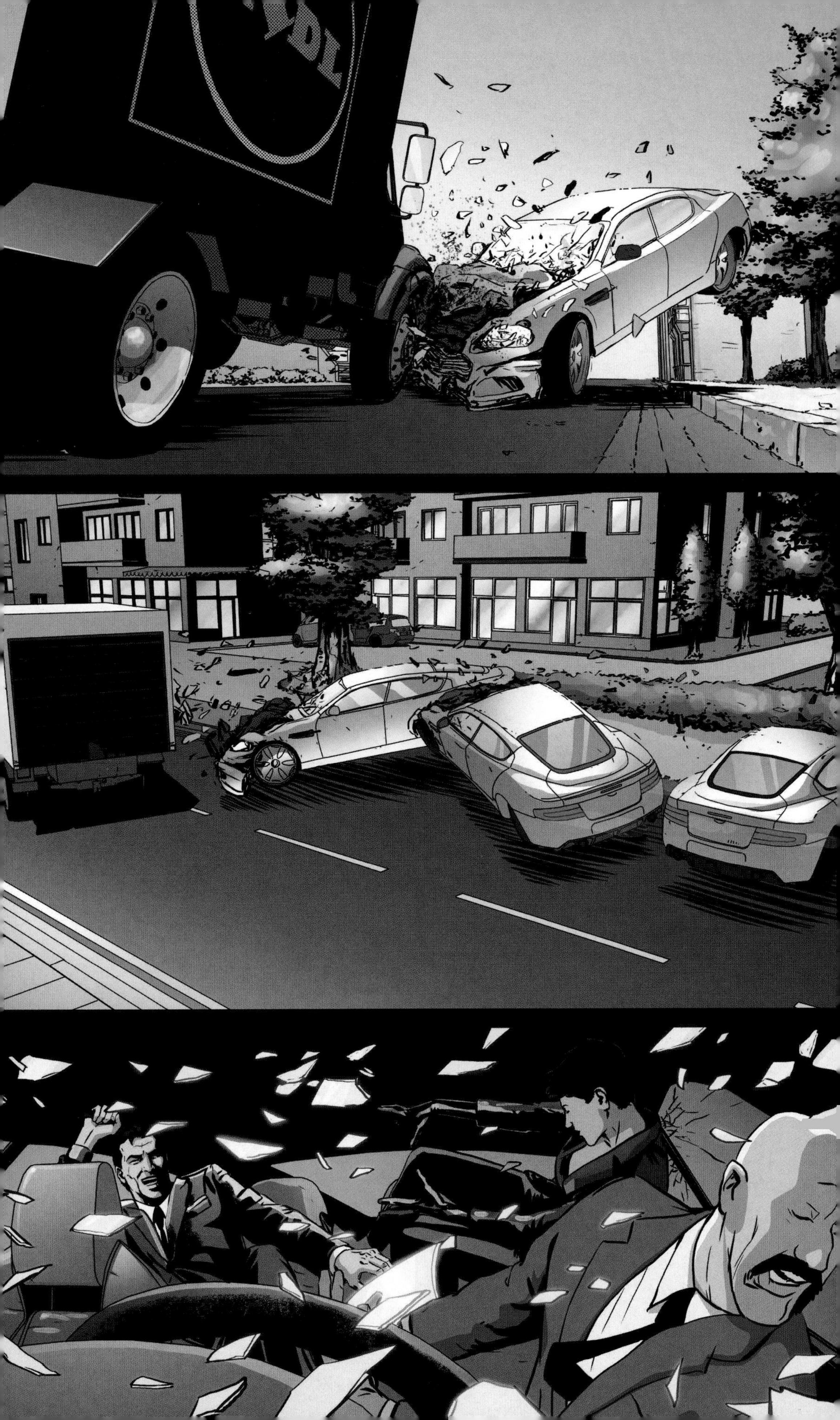

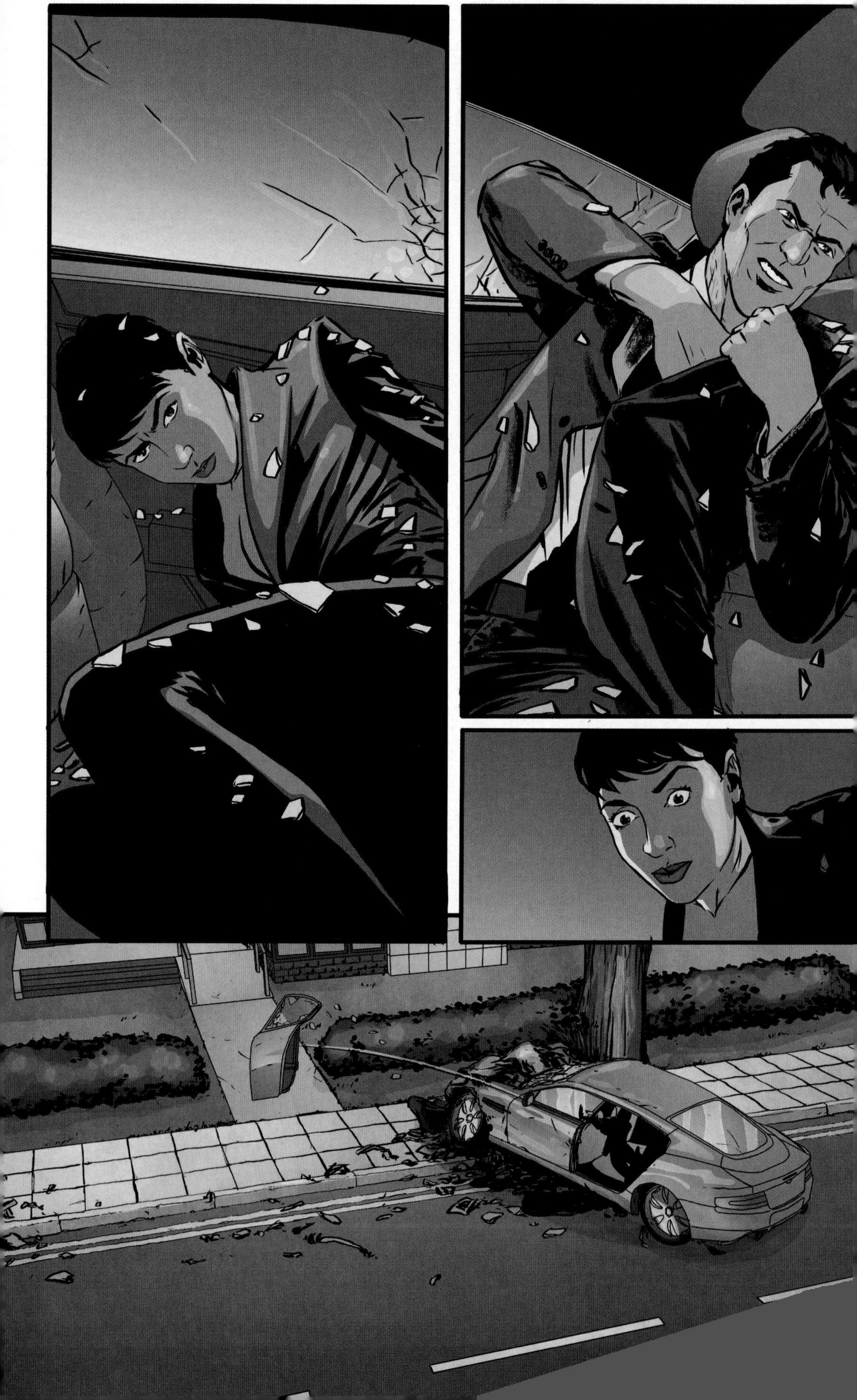

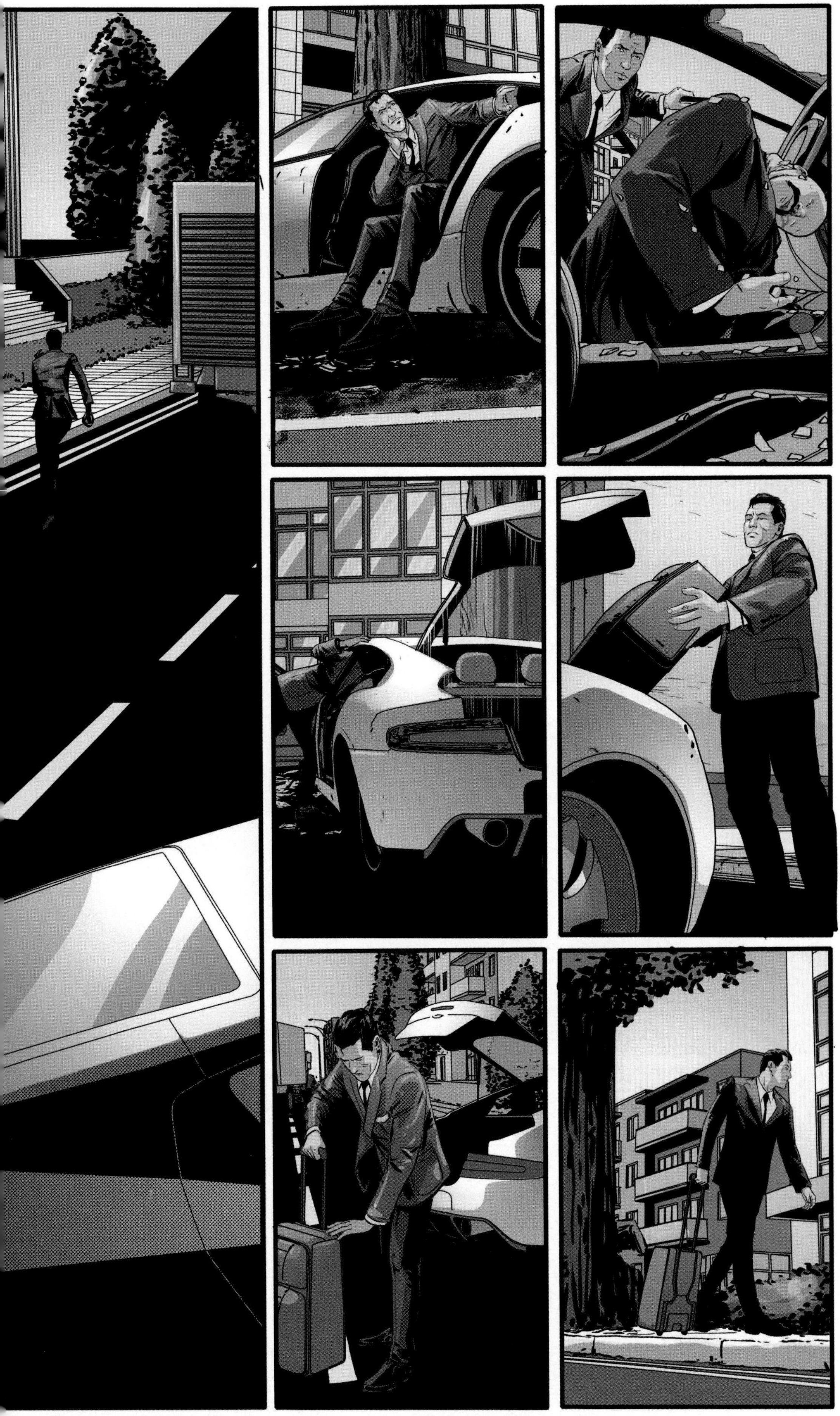

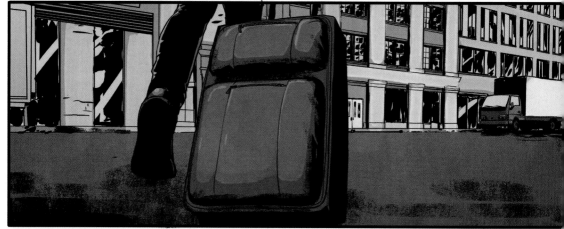

Mr. Hutcheon. We just learned your car was--

Replaced. Yes. Don't worry. It got me most of the way here. Shall we go in?

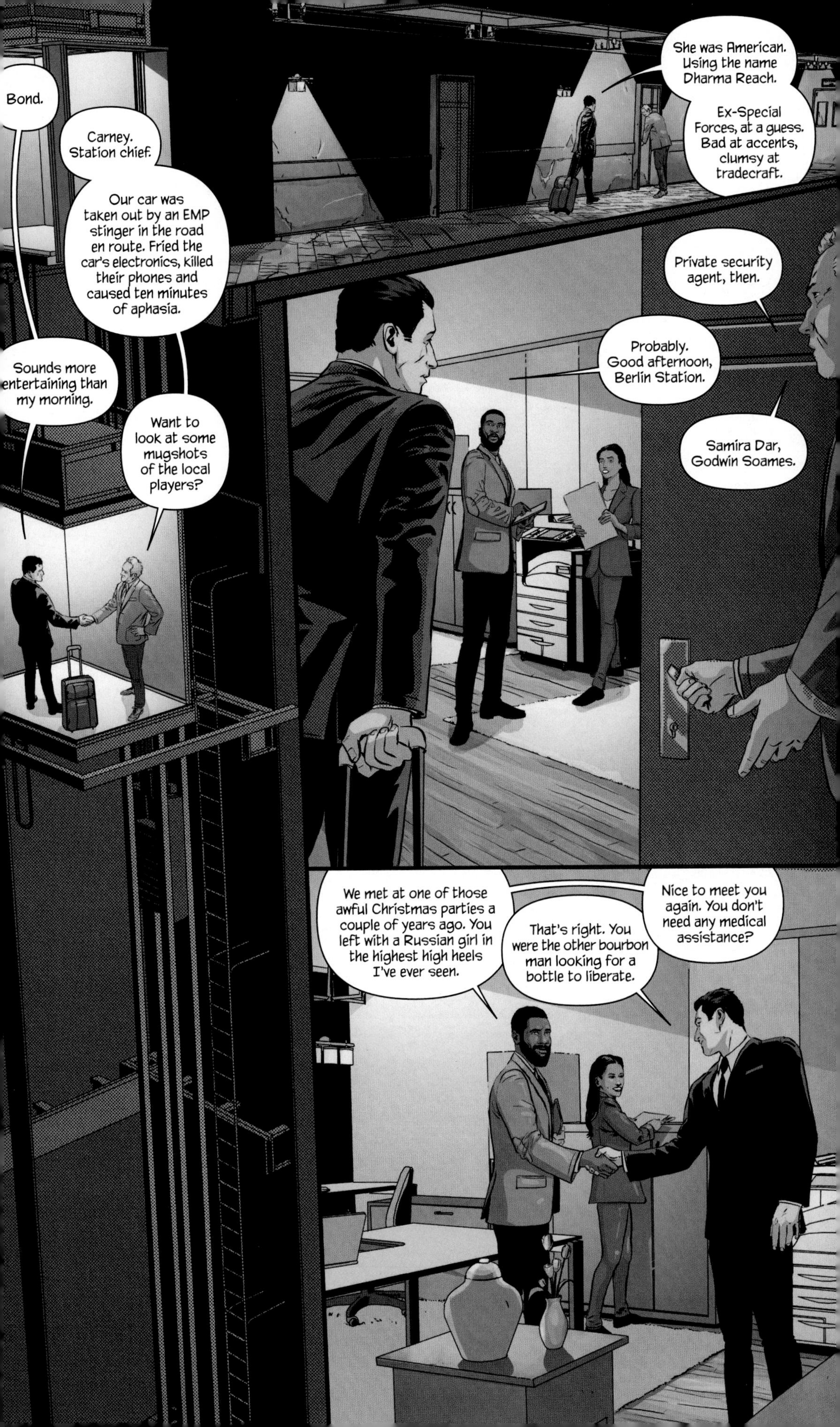
Bond.
Carney. Station chief.
Our car was taken out by an EMP stinger in the road en route. Fried the car's electronics, killed their phones and caused ten minutes of aphasia.
Sounds more entertaining than my morning.
Want to look at some mugshots of the local players?
She was American. Using the name Dharma Reach.
Ex-Special Forces, at a guess. Bad at accents, clumsy at tradecraft.
Private security agent, then.
Probably. Good afternoon, Berlin Station.
Samira Dar, Godwin Soames.
We met at one of those awful Christmas parties a couple of years ago. You left with a Russian girl in the highest high heels I've ever seen.
That's right. You were the other bourbon man looking for a bottle to liberate.
Nice to meet you again. You don't need any medical assistance?

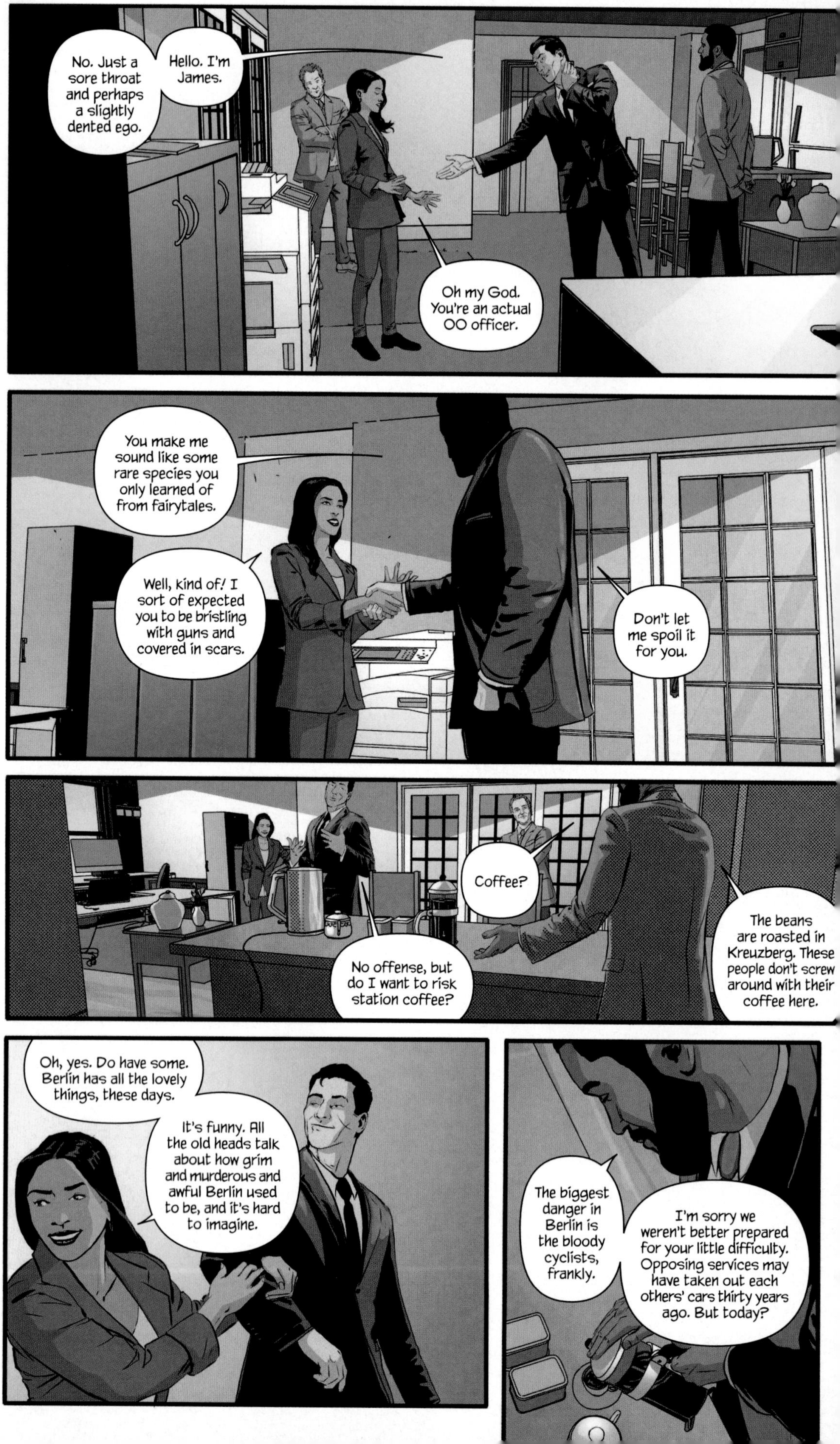
No. Just a sore throat and perhaps a slightly dented ego.
Hello. I'm James.
Oh my God. You're an actual 00 officer.
You make me sound like some rare species you only learned of from fairytales.
Well, kind of! I sort of expected you to be bristling with guns and covered in scars.
Don't let me spoil it for you.
Coffee?
No offense, but do I want to risk station coffee?
The beans are roasted in Kreuzberg. These people don't screw around with their coffee here.
Oh, yes. Do have some. Berlin has all the lovely things, these days.
It's funny. All the old heads talk about how grim and murderous and awful Berlin used to be, and it's hard to imagine.
The biggest danger in Berlin is the bloody cyclists, frankly.
I'm sorry we weren't better prepared for your little difficulty. Opposing services may have taken out each others' cars thirty years ago. But today?

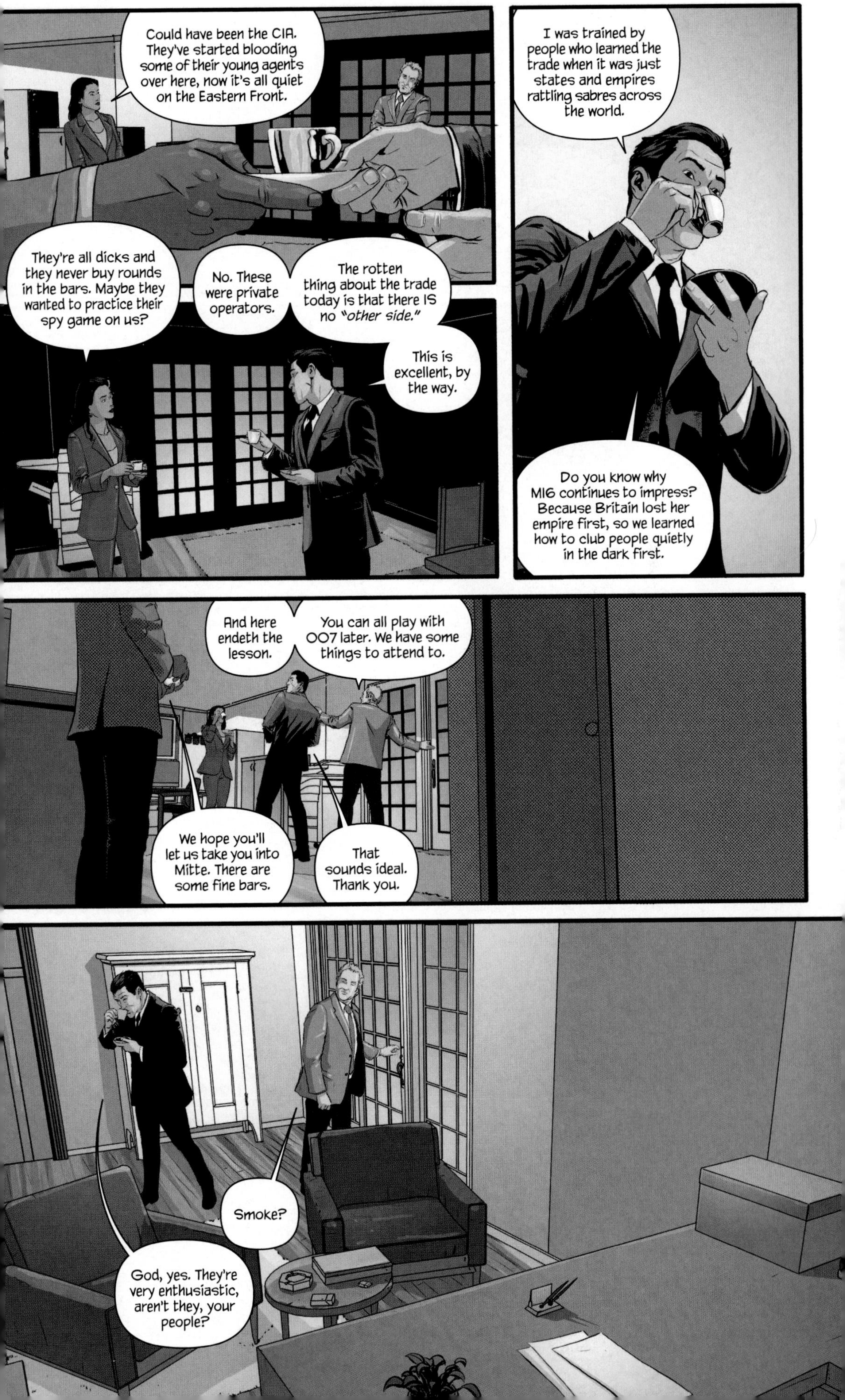
Could have been the CIA. They've started blooding some of their young agents over here, now it's all quiet on the Eastern Front.
I was trained by people who learned the trade when it was just states and empires rattling sabres across the world.
They're all dicks and they never buy rounds in the bars. Maybe they wanted to practice their spy game on us?
No. These were private operators.
The rotten thing about the trade today is that there IS no "other side."
This is excellent, by the way.
Do you know why MI6 continues to impress? Because Britain lost her empire first, so we learned how to club people quietly in the dark first.
And here endeth the lesson.
You can all play with 007 later. We have some things to attend to.
We hope you'll let us take you into Mitte. There are some fine bars.
That sounds ideal. Thank you.
Smoke?
God, yes. They're very enthusiastic, aren't they, your people?

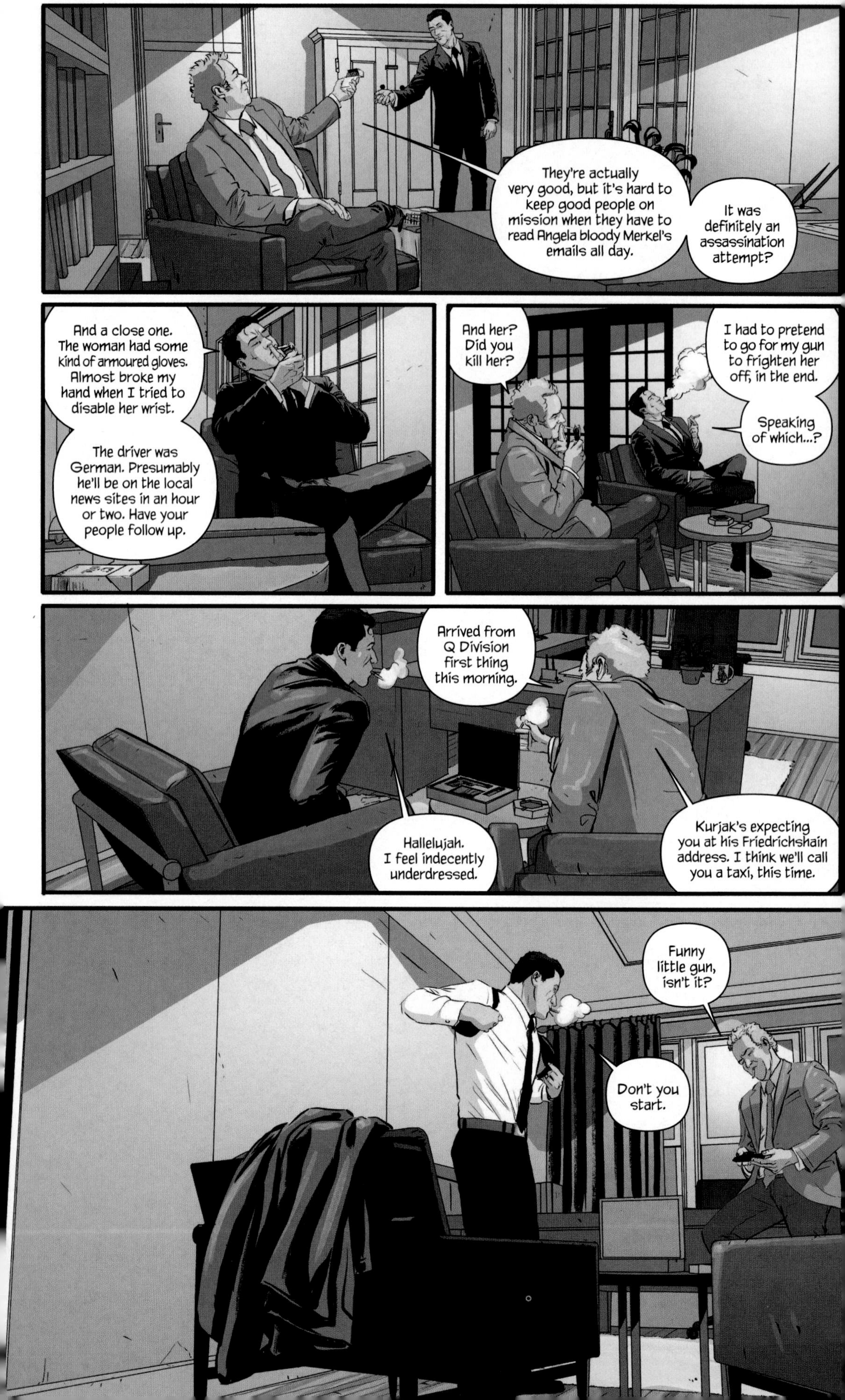
They're actually very good, but it's hard to keep good people on mission when they have to read Angela bloody Merkel's emails all day.
It was definitely an assassination attempt?
And a close one. The woman had some kind of armoured gloves. Almost broke my hand when I tried to disable her wrist.
The driver was German. Presumably he'll be on the local news sites in an hour or two. Have your people follow up.
And her? Did you kill her?
I had to pretend to go for my gun to frighten her off, in the end.
Speaking of which...?
Arrived from Q Division first thing this morning.
Hallelujah. I feel indecently underdressed.
Kurjak's expecting you at his Friedrichshain address. I think we'll call you a taxi, this time.
Funny little gun, isn't it?
Don't you start.

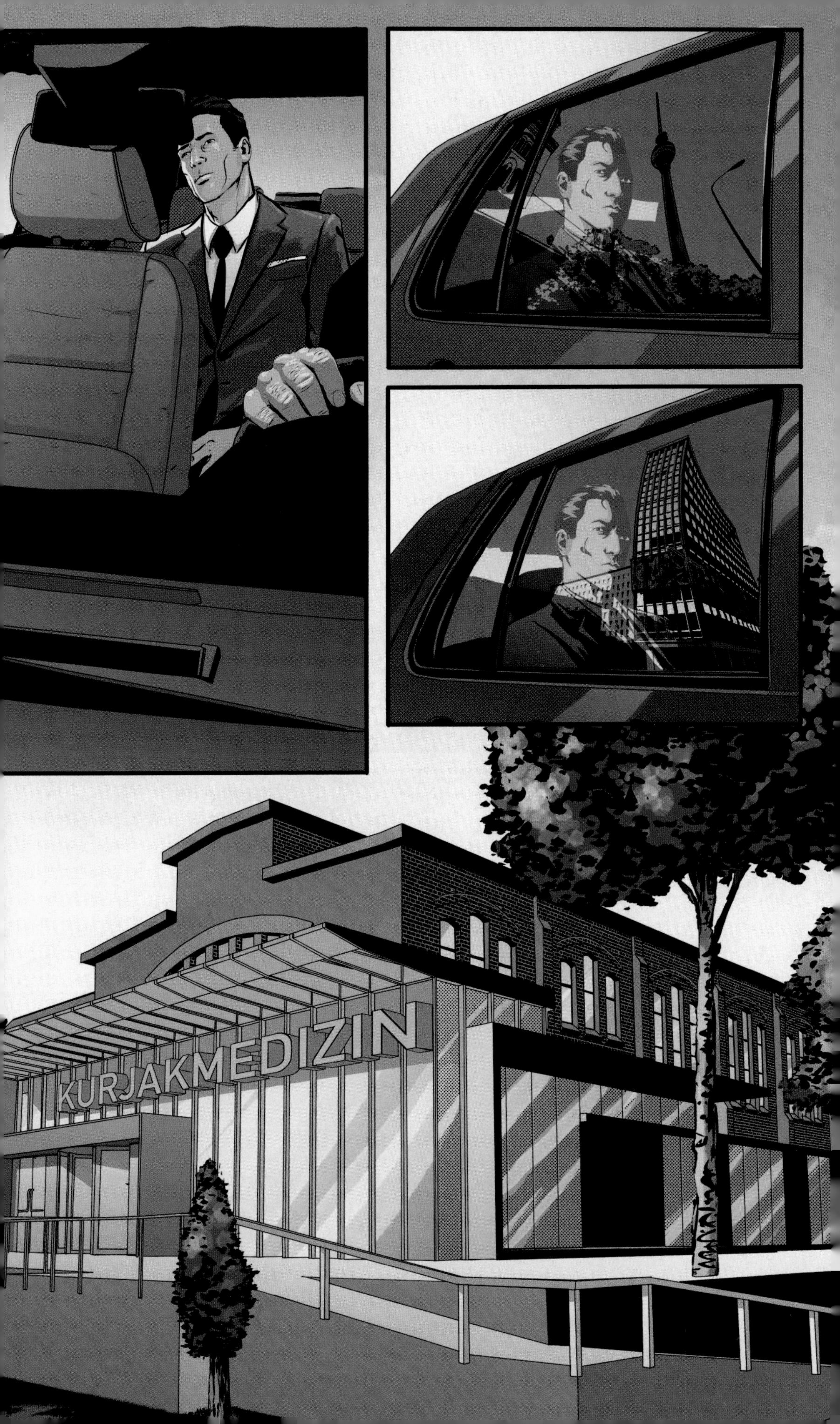
KURJAKMEDIZIN

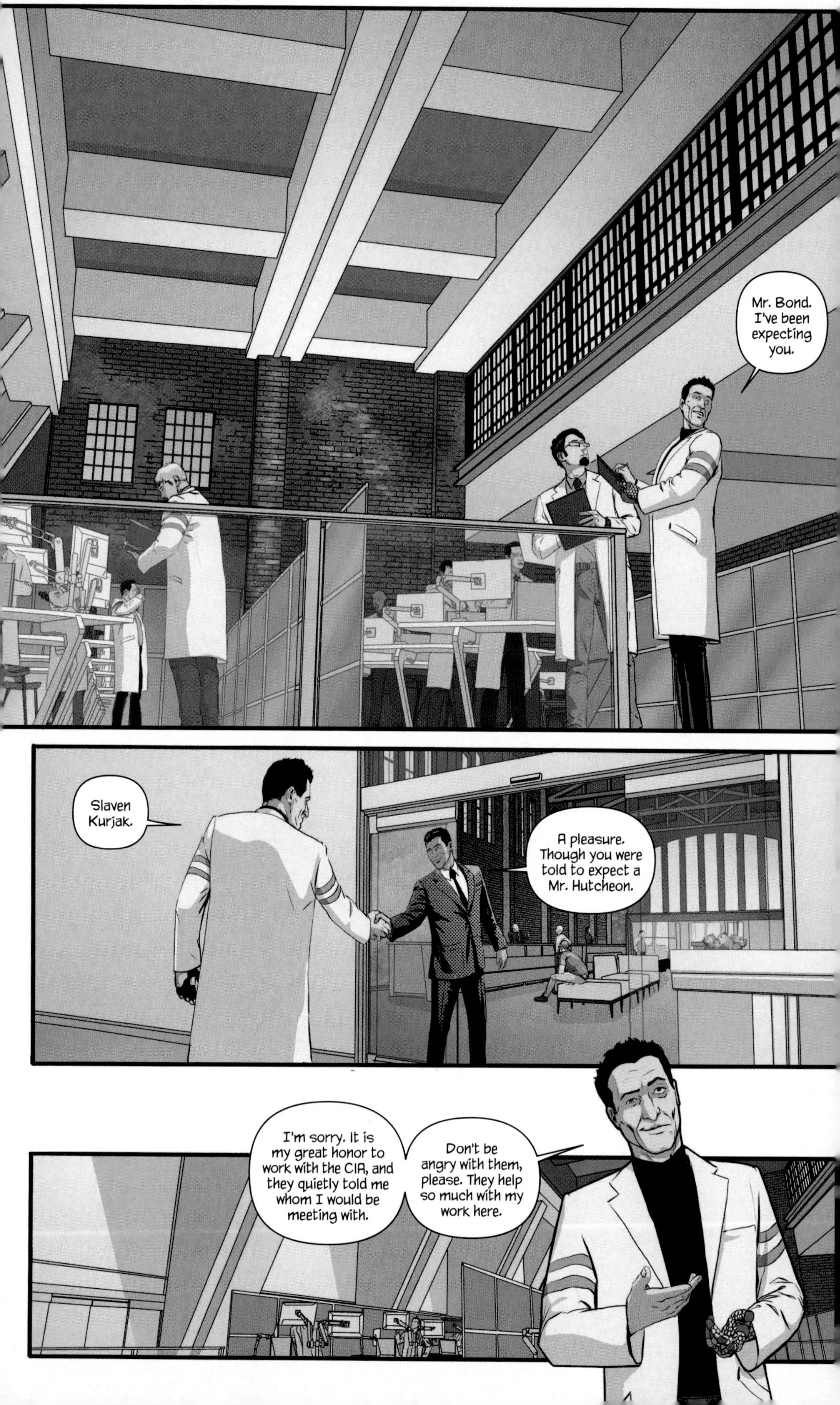
Mr. Bond. I've been expecting you.
Slaven Kurjak.
A pleasure. Though you were told to expect a Mr. Hutcheon.
I'm sorry. It is my great honor to work with the CIA, and they quietly told me whom I would be meeting with.
Don't be angry with them, please. They help so much with my work here.

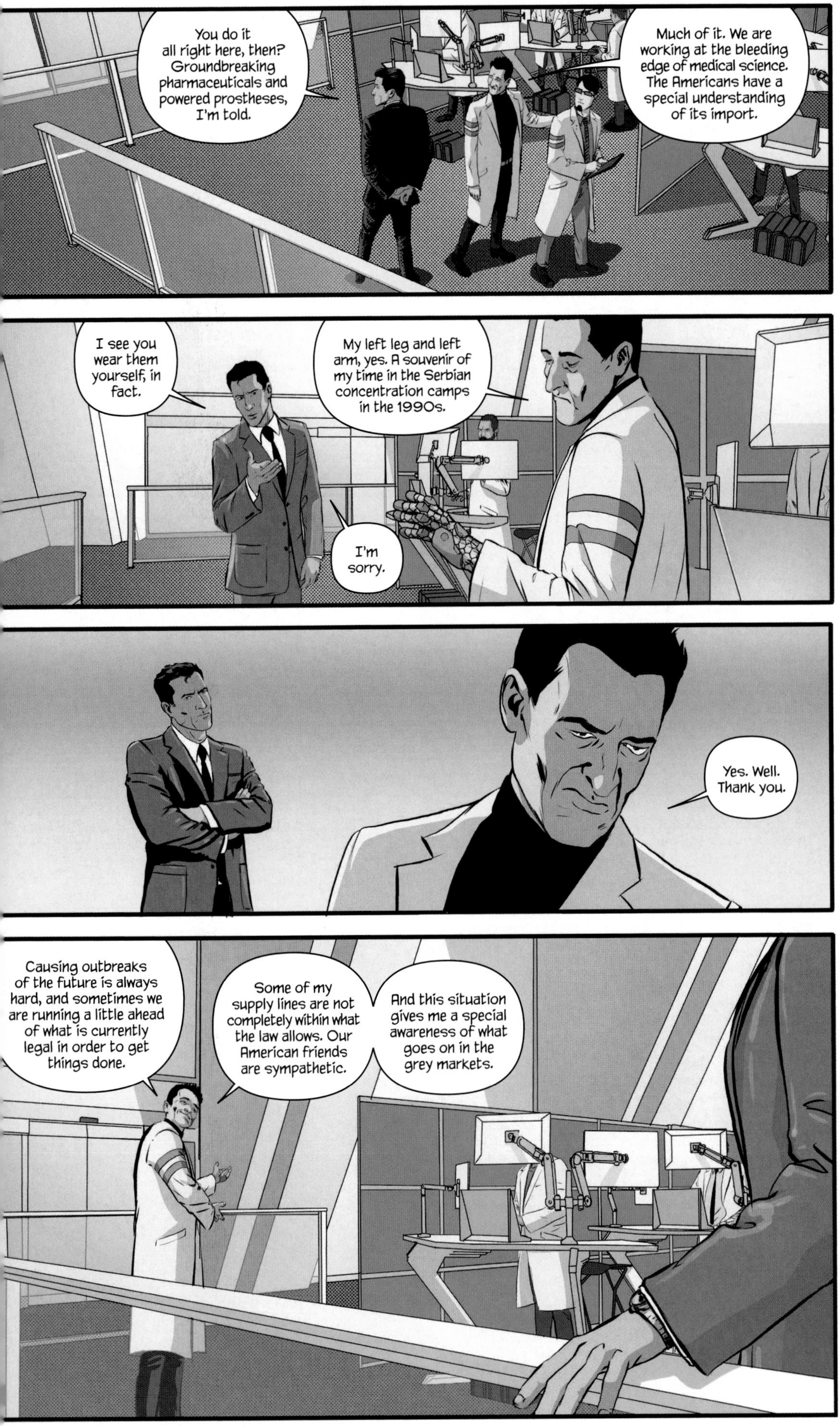
You do it all right here, then? Groundbreaking pharmaceuticals and powered prostheses, I'm told.
Much of it. We are working at the bleeding edge of medical science. The Americans have a special understanding of its import.
I see you wear them yourself, in fact.
My left leg and left arm, yes. A souvenir of my time in the Serbian concentration camps in the 1990s.
I'm sorry.
Yes. Well. Thank you.
Causing outbreaks of the future is always hard, and sometimes we are running a little ahead of what is currently legal in order to get things done.
Some of my supply lines are not completely within what the law allows. Our American friends are sympathetic.
And this situation gives me a special awareness of what goes on in the grey markets.

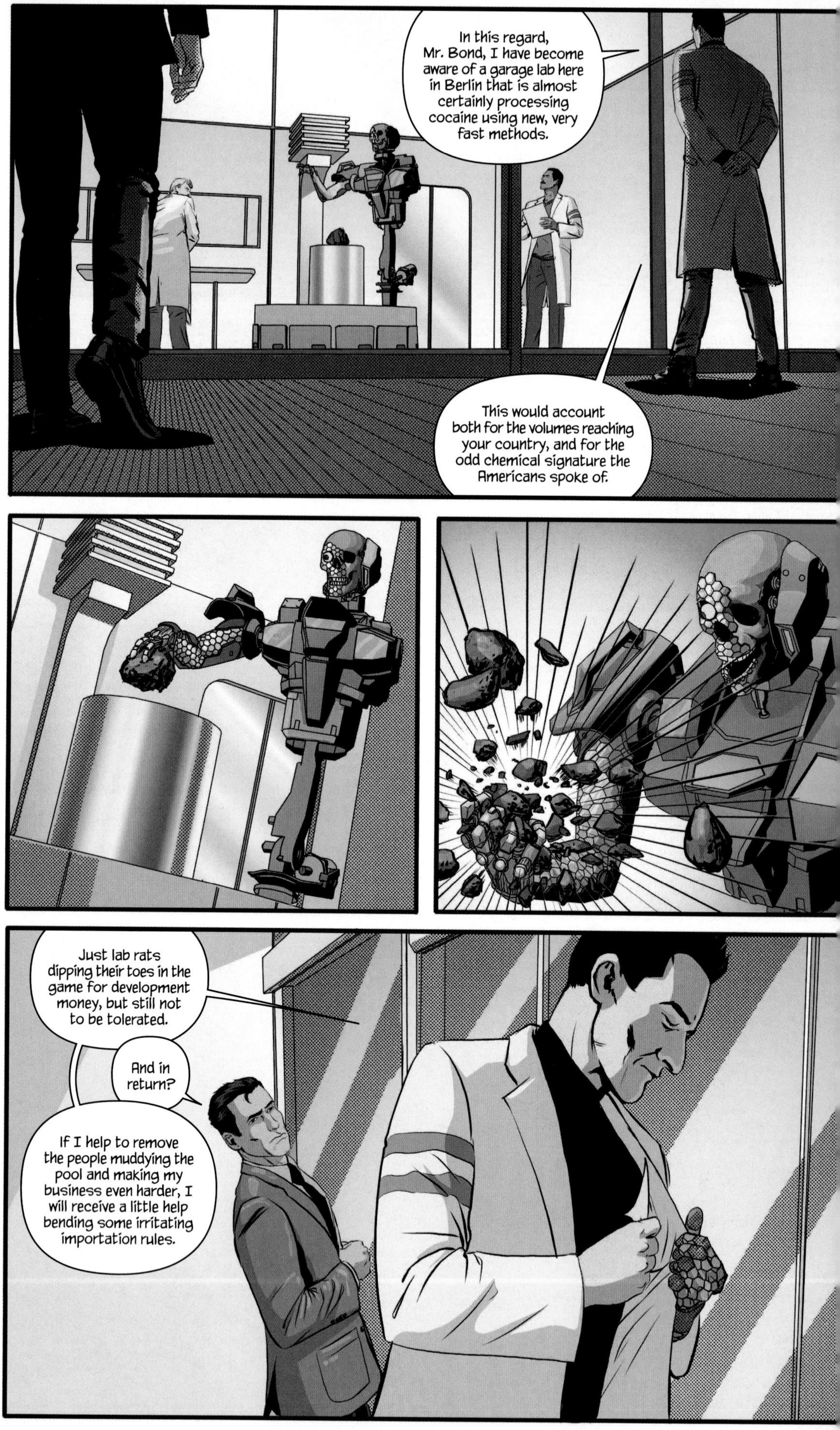
In this regard, Mr. Bond, I have become aware of a garage lab here in Berlin that is almost certainly processing cocaine using new, very fast methods.
This would account both for the volumes reaching your country, and for the odd chemical signature the Americans spoke of.
Just lab rats dipping their toes in the game for development money, but still not to be tolerated.
And in return?
If I help to remove the people muddying the pool and making my business even harder, I will receive a little help bending some irritating importation rules.

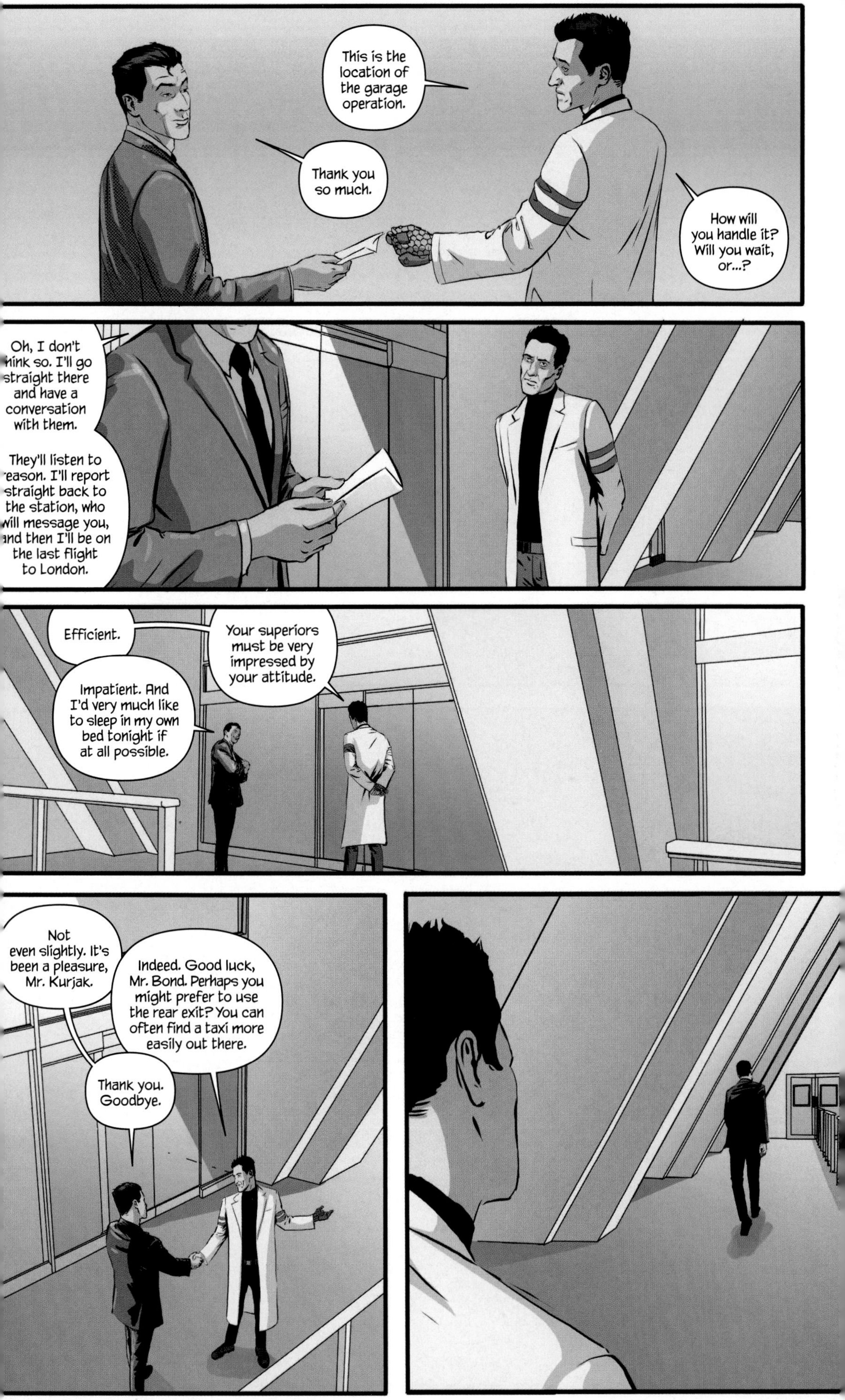
This is the location of the garage operation.
Thank you so much.
How will you handle it? Will you wait, or...?
Oh, I don't hink so. I'll go straight there and have a conversation with them.
They'll listen to eason. I'll report straight back to the station, who vill message you, and then I'll be on the last flight to London.
Efficient.
Your superiors must be very impressed by your attitude.
Impatient. And I'd very much like to sleep in my own bed tonight if at all possible.
Not even slightly. It's been a pleasure, Mr. Kurjak.
Indeed. Good luck, Mr. Bond. Perhaps you might prefer to use the rear exit? You can often find a taxi more easily out there.
Thank you. Goodbye.

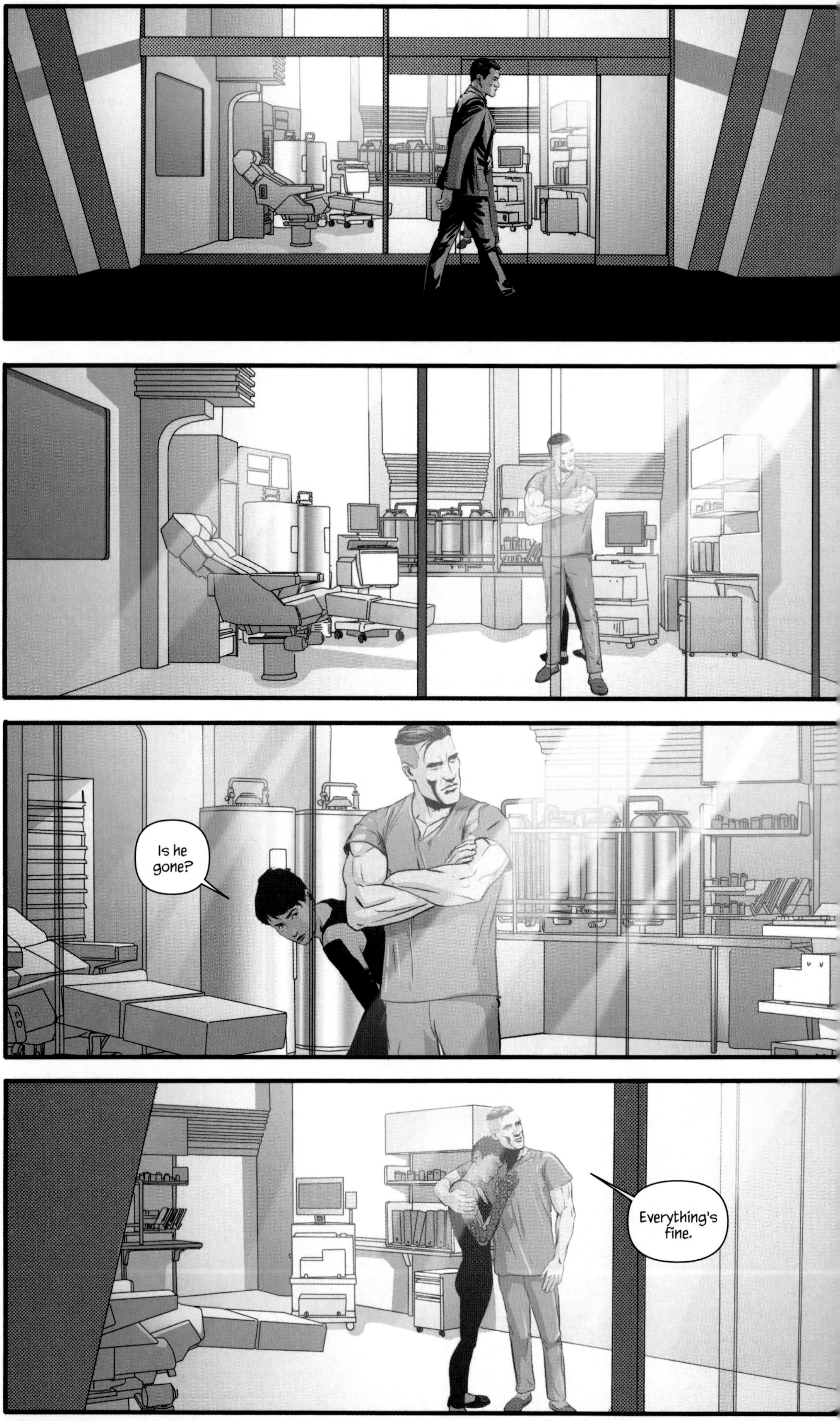
Is he gone?
Everything's fine.

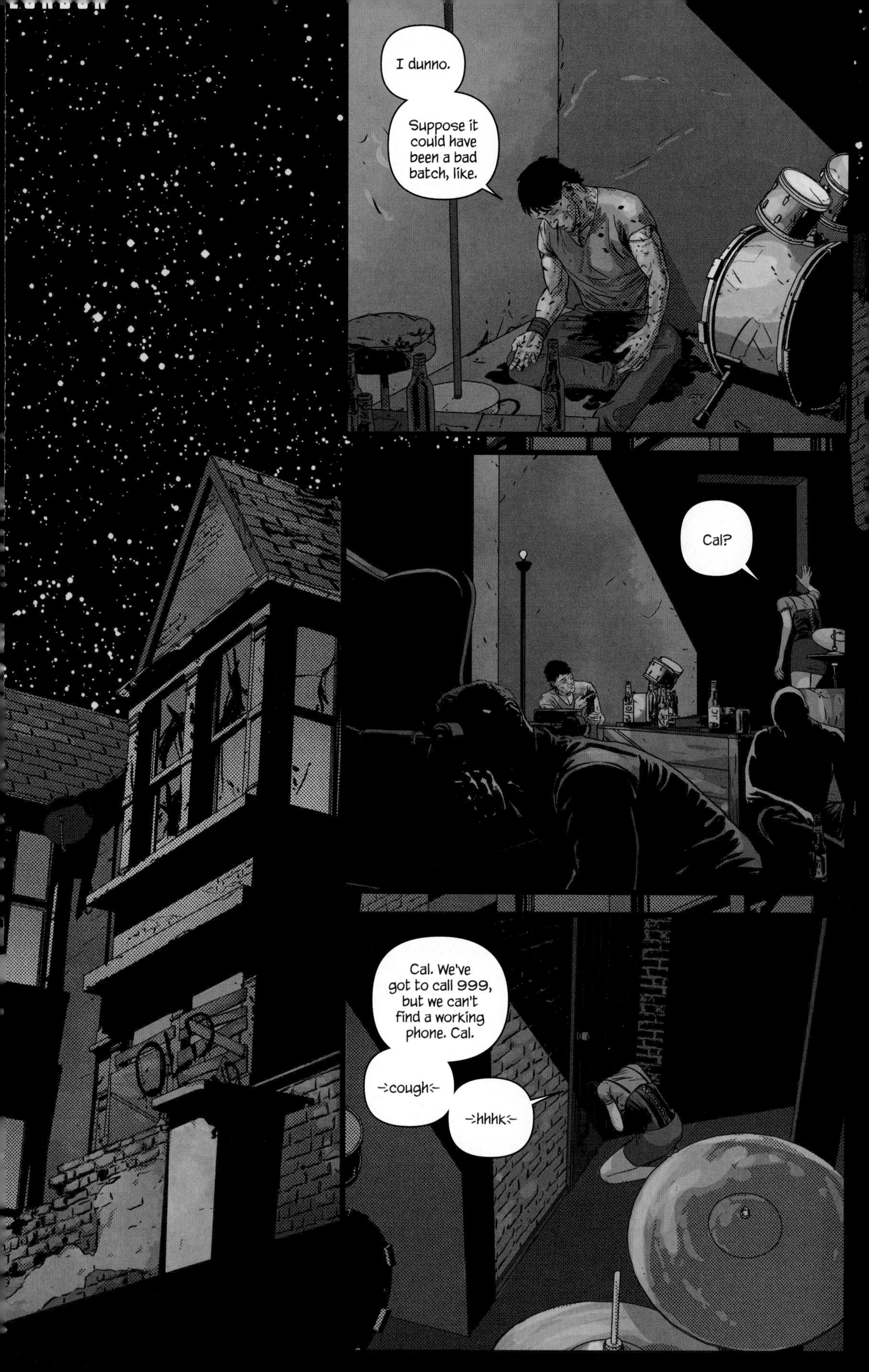
I dunno.
Suppose it could have been a bad batch, like.
Cal?
Cal. We've got to call 999, but we can't find a working phone. Cal.
-cough-
-hhhk-

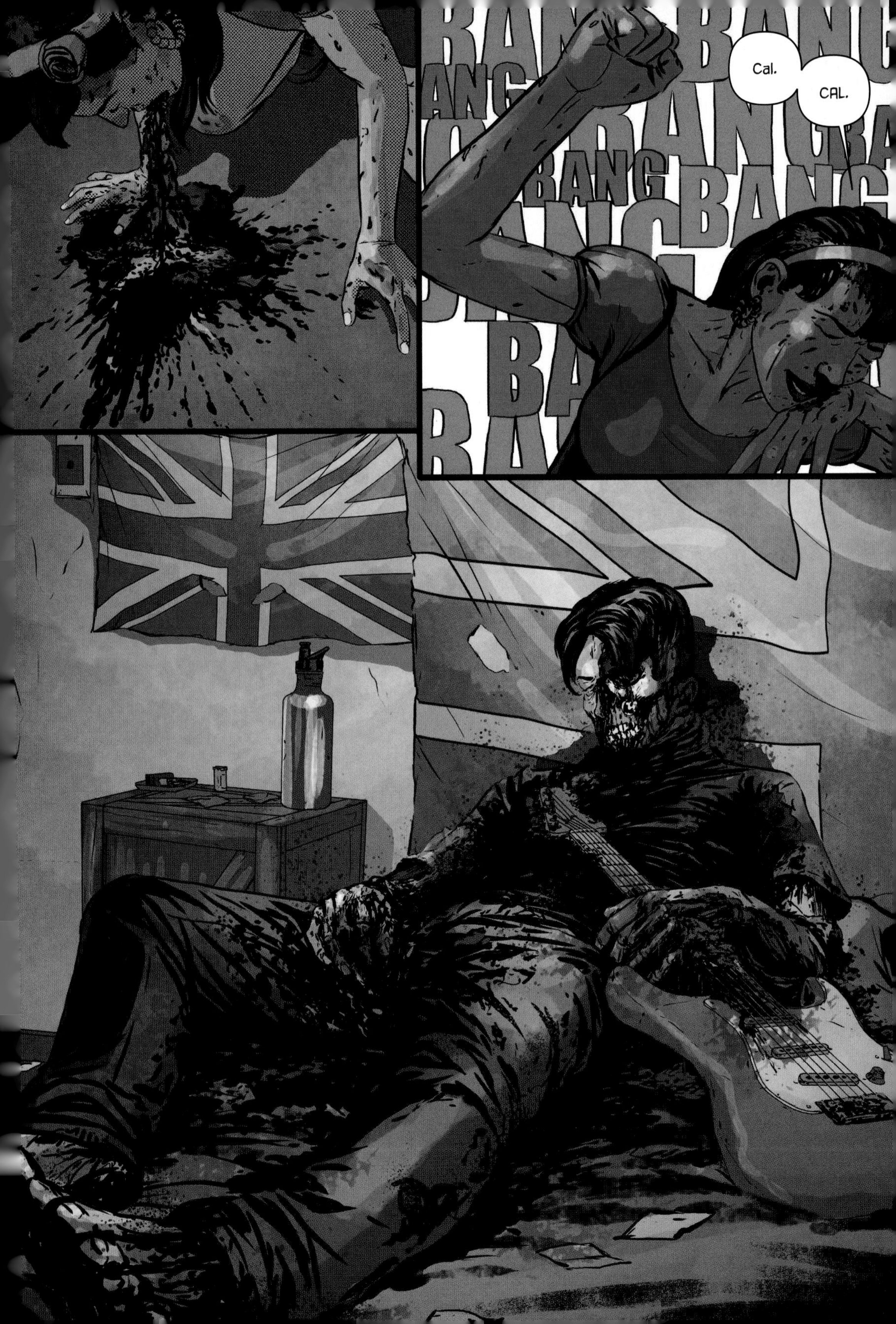
BANG
BANG
Cal.
CAL.

ISSUE 003

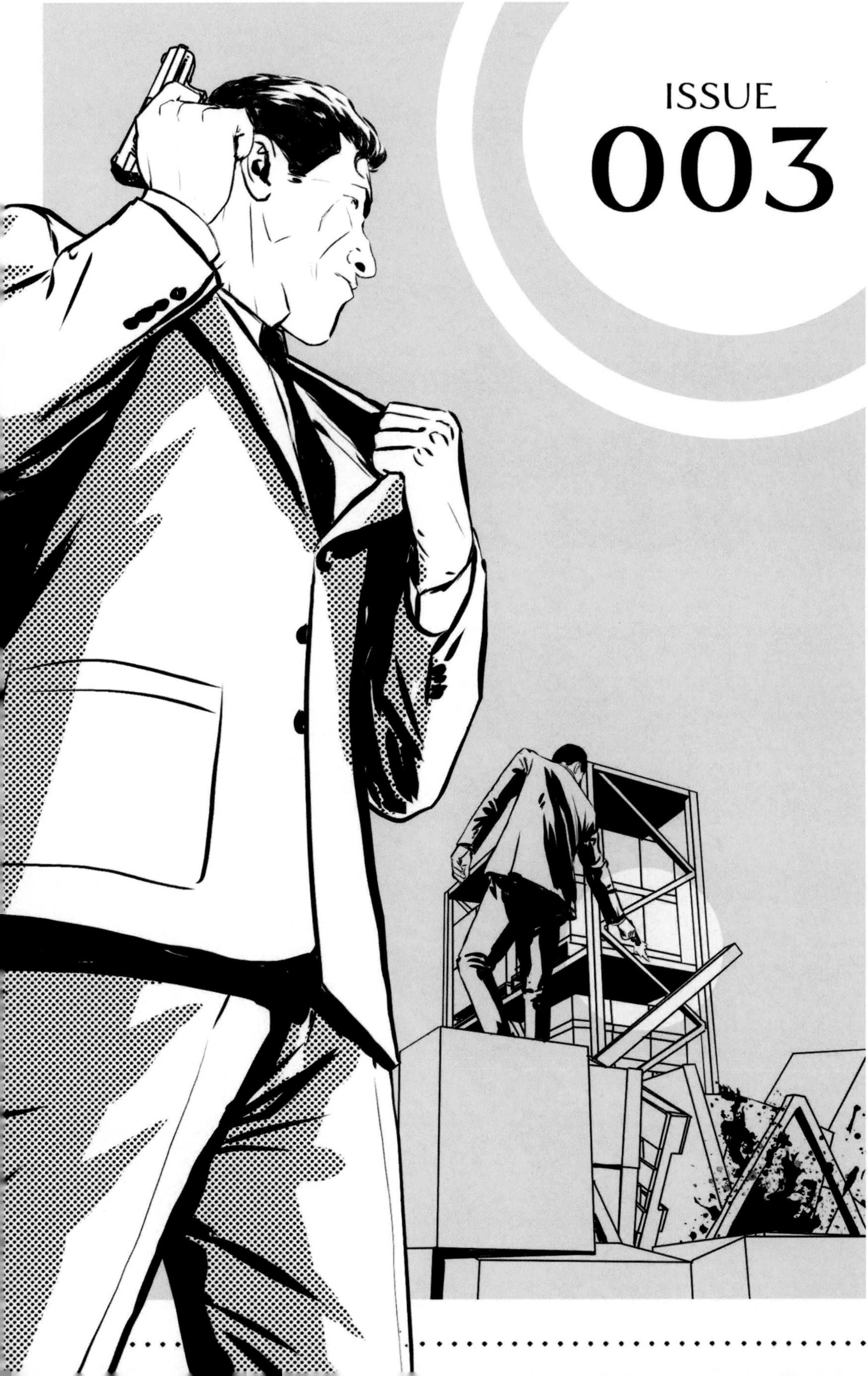

issue #3 main cover by **DOM REARDON**

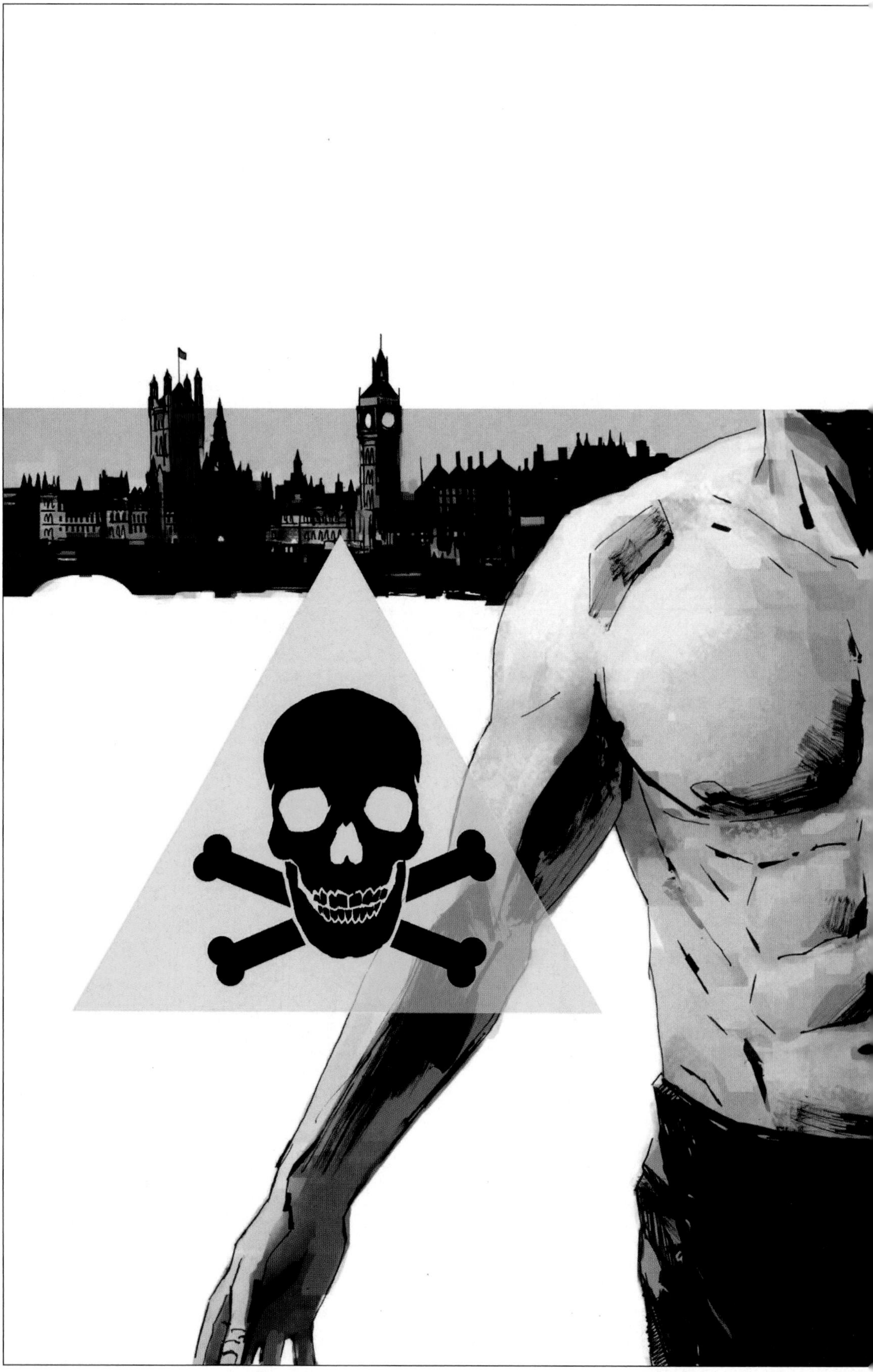

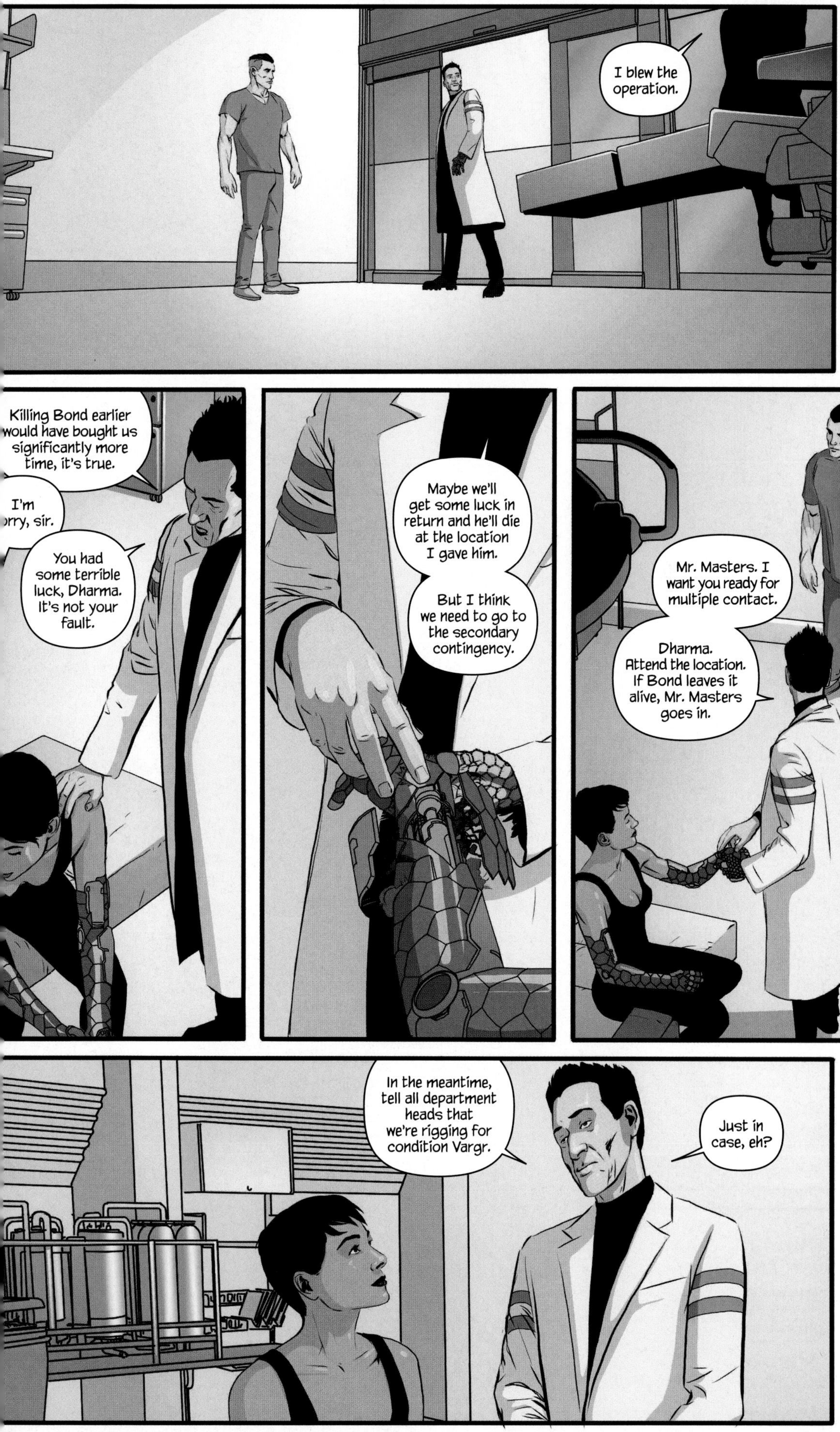
I blew the operation.
Killing Bond earlier would have bought us significantly more time, it's true.
I'm orry, sir.
You had some terrible luck, Dharma. It's not your fault.
Maybe we'll get some luck in return and he'll die at the location I gave him.
But I think we need to go to the secondary contingency.
Mr. Masters. I want you ready for multiple contact.
Dharma. Attend the location. If Bond leaves it alive, Mr. Masters goes in.
In the meantime, tell all department heads that we're rigging for condition Vargr.
Just in case, eh?

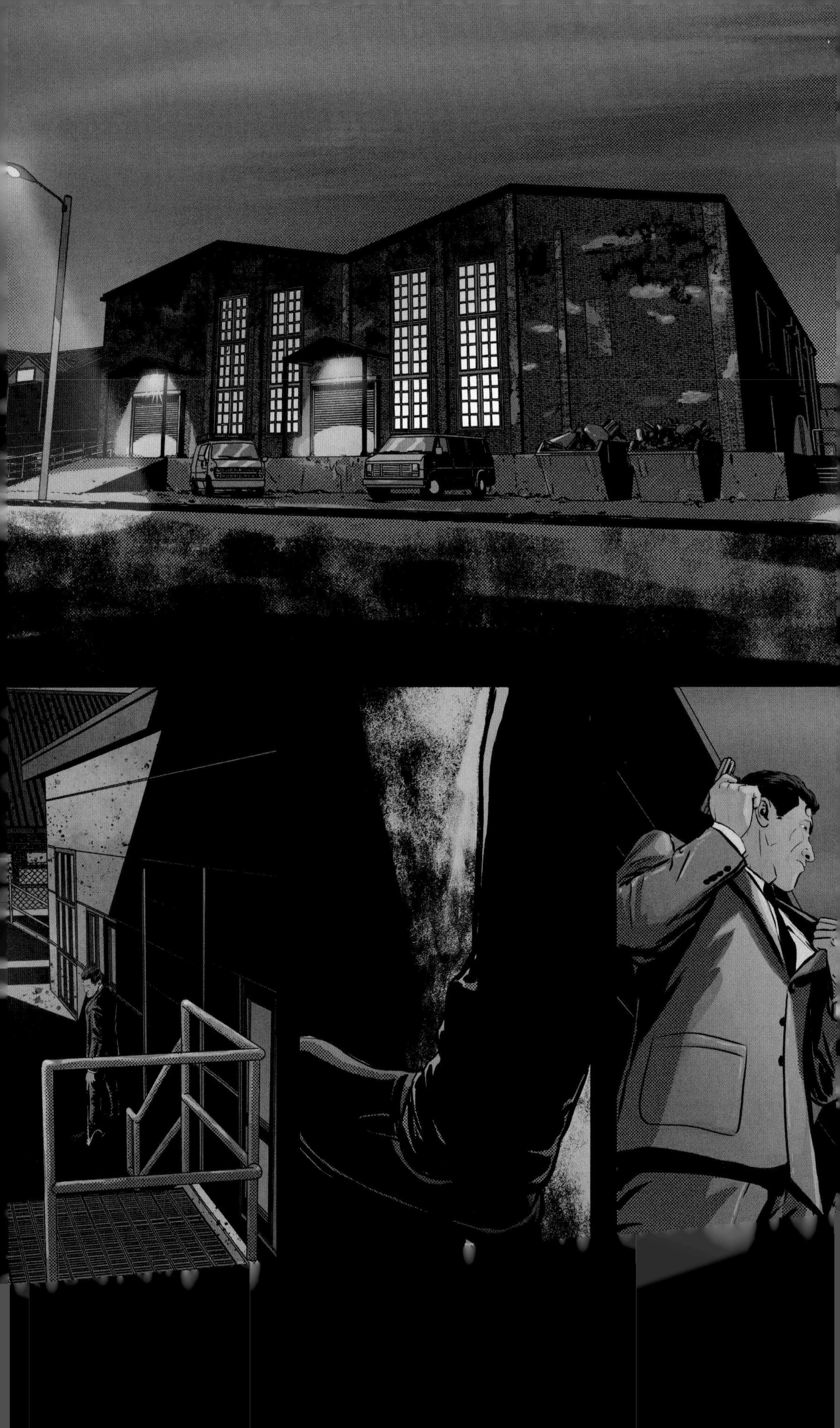

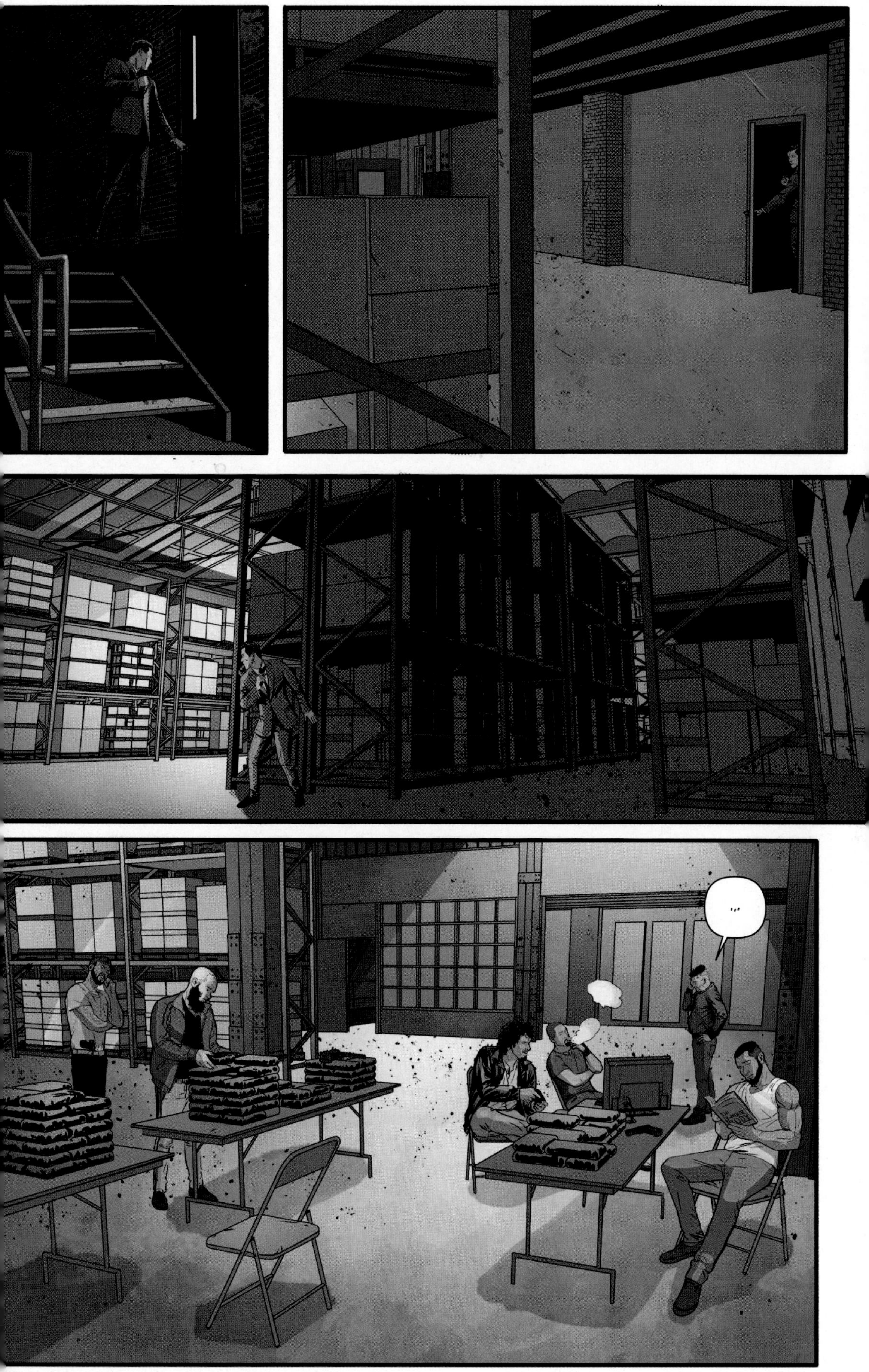
...

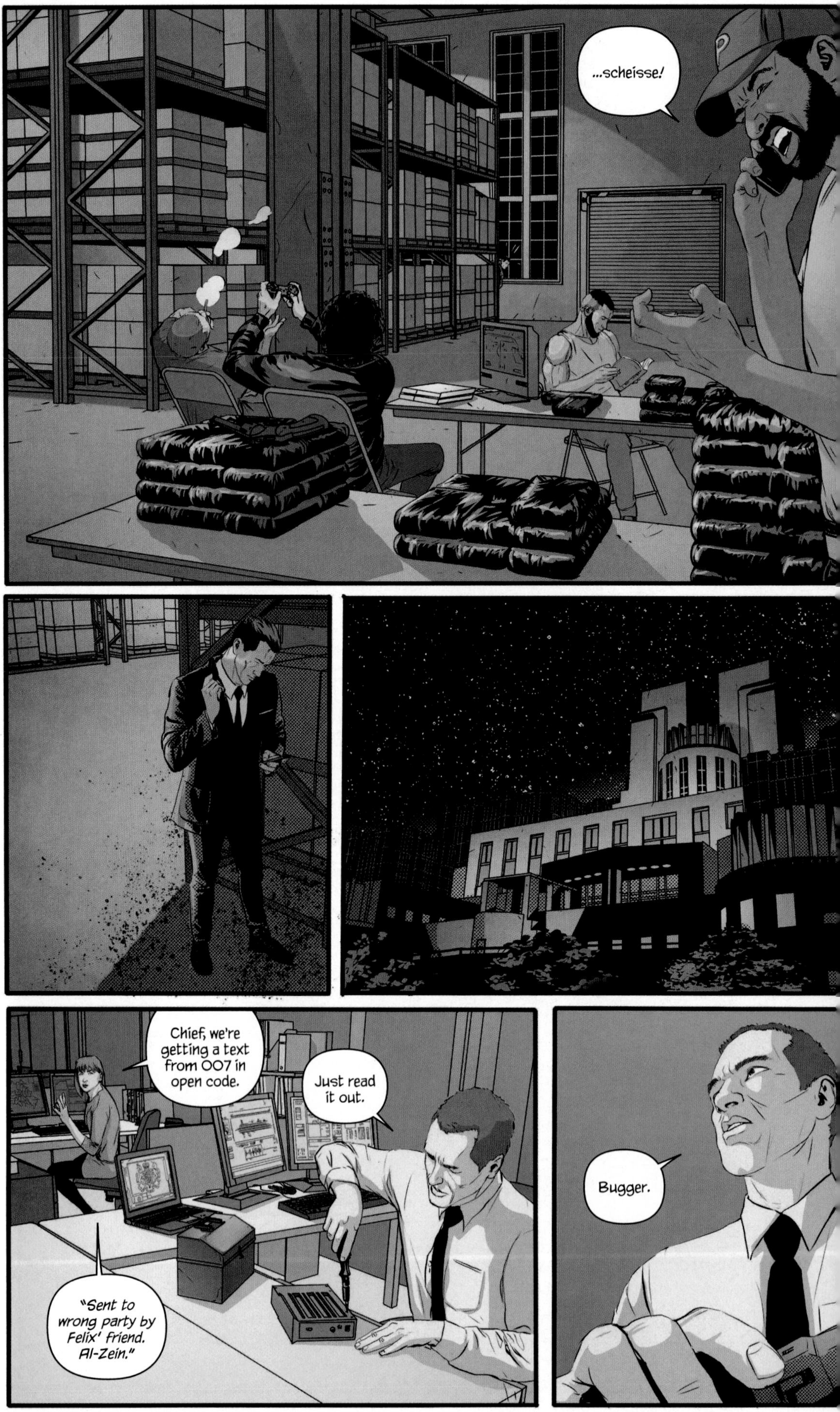
...scheisse!
Chief, we're getting a text from 007 in open code.
Just read it out.
"Sent to wrong party by Felix' friend. Al-Zein."
Bugger.

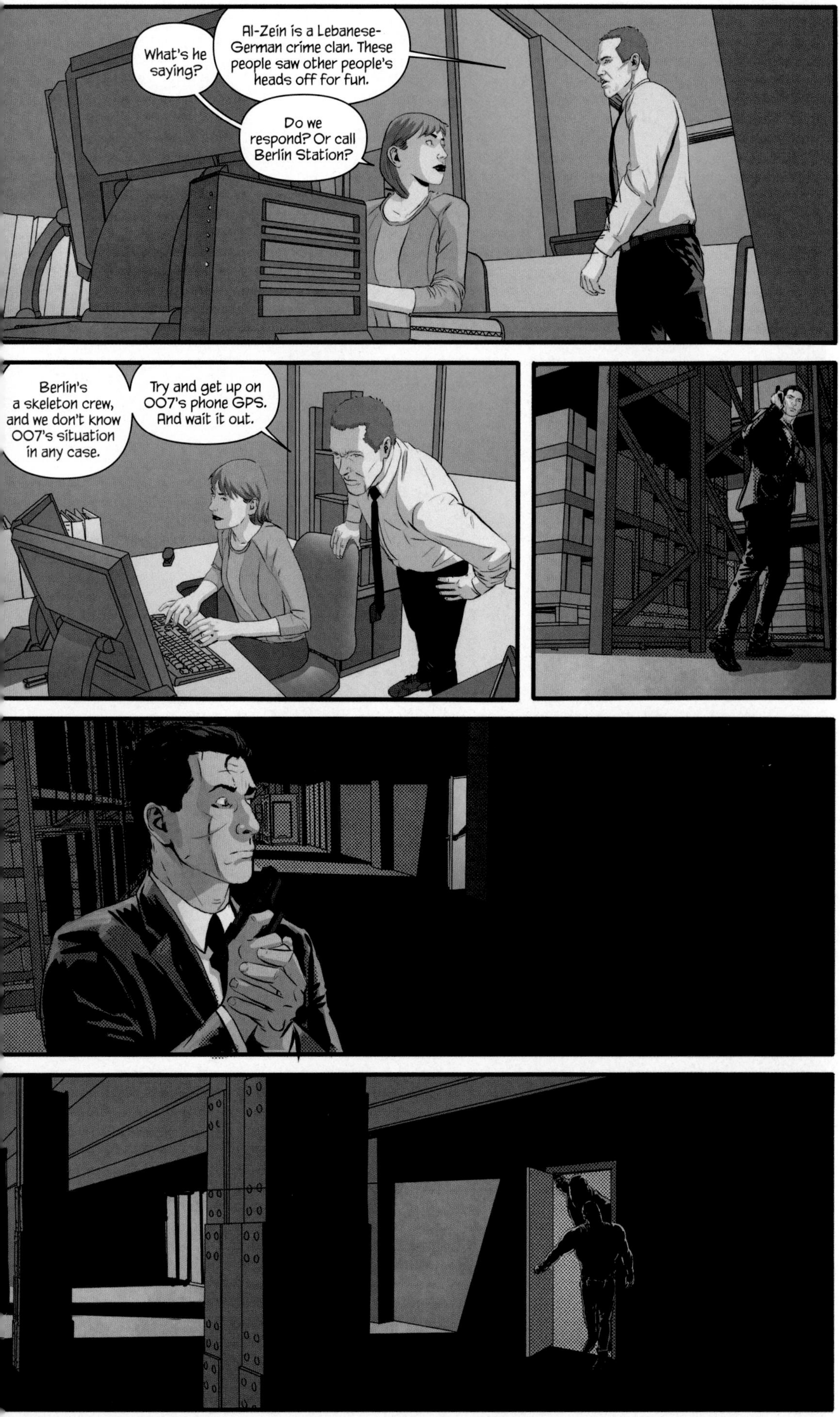
What's he saying?
Al-Zein is a Lebanese-German crime clan. These people saw other people's heads off for fun.
Do we respond? Or call Berlin Station?
Berlin's a skeleton crew, and we don't know 007's situation in any case.
Try and get up on 007's phone GPS. And wait it out.

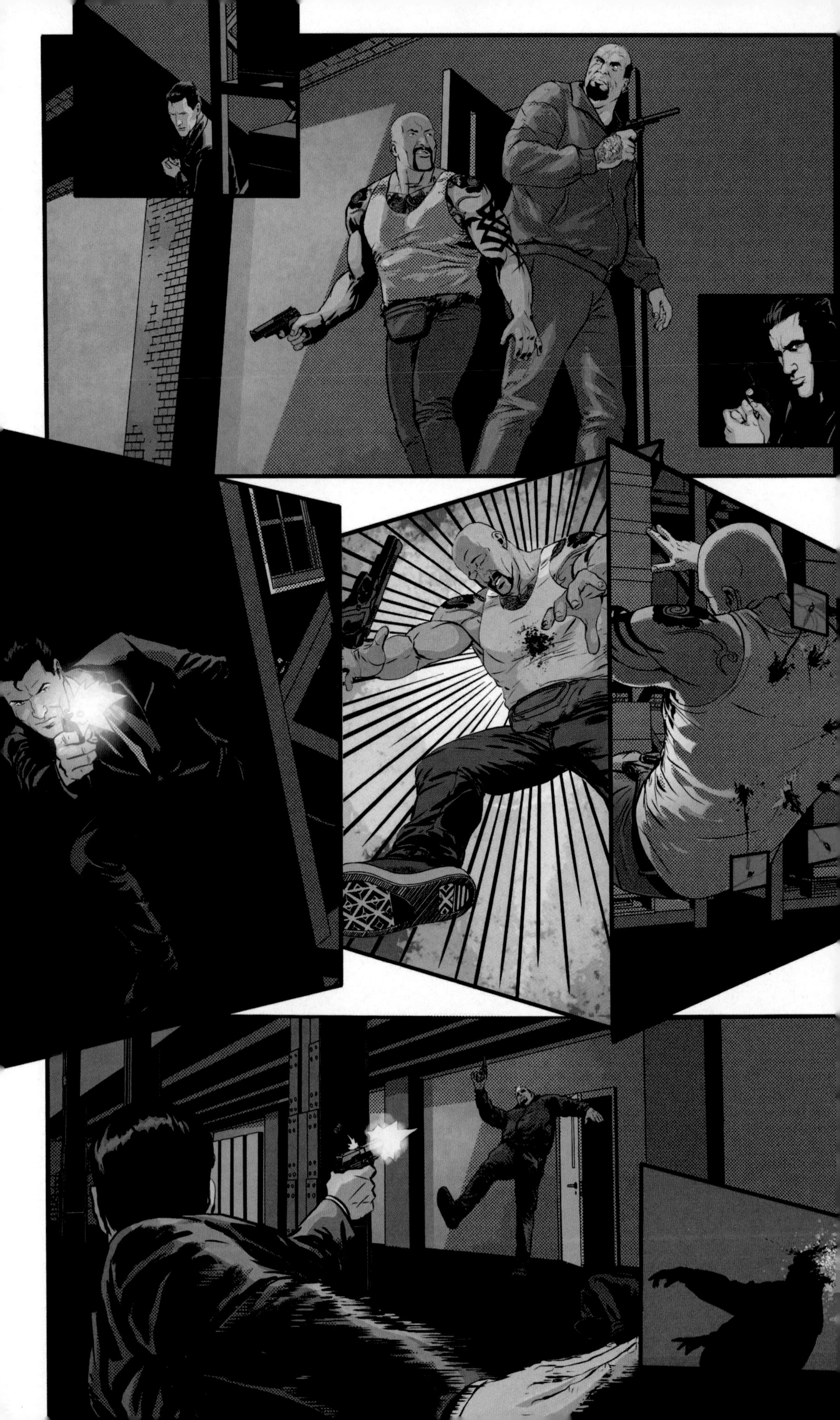

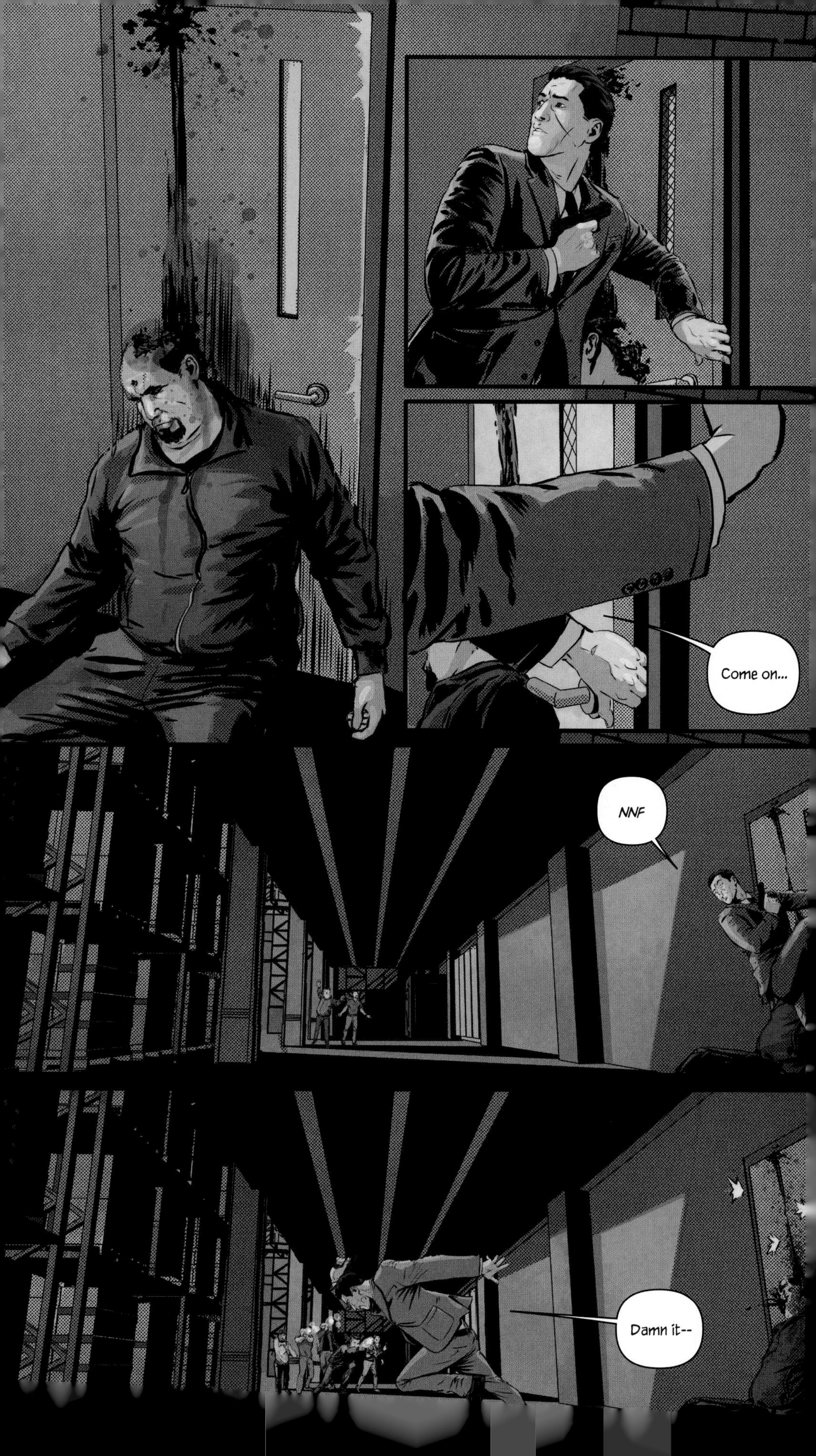
Come on...
NNF
Damn it--

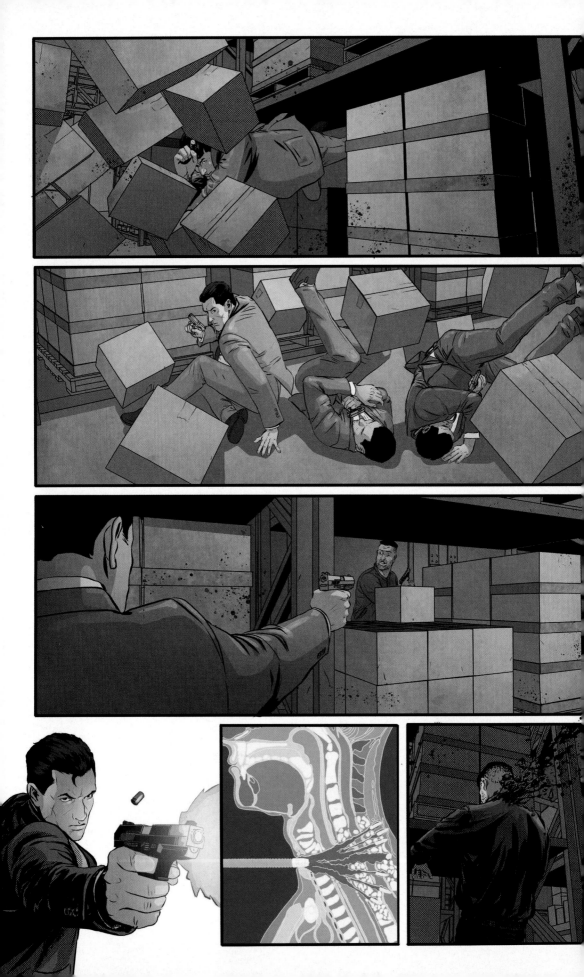

Wo is der Bastard...

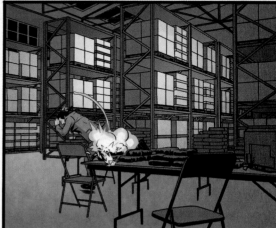

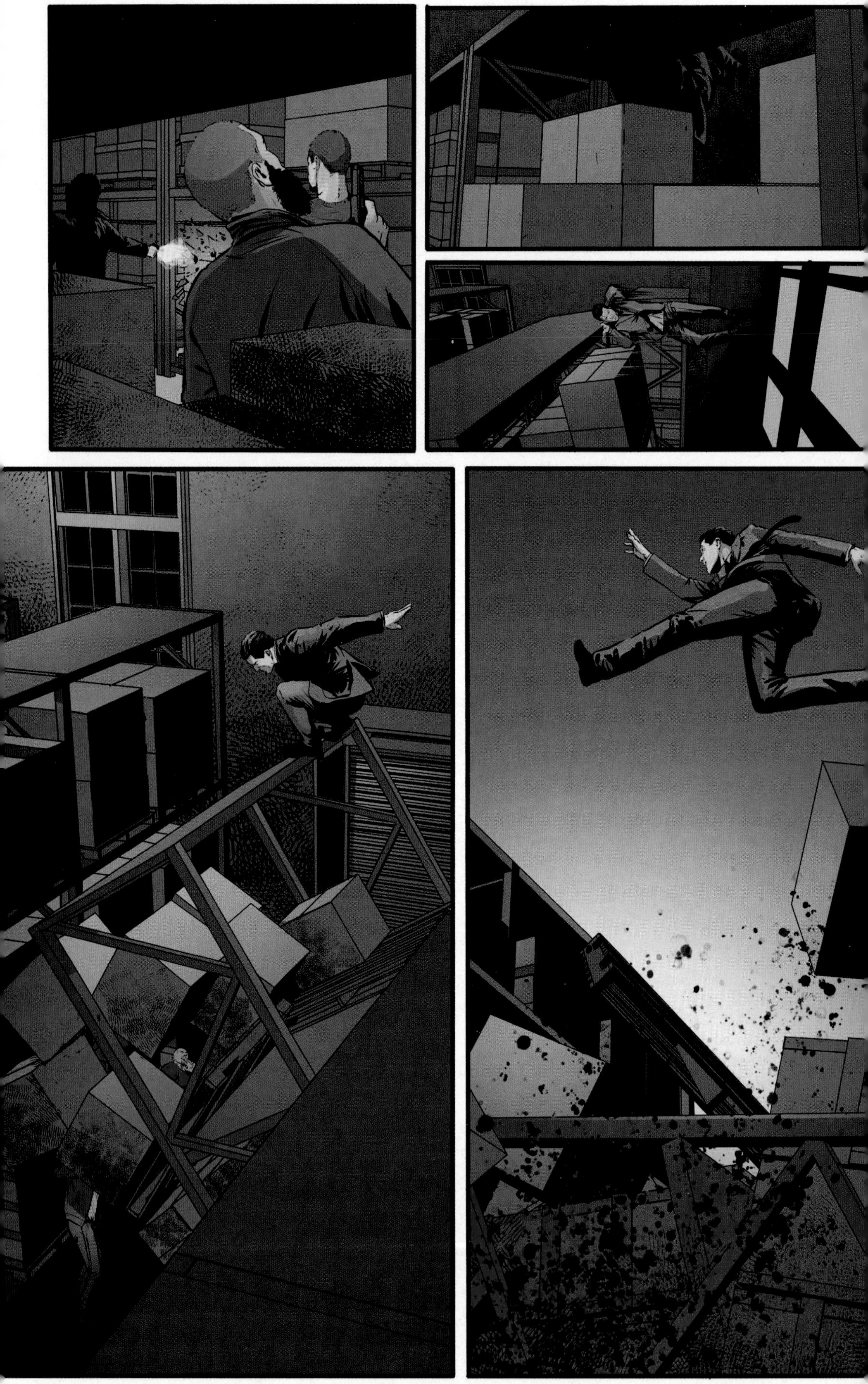

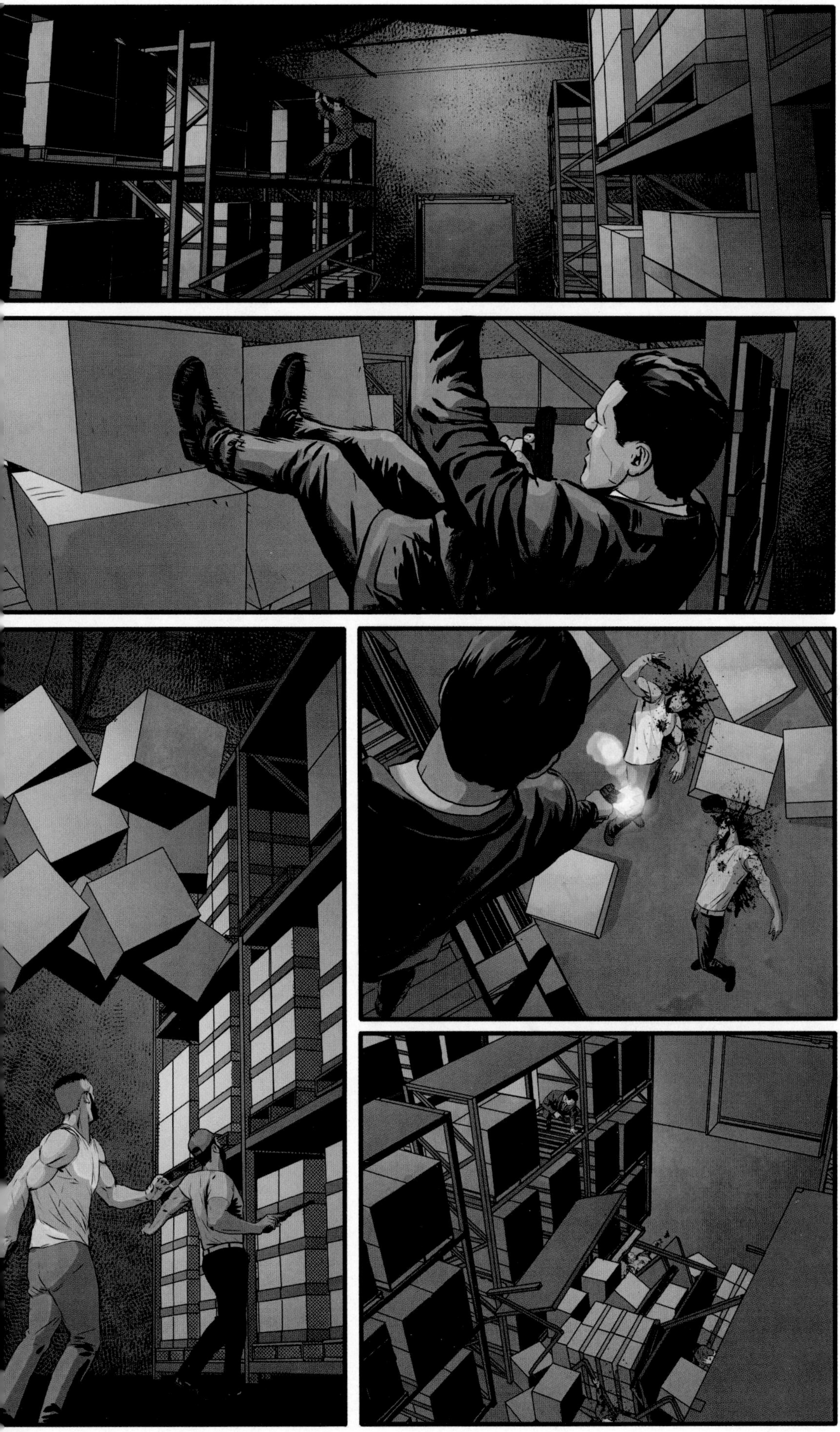

BASTARD!

You speak English?

Grew up in Birmingham. Give me my bloody gun.

Your guts are leaking out.

Tell me something I don't know. Give me my gun.

You're Al-Zein, yes? Are you trafficking to London?

You're having a laugh. Why would we? All the bloody money's in Europe.

Do you know a Slaven Kurjak? The truth wins you your gun back.

Never heard of him. Straight up. Sounds like a bloody Serbian. Zemun Clan are Serbians. We don't deal with them.

And I'm not going to bloo prison, so gi me that.

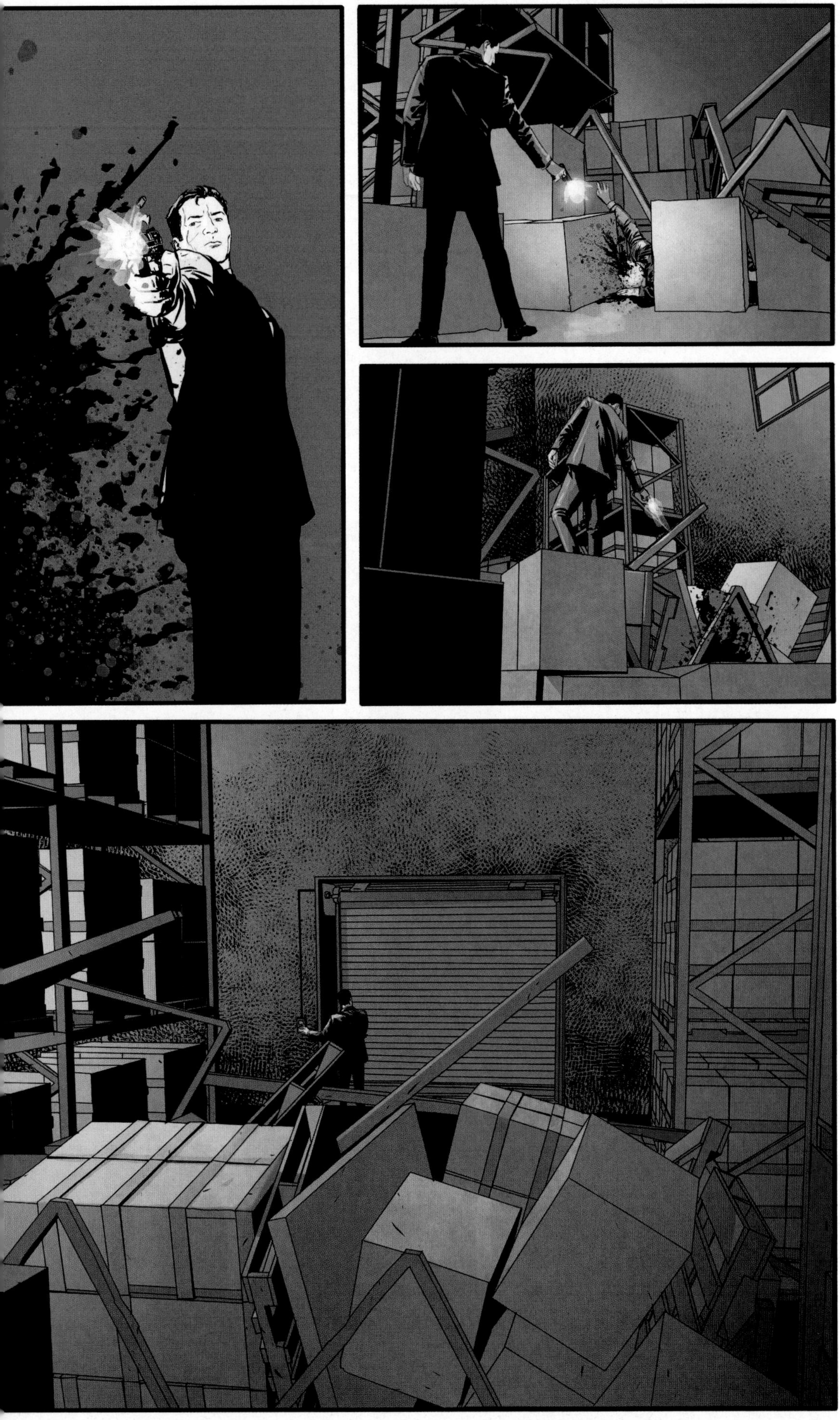

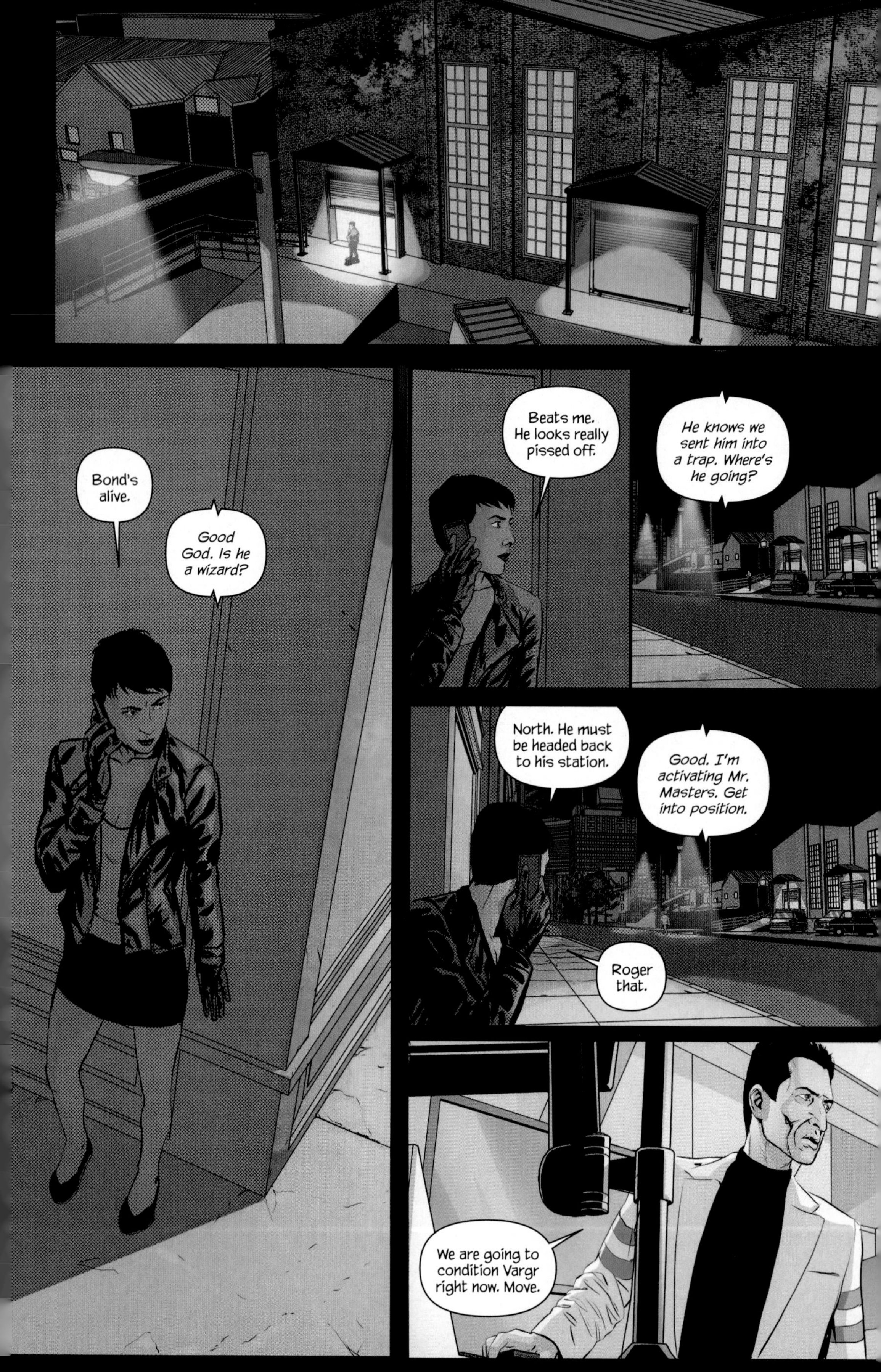
Bond's alive.
Good God. Is he a wizard?
Beats me. He looks really pissed off.
He knows we sent him into a trap. Where's he going?
North. He must be headed back to his station.
Good. I'm activating Mr. Masters. Get into position.
Roger that.
We are going to condition Vargr right now. Move.

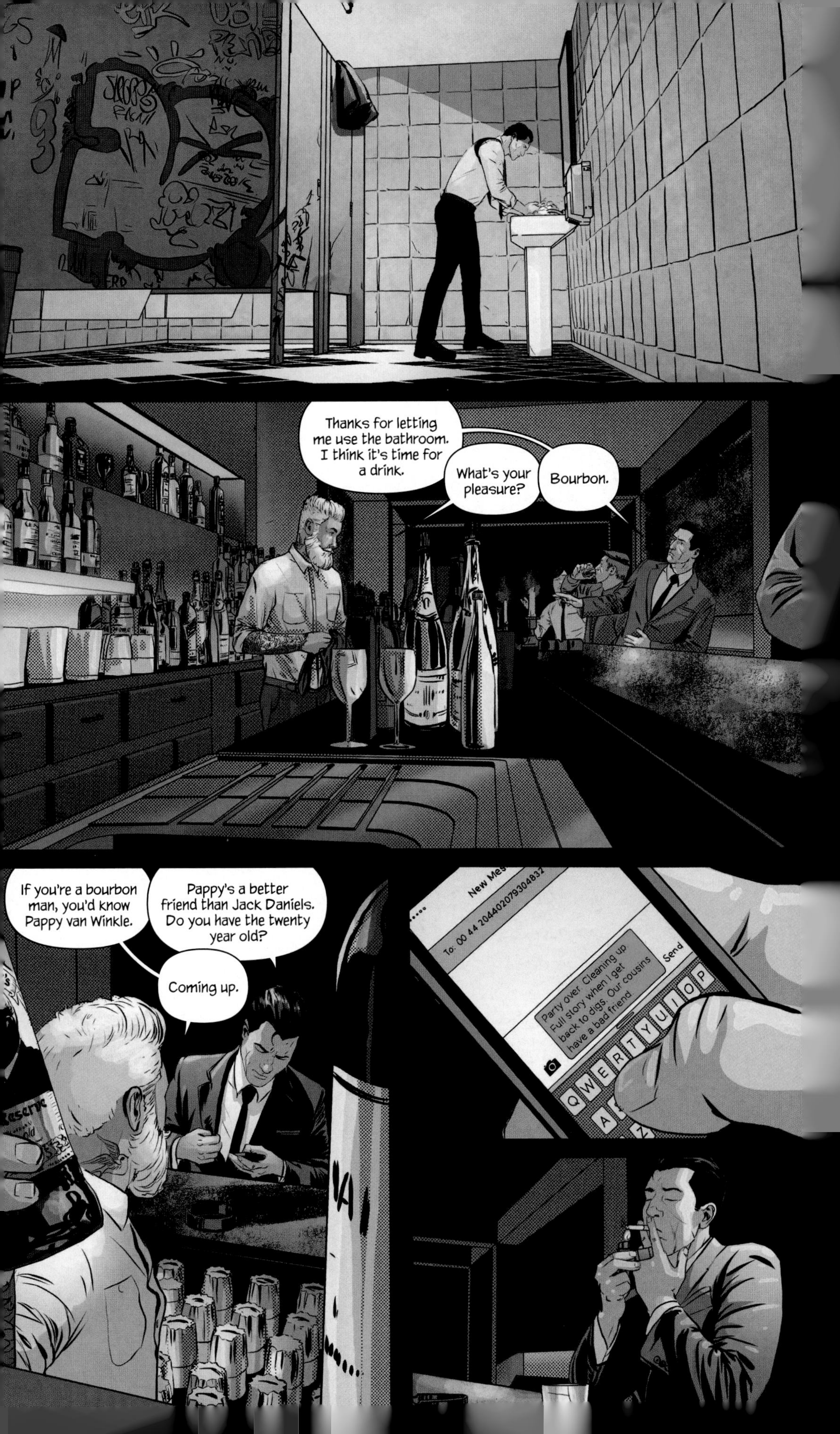
Thanks for letting me use the bathroom. I think it's time for a drink.
What's your pleasure?
Bourbon.
If you're a bourbon man, you'd know Pappy van Winkle.
Pappy's a better friend than Jack Daniels. Do you have the twenty year old?
Coming up.
To: 00 44 2044020793048322
Party over. Cleaning up. Full story when I get back to digs. Our cousins have a bad friend.
Send

An actual OO agent.

In Berlin, even. Kind of surreal. You get that little chill from the Cold War when you think about it.

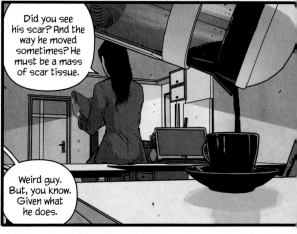

Did you see his scar? And the way he moved sometimes? He must be a mass of scar tissue.

Weird guy. But, you know. Given what he does.

I kind of liked him.

I'll bet.

Didn't he seem just a little bit sad to you? Like his smile didn't reach all the way up to his eyes?

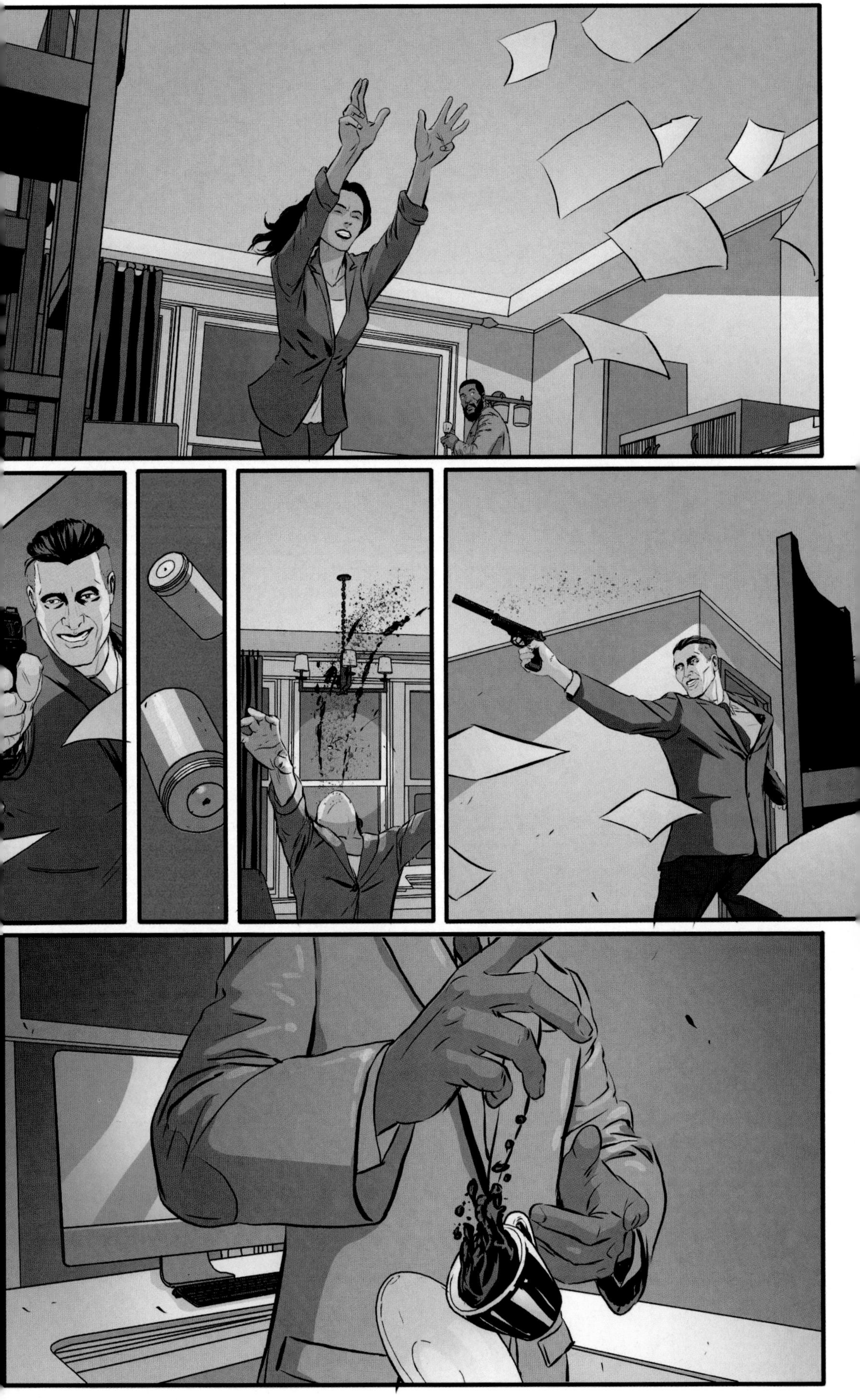

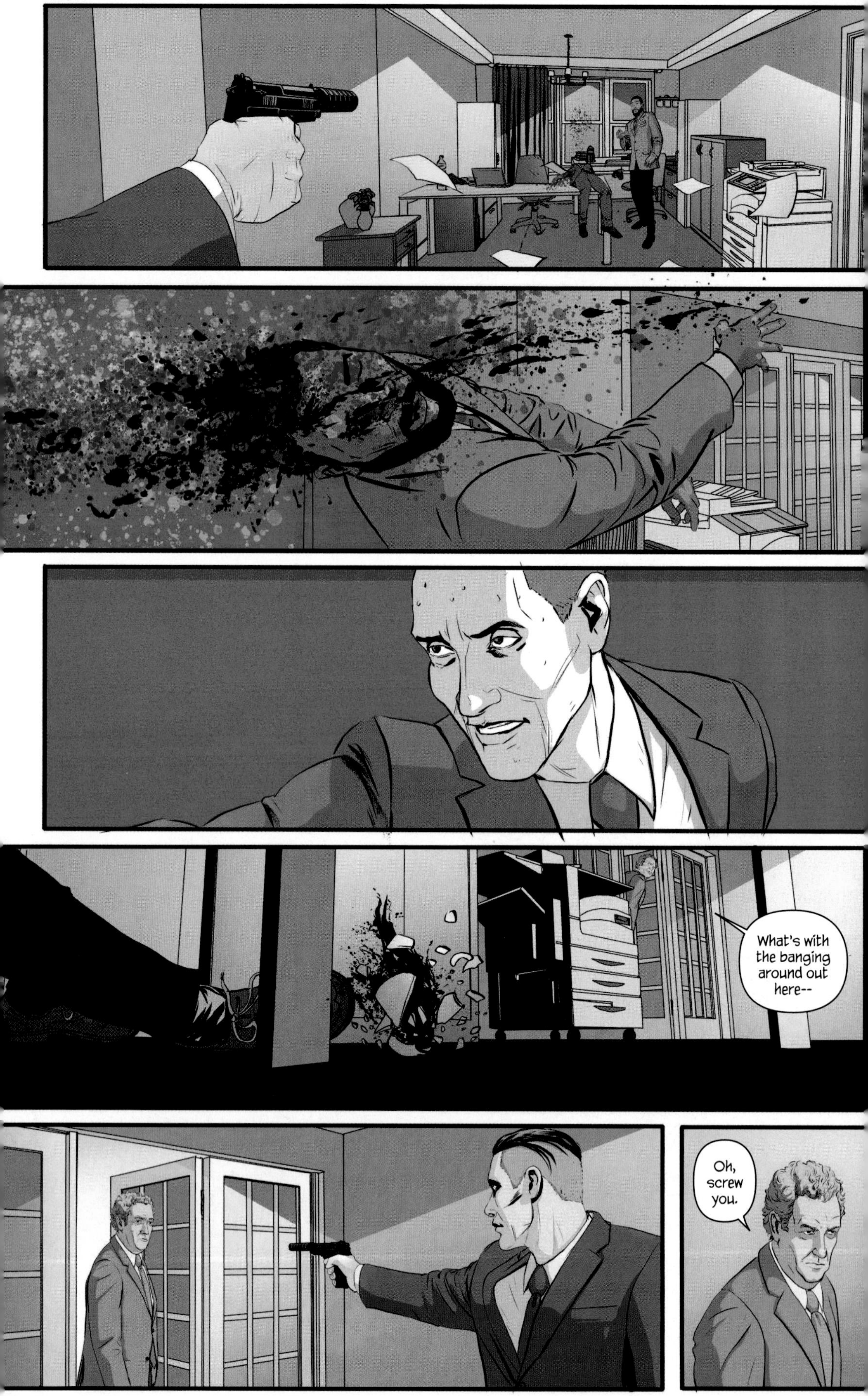
What's with the banging around out here--
Oh, screw you.

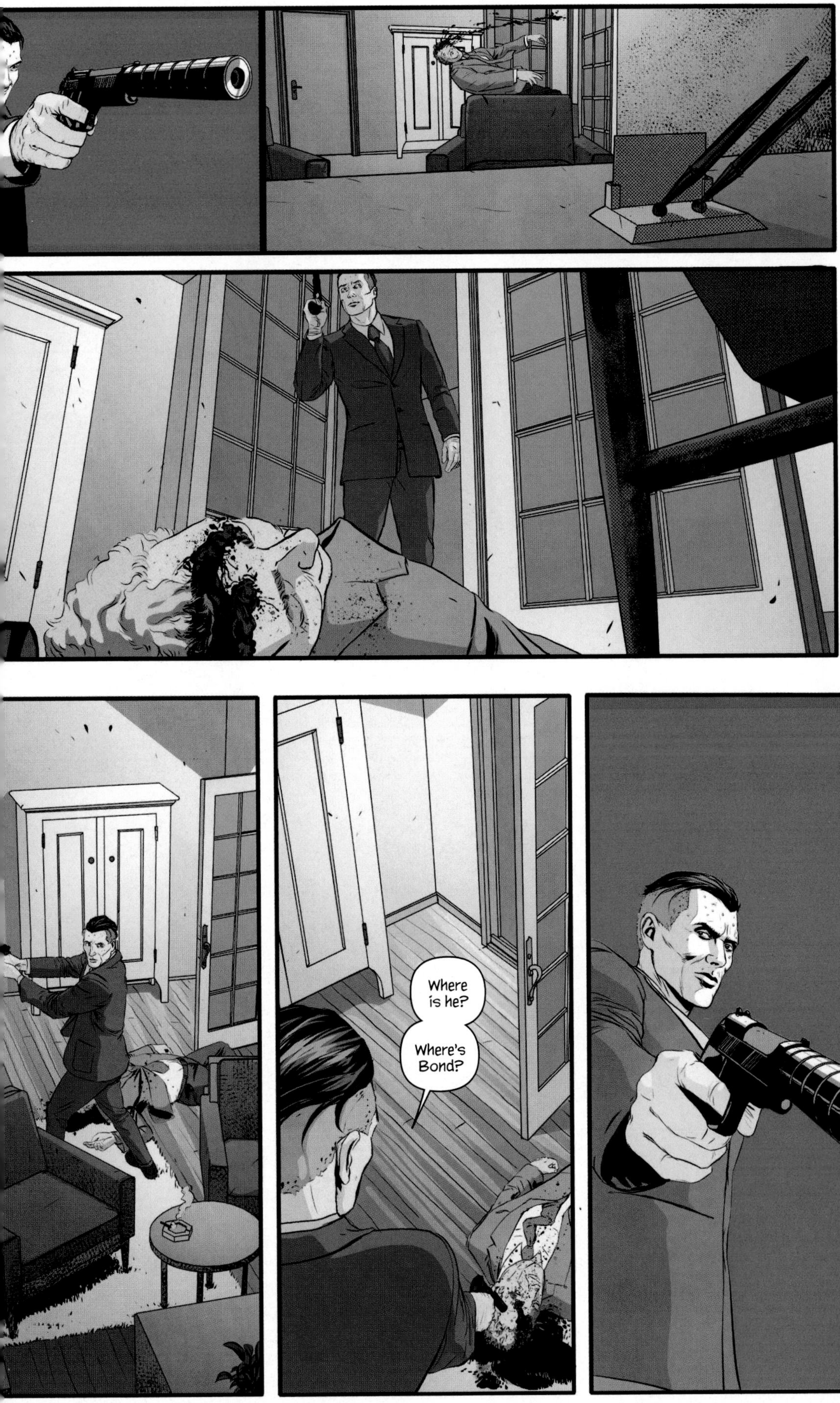
Where is he?
Where's Bond?

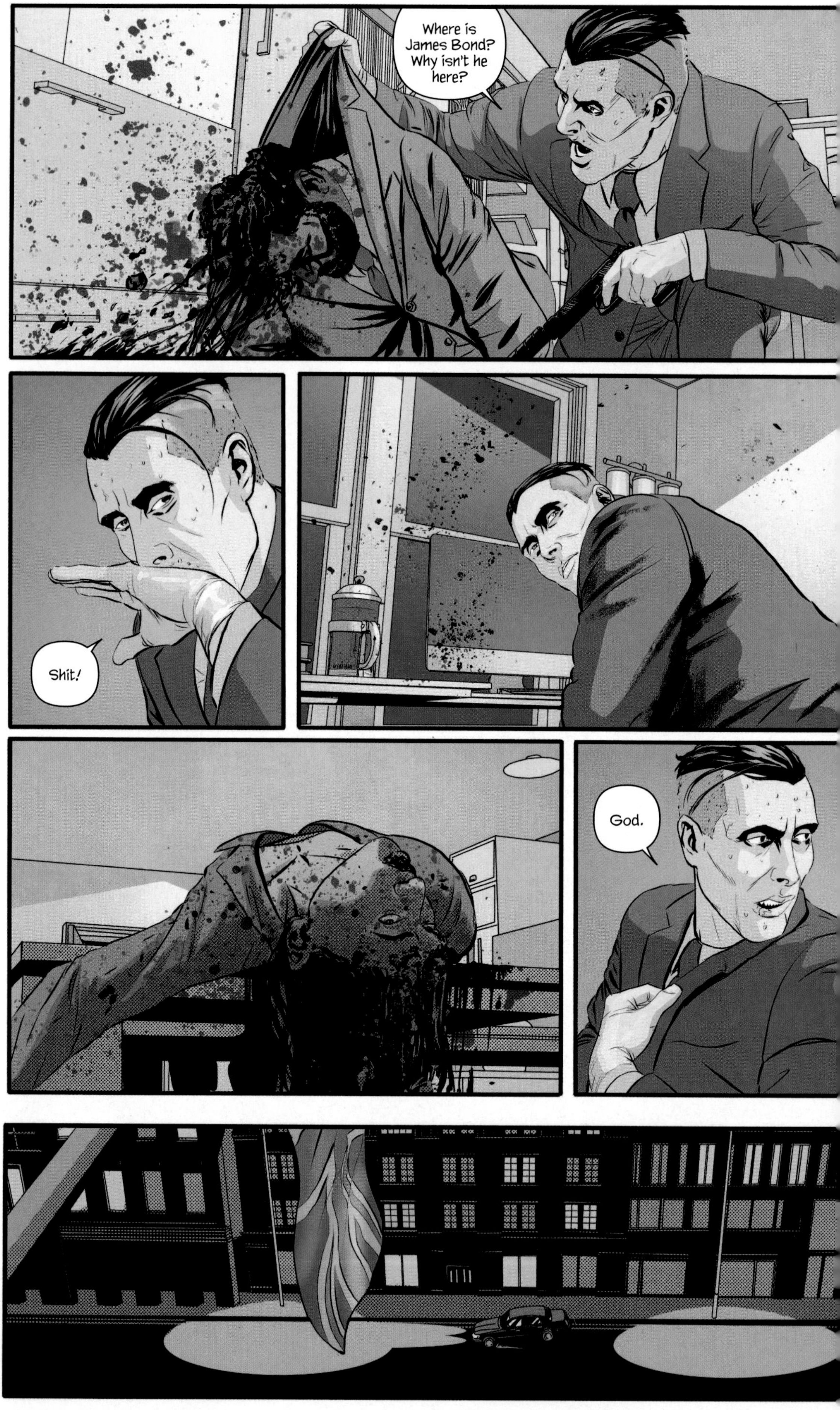
Where is James Bond? Why isn't he here?
Shit!
God.

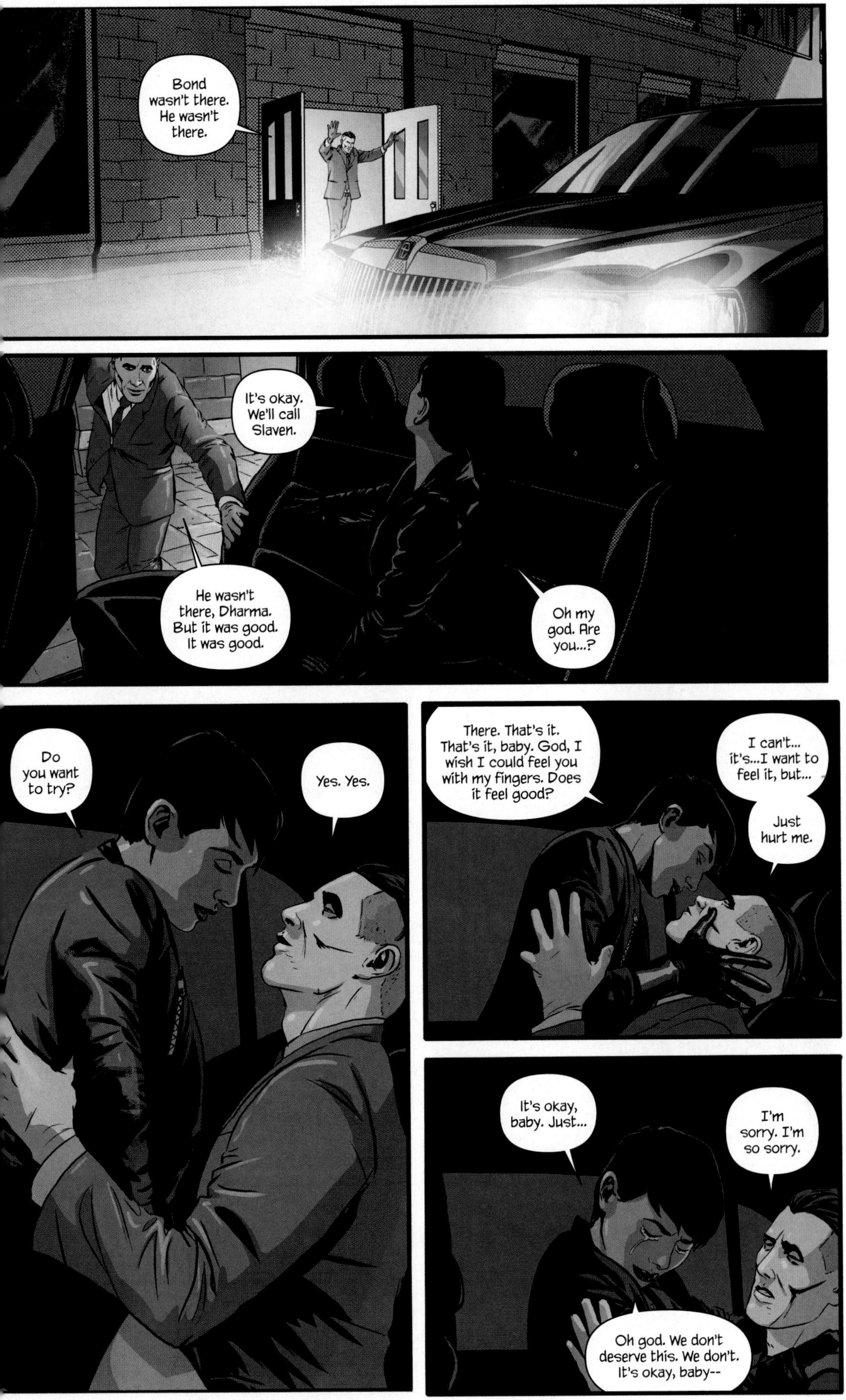
Bond wasn't there. He wasn't there.
It's okay. We'll call Slaven.
He wasn't there, Dharma. But it was good. It was good.
Oh my god. Are you...?
Do you want to try?
Yes. Yes.
There. That's it. That's it, baby. God, I wish I could feel you with my fingers. Does it feel good?
I can't... it's...I want to feel it, but...
Just hurt me.
It's okay, baby. Just...
I'm sorry. I'm so sorry.
Oh god. We don't deserve this. We don't. It's okay, baby--

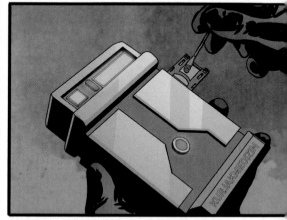

Call Joint Intelligence.

The drugs aren't infected. It's something much worse.

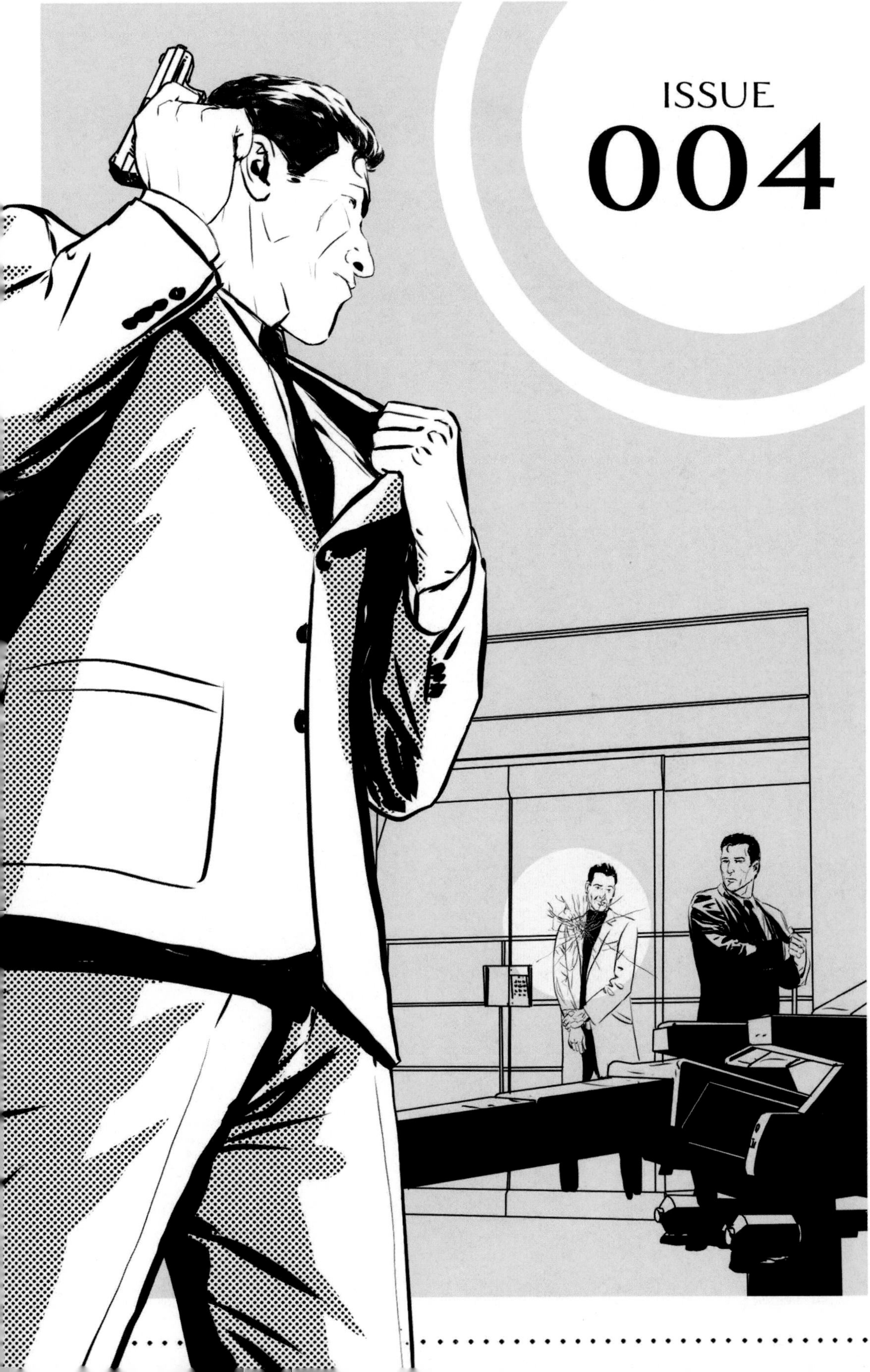
ISSUE
004

issue #4 main cover by **DOM REARDON**

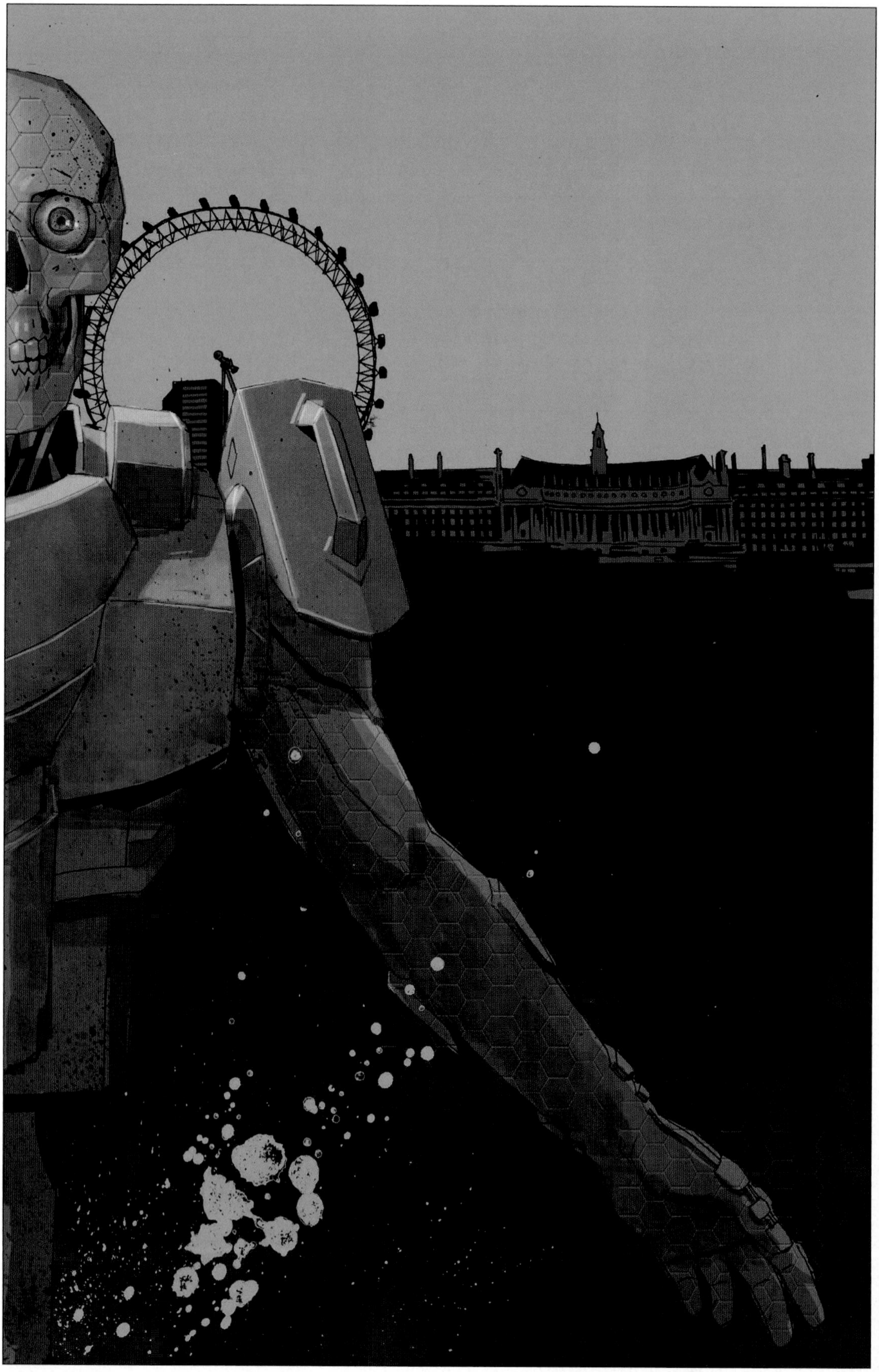

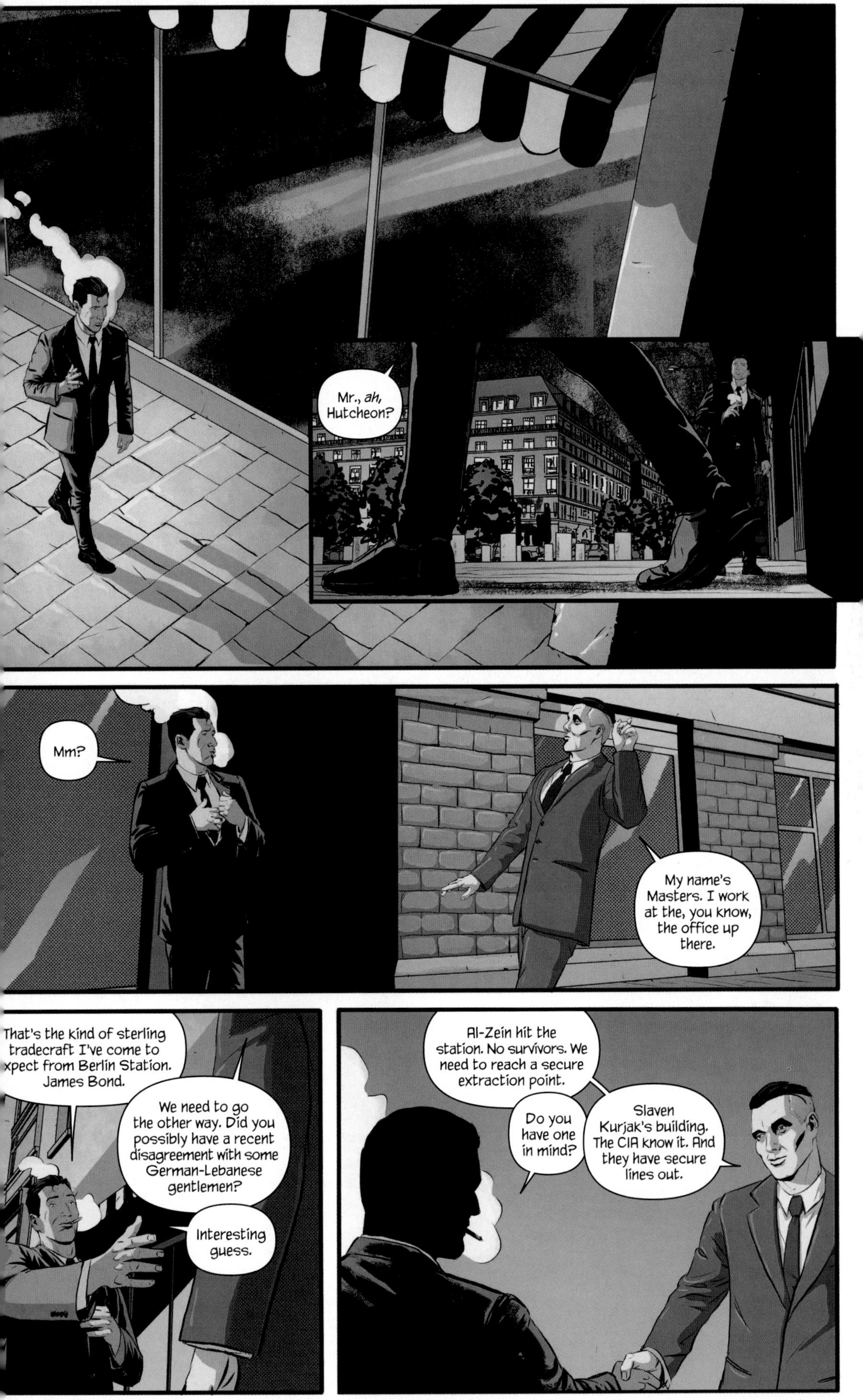
Mr., *ah*, Hutcheon?
Mm?
My name's Masters. I work at the, you know, the office up there.
That's the kind of sterling tradecraft I've come to xpect from Berlin Station. James Bond.
We need to go the other way. Did you possibly have a recent disagreement with some German-Lebanese gentlemen?
Interesting guess.
Al-Zein hit the station. No survivors. We need to reach a secure extraction point.
Do you have one in mind?
Slaven Kurjak's building. The CIA know it. And they have secure lines out.

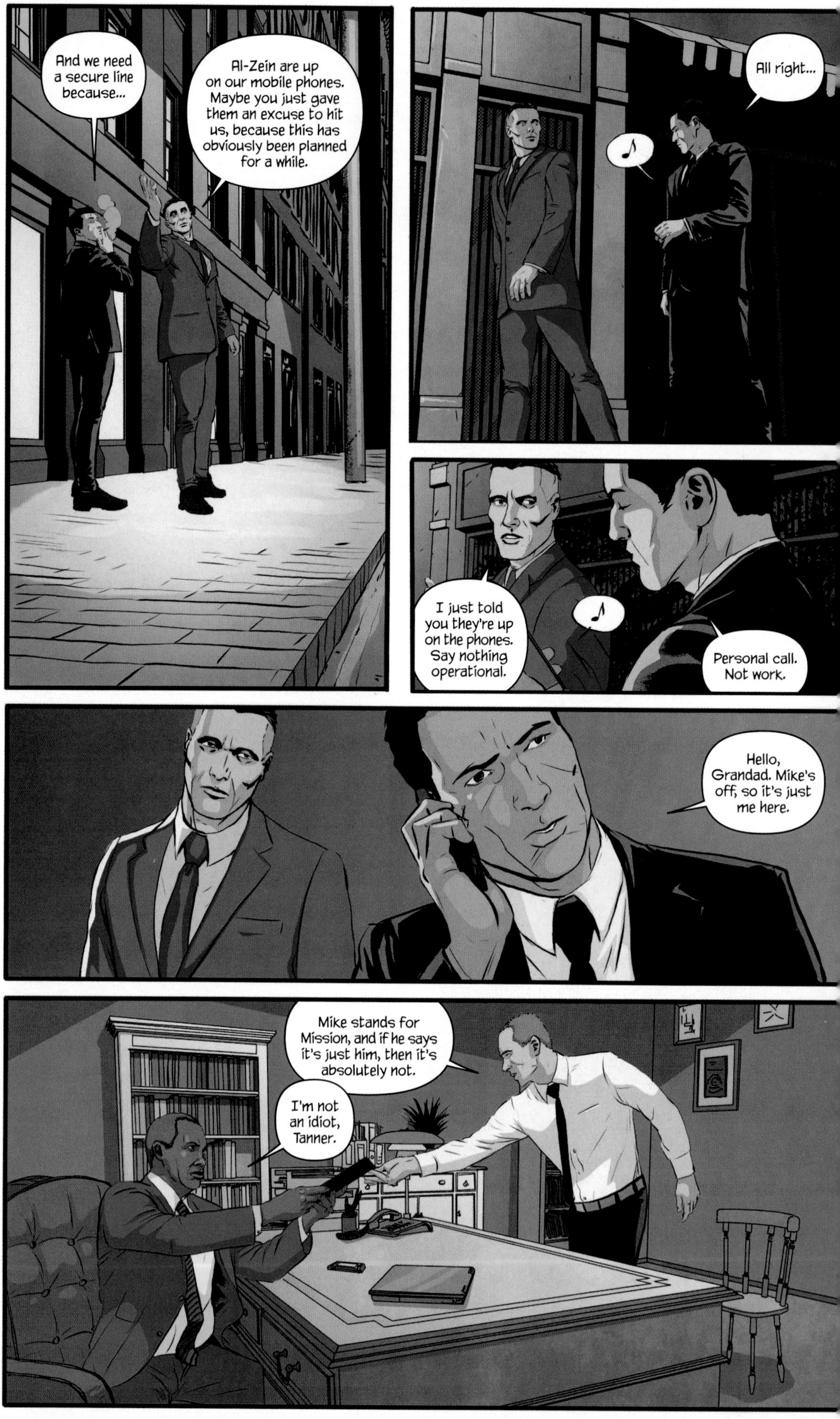
And we need a secure line because...
Al-Zein are up on our mobile phones. Maybe you just gave them an excuse to hit us, because this has obviously been planned for a while.
All right...
♪
I just told you they're up on the phones. Say nothing operational.
♪
Personal call. Not work.
Hello, Grandad. Mike's off, so it's just me here.
Mike stands for Mission, and if he says it's just him, then it's absolutely not.
I'm not an idiot, Tanner.

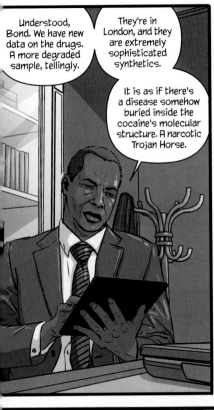

Understood, Bond. We have new data on the drugs. A more degraded sample, tellingly.

They're in London, and they are extremely sophisticated synthetics.

It is as if there's a disease somehow buried inside the cocaine's molecular structure. A narcotic Trojan Horse.

Well, that makes a disturbing amount of sense.

Listen, the other party was useless, but I think my cousin's friend might be the better bet.

I've bumped into someone who claims he's from our firm. Going to visit our cousin's friend now. At his office.

Very well. We can't raise Berlin Station, so we're about to get some local aid drafted.

Yeah, that old house is apparently closed now. Talk soon.

Shall we?

It would be a pleasure.

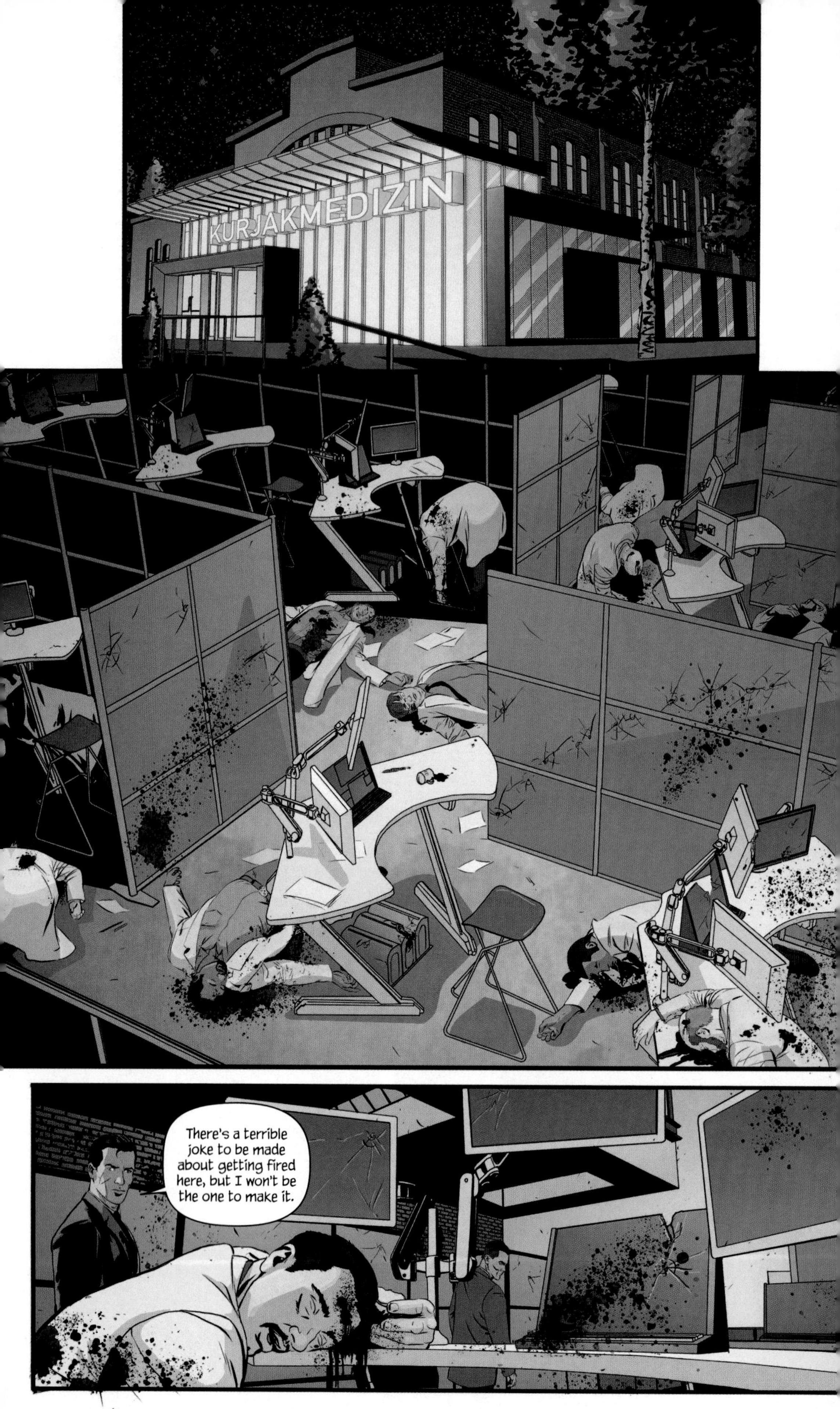
KURJAKMEDIZIN
There's a terrible joke to be made about getting fired here, but I won't be the one to make it.

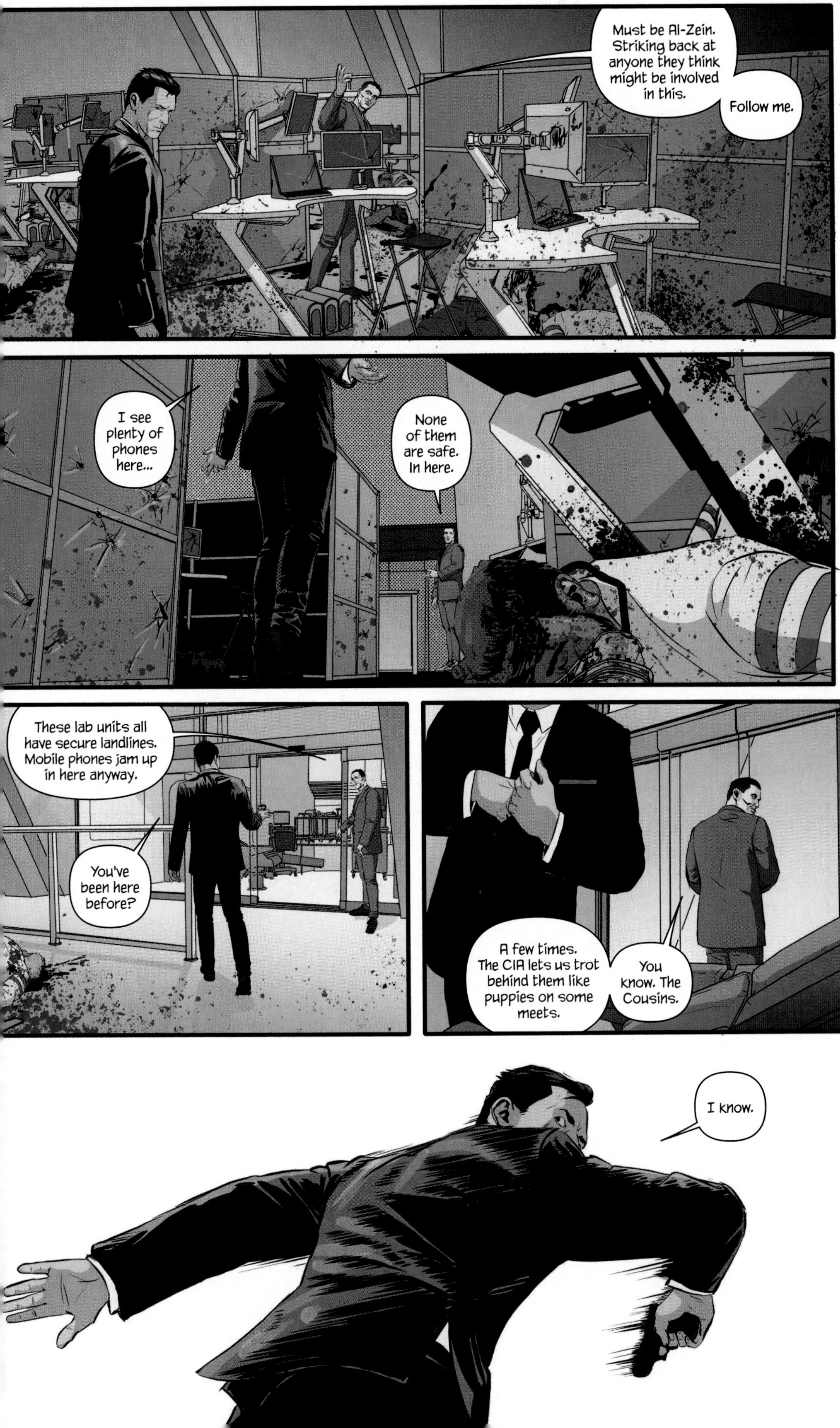

Must be Al-Zein. Striking back at anyone they think might be involved in this.
Follow me.
I see plenty of phones here...
None of them are safe. In here.
These lab units all have secure landlines. Mobile phones jam up in here anyway.
You've been here before?
A few times. The CIA lets us trot behind them like puppies on some meets.
You know. The Cousins.
I know.

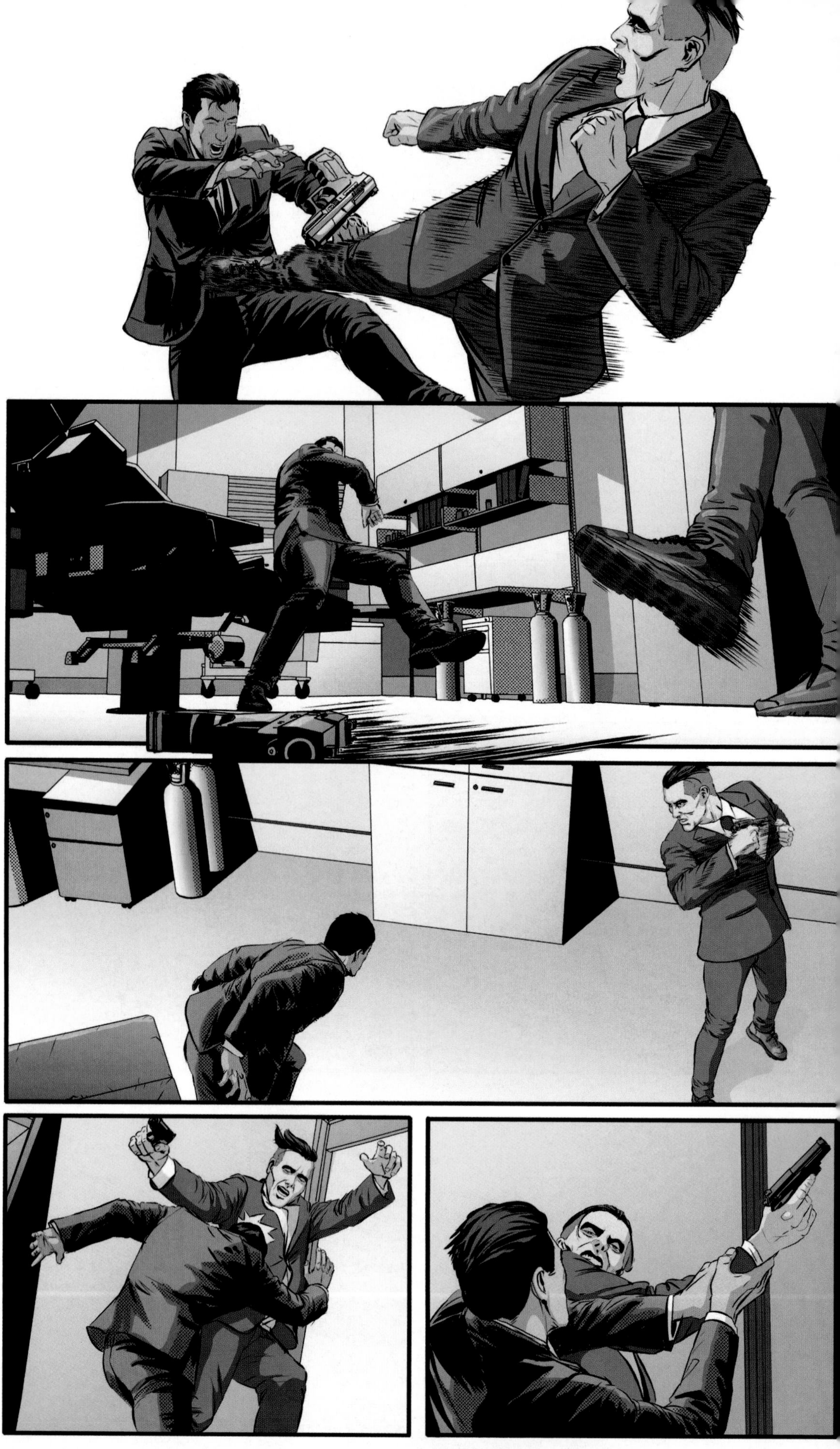

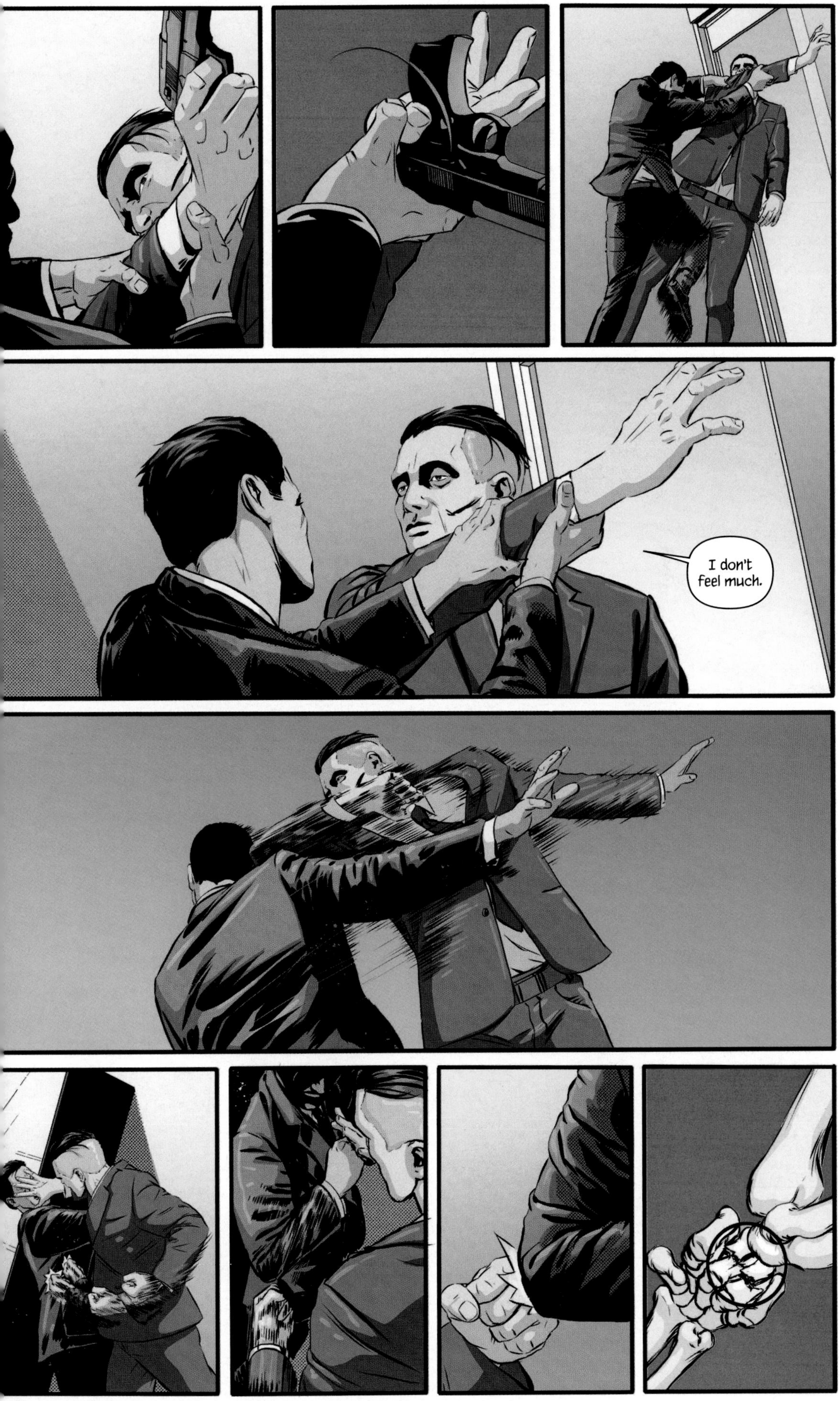
I don't feel much.

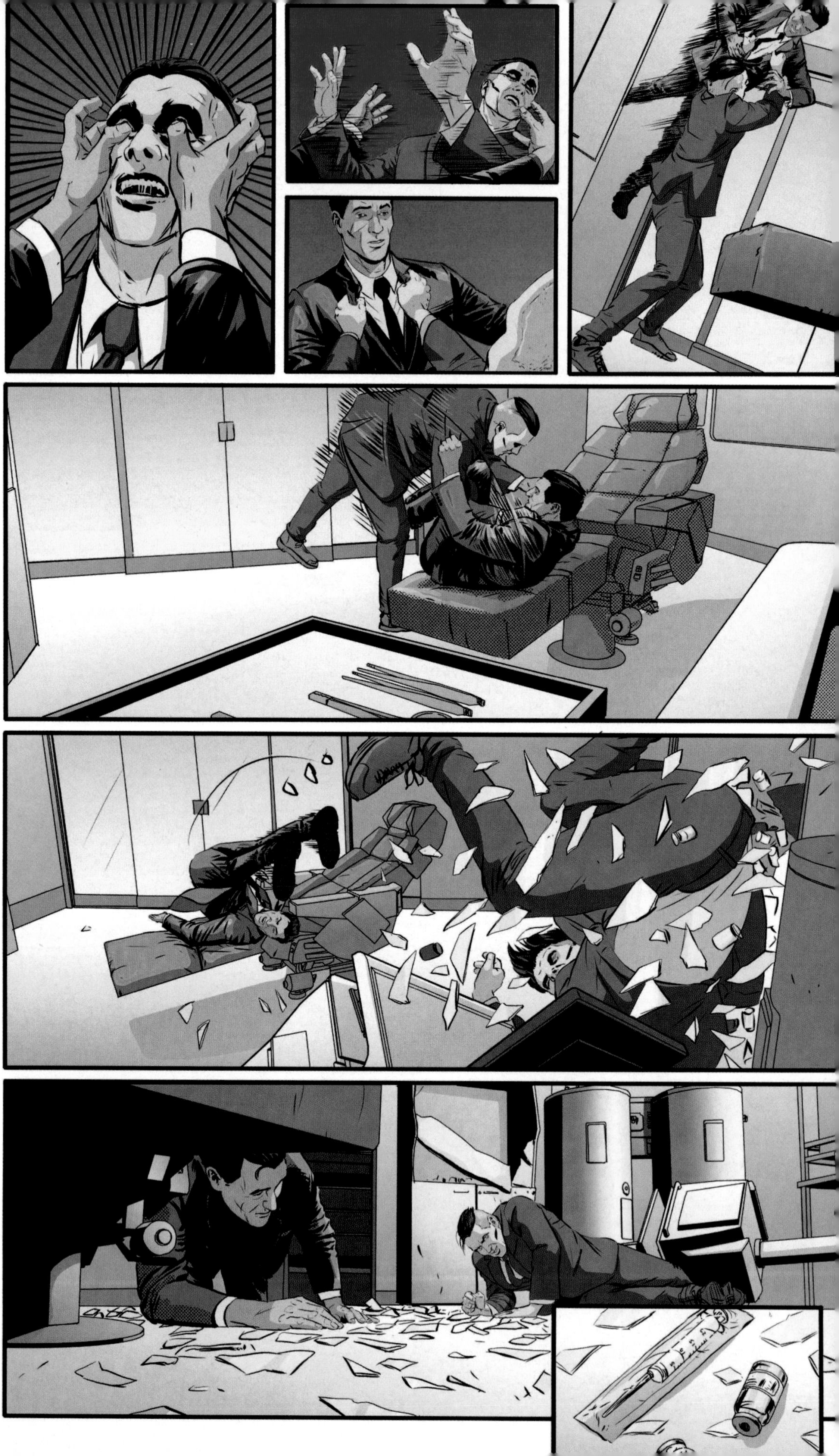

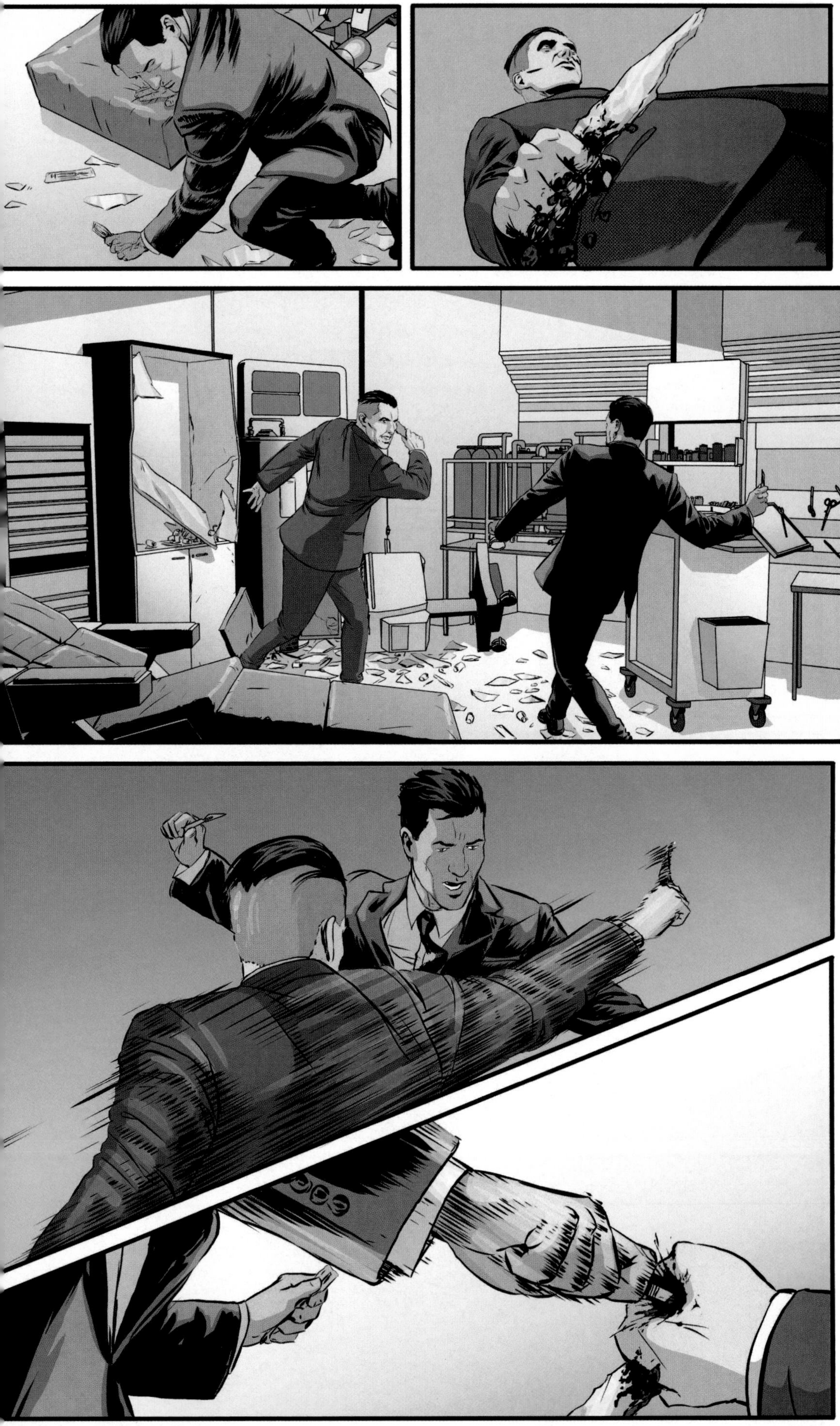

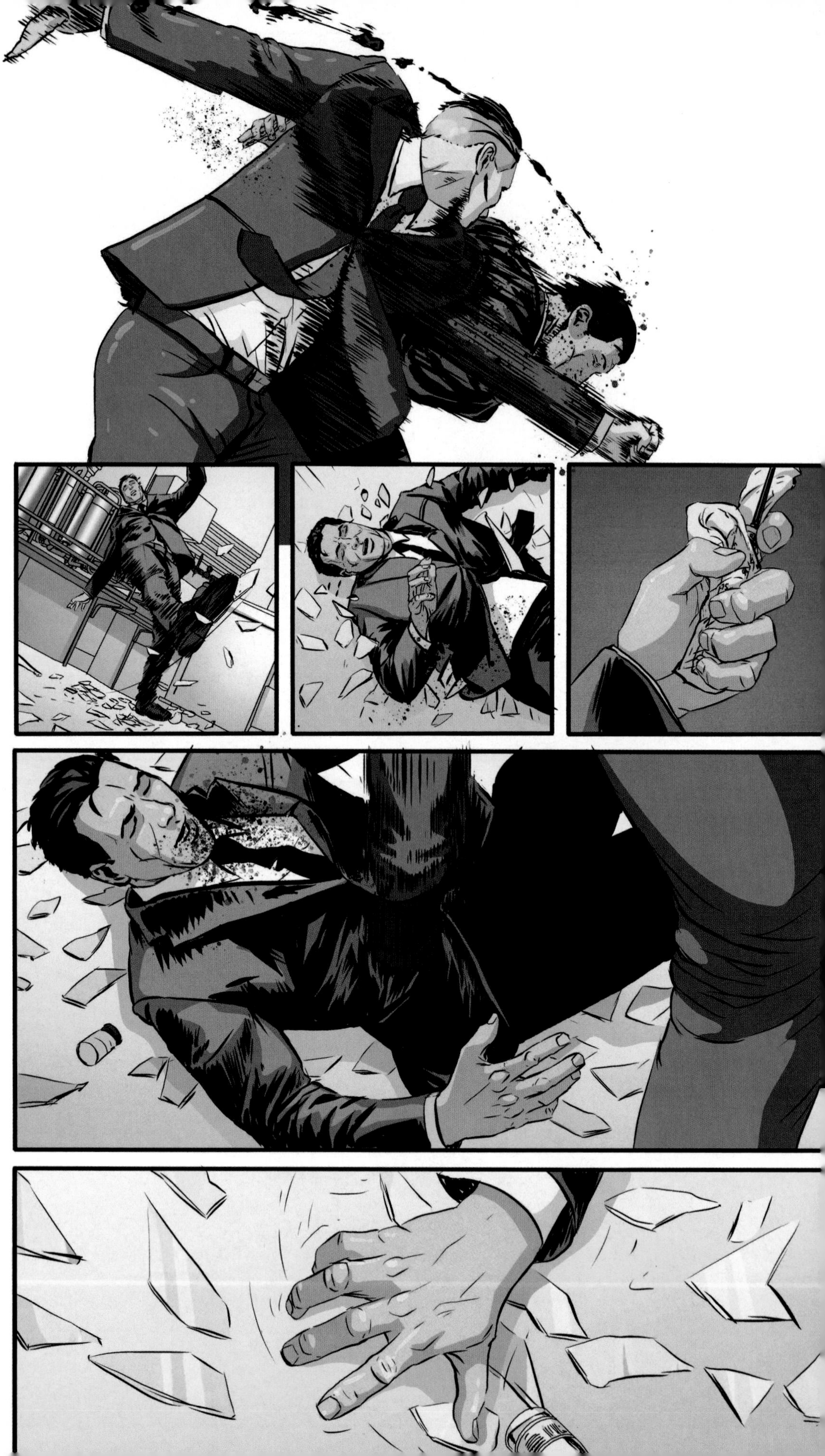

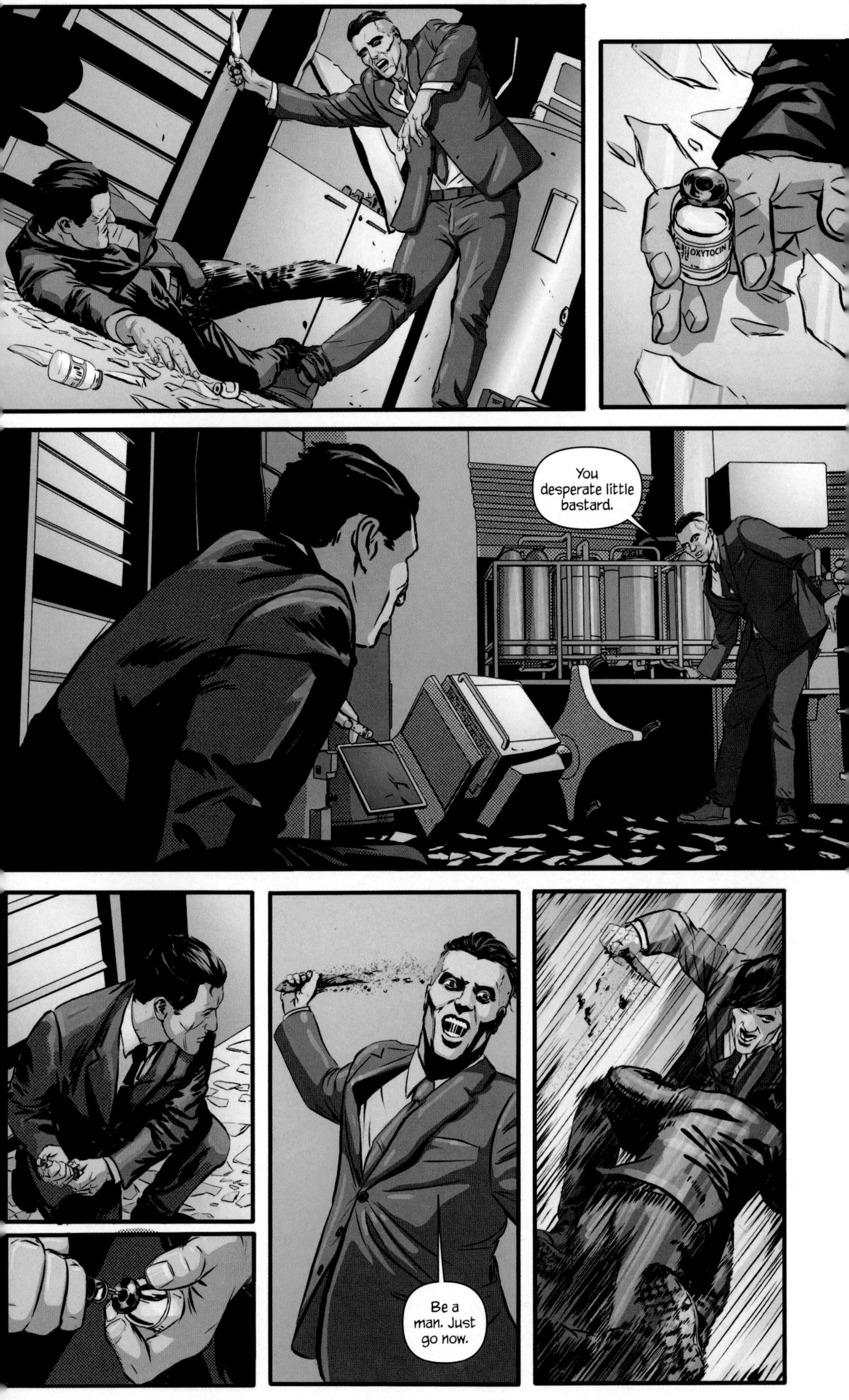
OXYTOCIN
You desperate little bastard.
Be a man. Just go now.

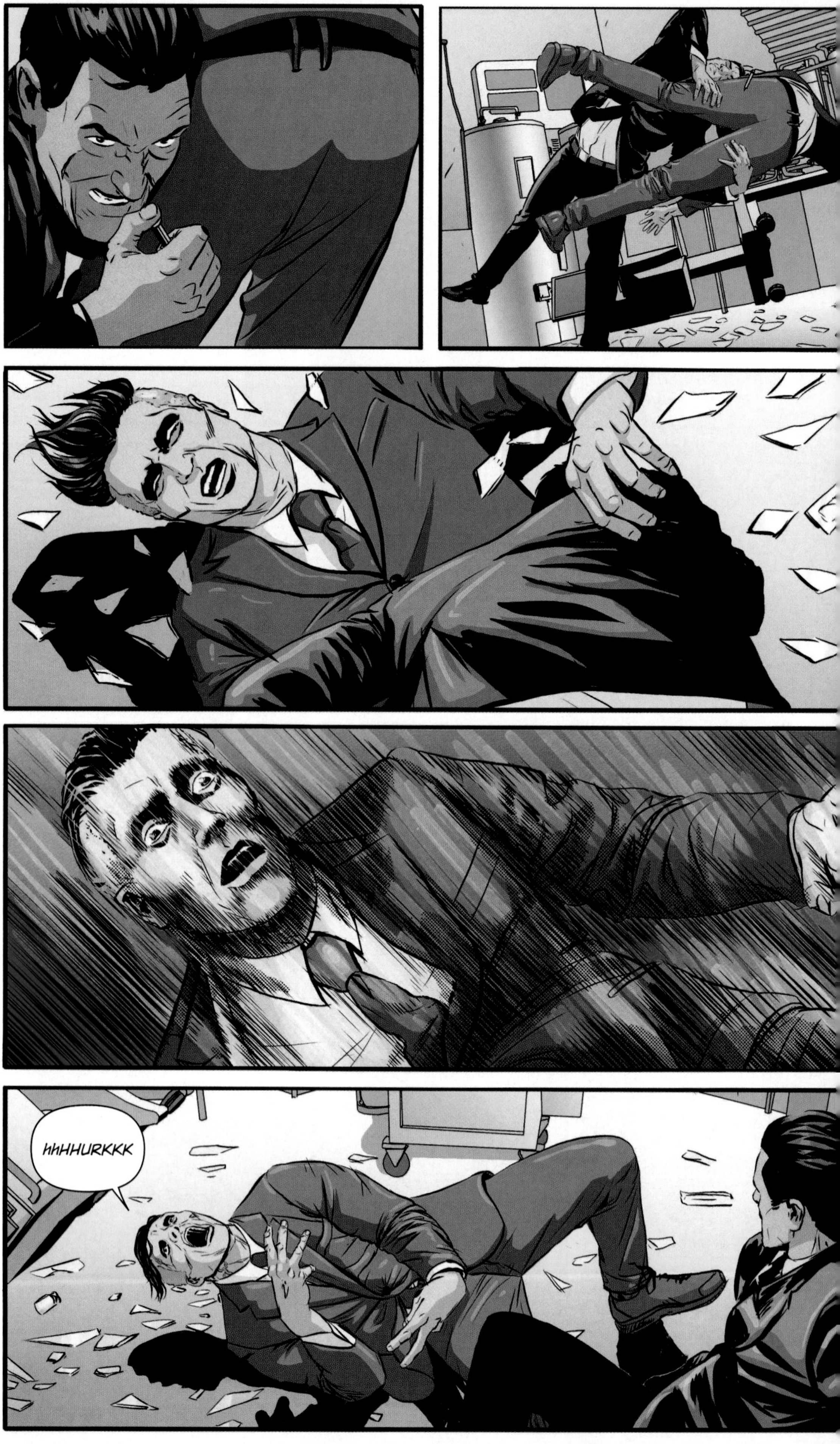
hhHHURKKK

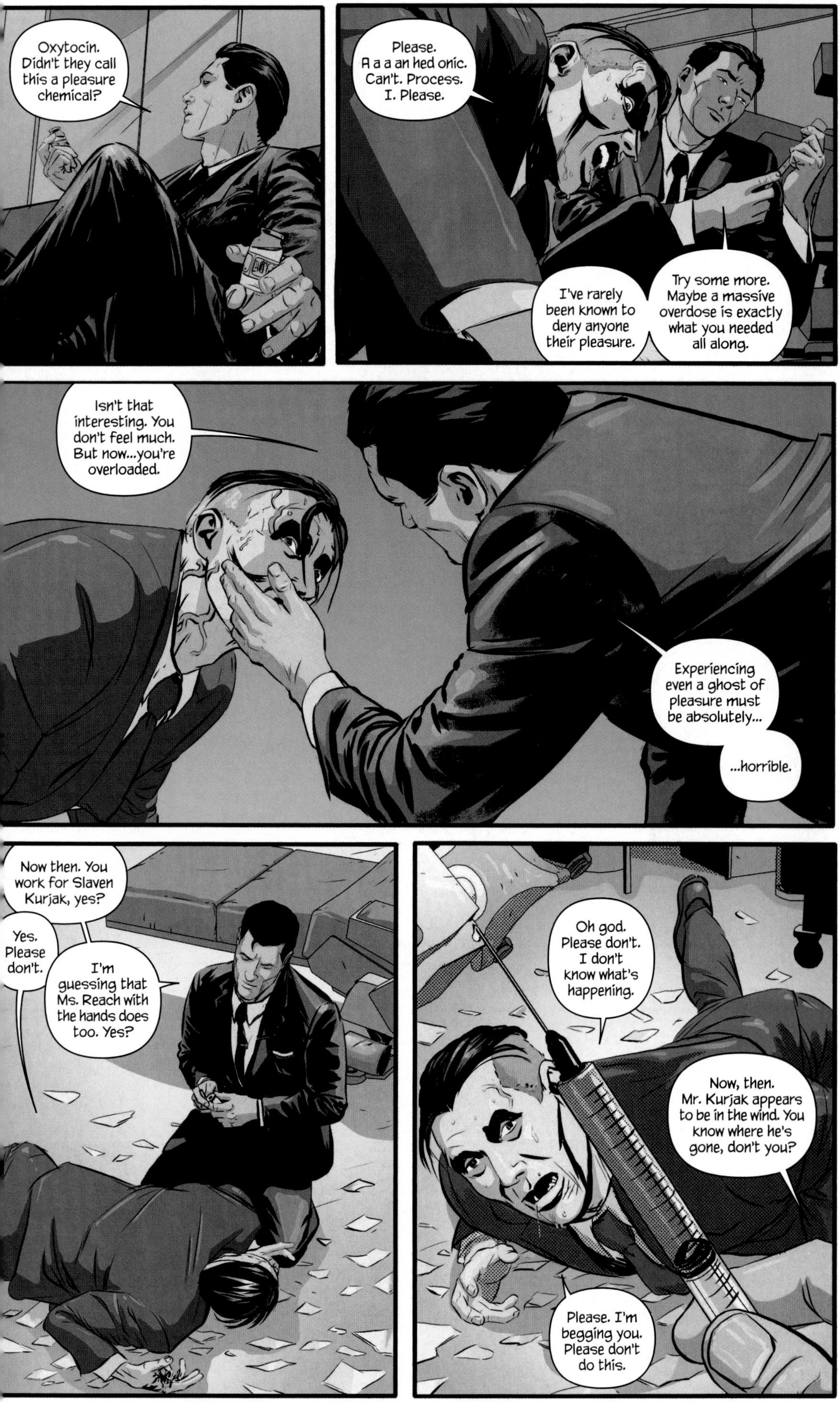
Oxytocin. Didn't they call this a pleasure chemical?
Please. A a a an hed onic. Can't. Process. I. Please.
I've rarely been known to deny anyone their pleasure.
Try some more. Maybe a massive overdose is exactly what you needed all along.
Isn't that interesting. You don't feel much. But now...you're overloaded.
Experiencing even a ghost of pleasure must be absolutely...
...horrible.
Now then. You work for Slaven Kurjak, yes?
Yes. Please don't.
I'm guessing that Ms. Reach with the hands does too. Yes?
Oh god. Please don't. I don't know what's happening.
Now, then. Mr. Kurjak appears to be in the wind. You know where he's gone, don't you?
Please. I'm begging you. Please don't do this.

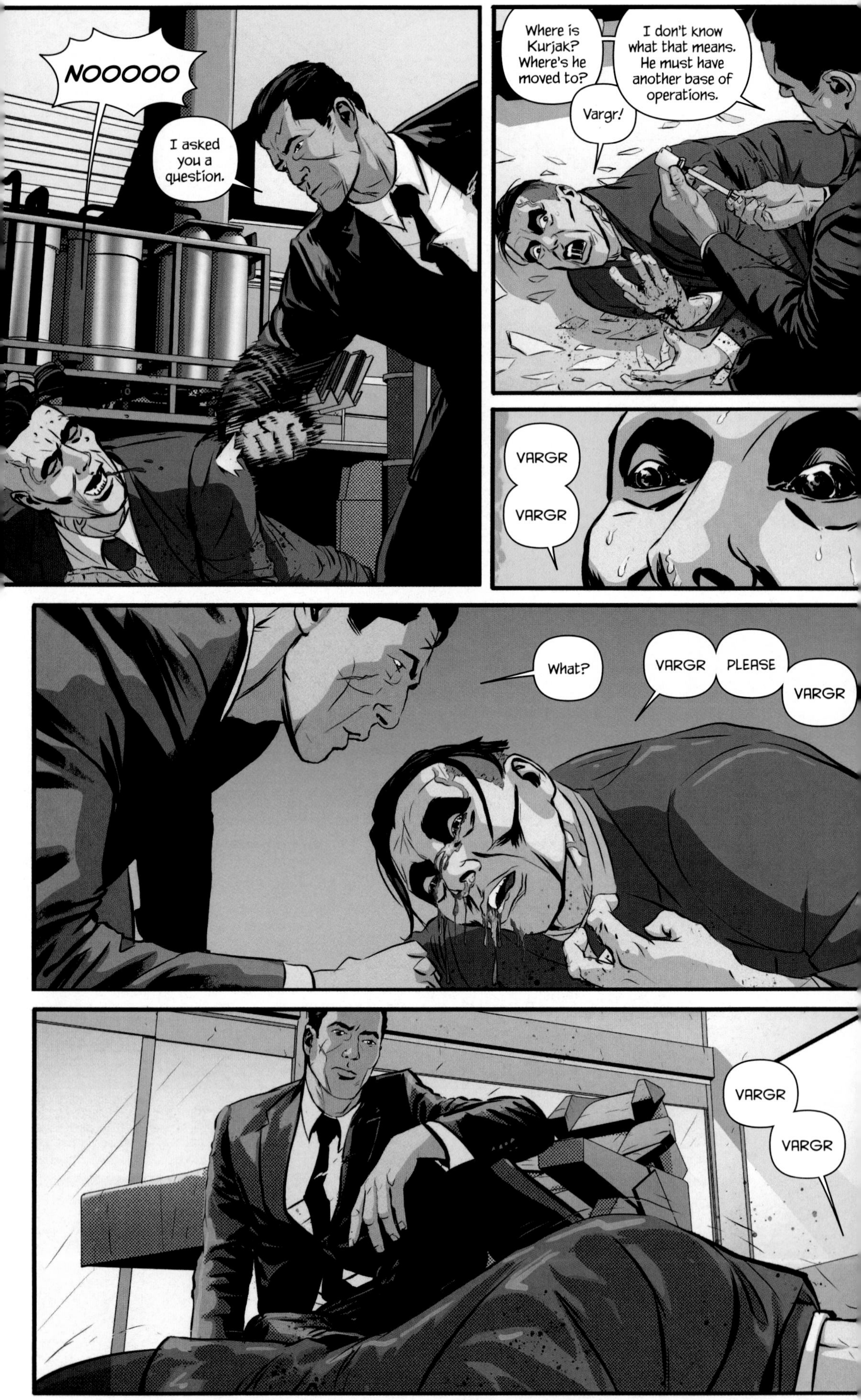
NOOOOO
I asked you a question.
Where is Kurjak? Where's he moved to?
Vargr!
I don't know what that means. He must have another base of operations.
VARGR
VARGR
What?
VARGR
PLEASE
VARGR
VARGR
VARGR

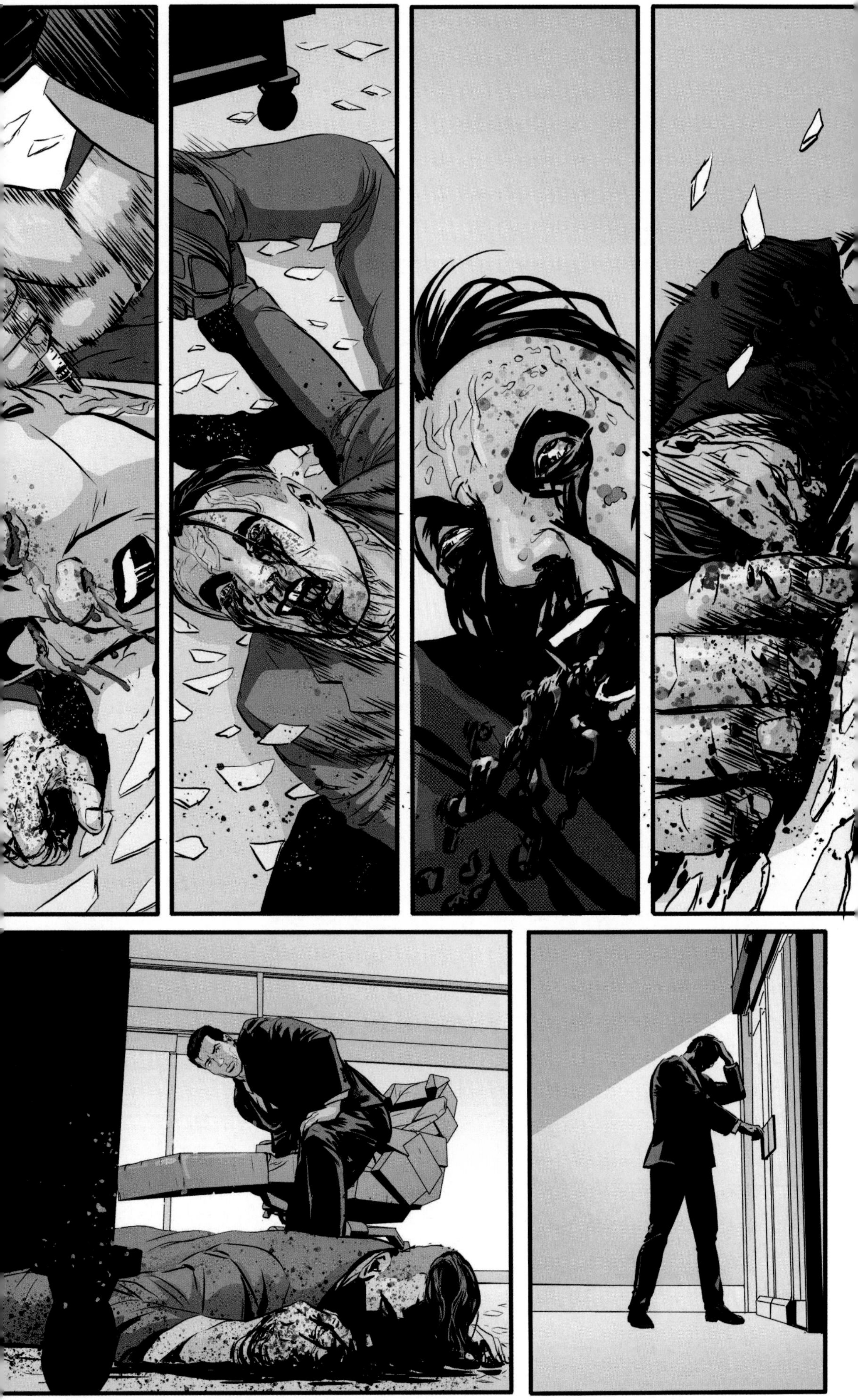

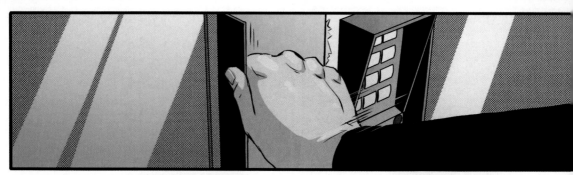

The hard seal is a safety feature.

Hello again.

I'll be right with you, Mr. Kurjak.

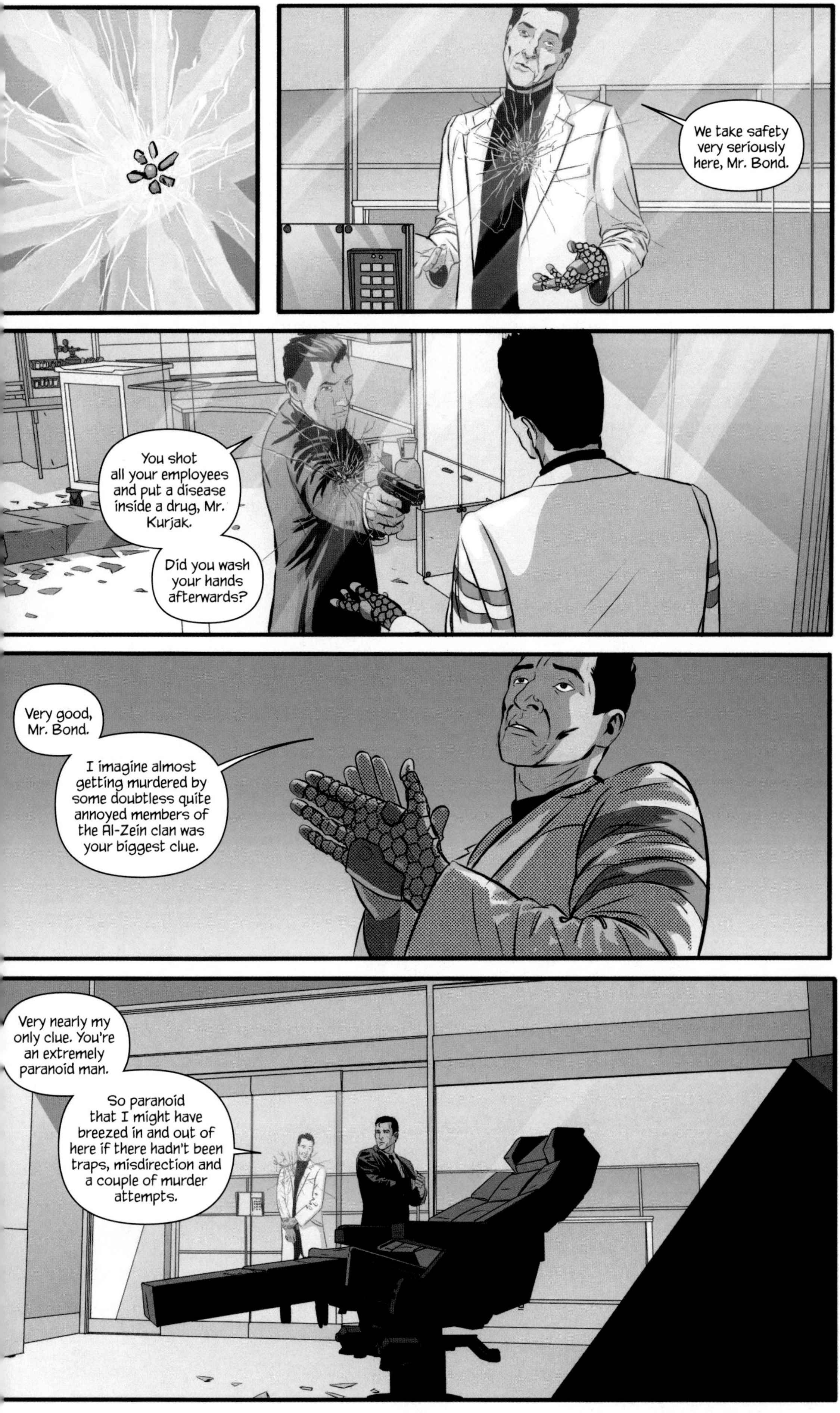
We take safety very seriously here, Mr. Bond.
You shot all your employees and put a disease inside a drug, Mr. Kurjak.
Did you wash your hands afterwards?
Very good, Mr. Bond.
I imagine almost getting murdered by some doubtless quite annoyed members of the Al-Zein clan was your biggest clue.
Very nearly my only clue. You're an extremely paranoid man.
So paranoid that I might have breezed in and out of here if there hadn't been traps, misdirection and a couple of murder attempts.

I would have thought someone who grew up in a concentration camp would be a little more circumspect about drawing attention to themselves.

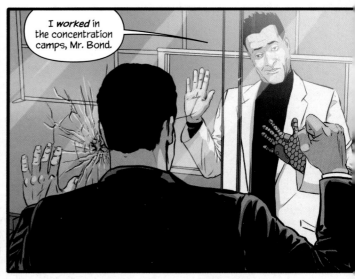

I *worked* in the concentration camps, Mr. Bond.

It was a wondrous playground for a teenager. Complete control of contained systems.

The inmates would have to drink from the contaminated river nearby, and I could watch to see who got sick, and how the dysentery would spread, and it fascinated me.

It was so beautiful.

I thought to myself, this is how the world should be run. Controlled. With experiments.

Britain is an island. The ways to get off it--sea, air, train-are quite limited. It's perfect test bed.

A giant concentration camp with very few vectors for travel.

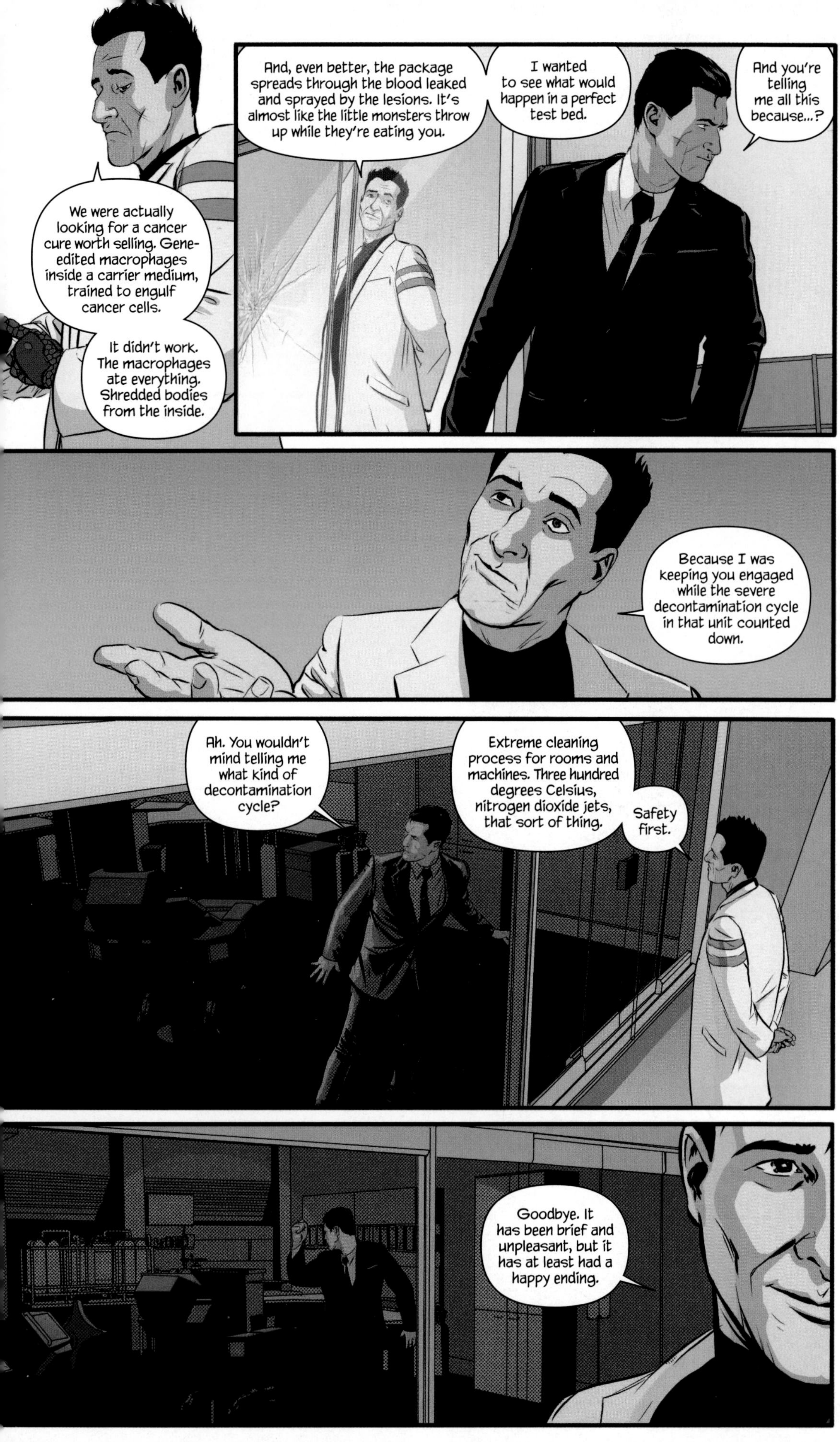
We were actually looking for a cancer cure worth selling. Gene-edited macrophages inside a carrier medium, trained to engulf cancer cells.
It didn't work. The macrophages ate everything. Shredded bodies from the inside.
And, even better, the package spreads through the blood leaked and sprayed by the lesions. It's almost like the little monsters throw up while they're eating you.
I wanted to see what would happen in a perfect test bed.
And you're telling me all this because...?
Because I was keeping you engaged while the severe decontamination cycle in that unit counted down.
Ah. You wouldn't mind telling me what kind of decontamination cycle?
Extreme cleaning process for rooms and machines. Three hundred degrees Celsius, nitrogen dioxide jets, that sort of thing.
Safety first.
Goodbye. It has been brief and unpleasant, but it has at least had a happy ending.

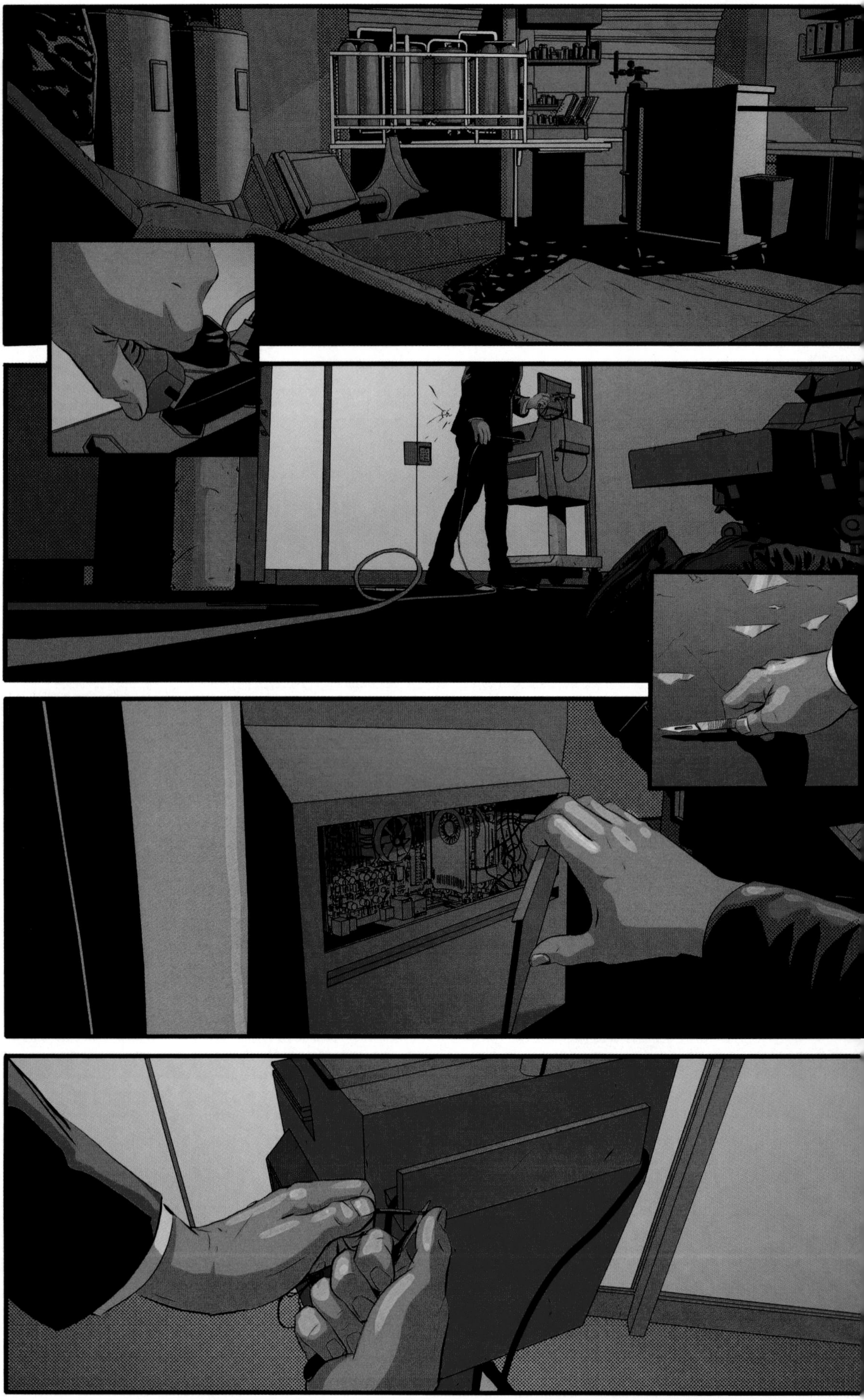

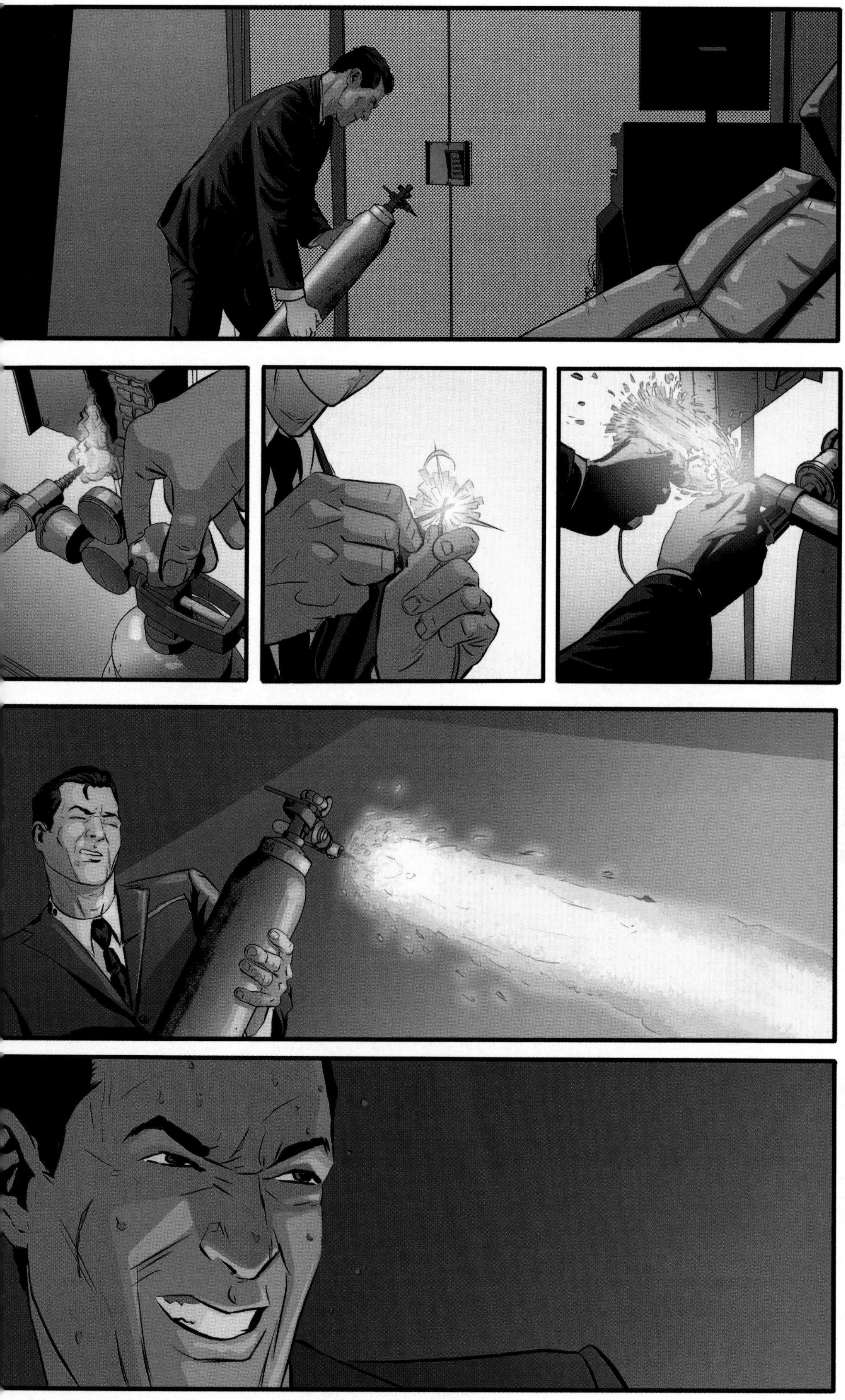

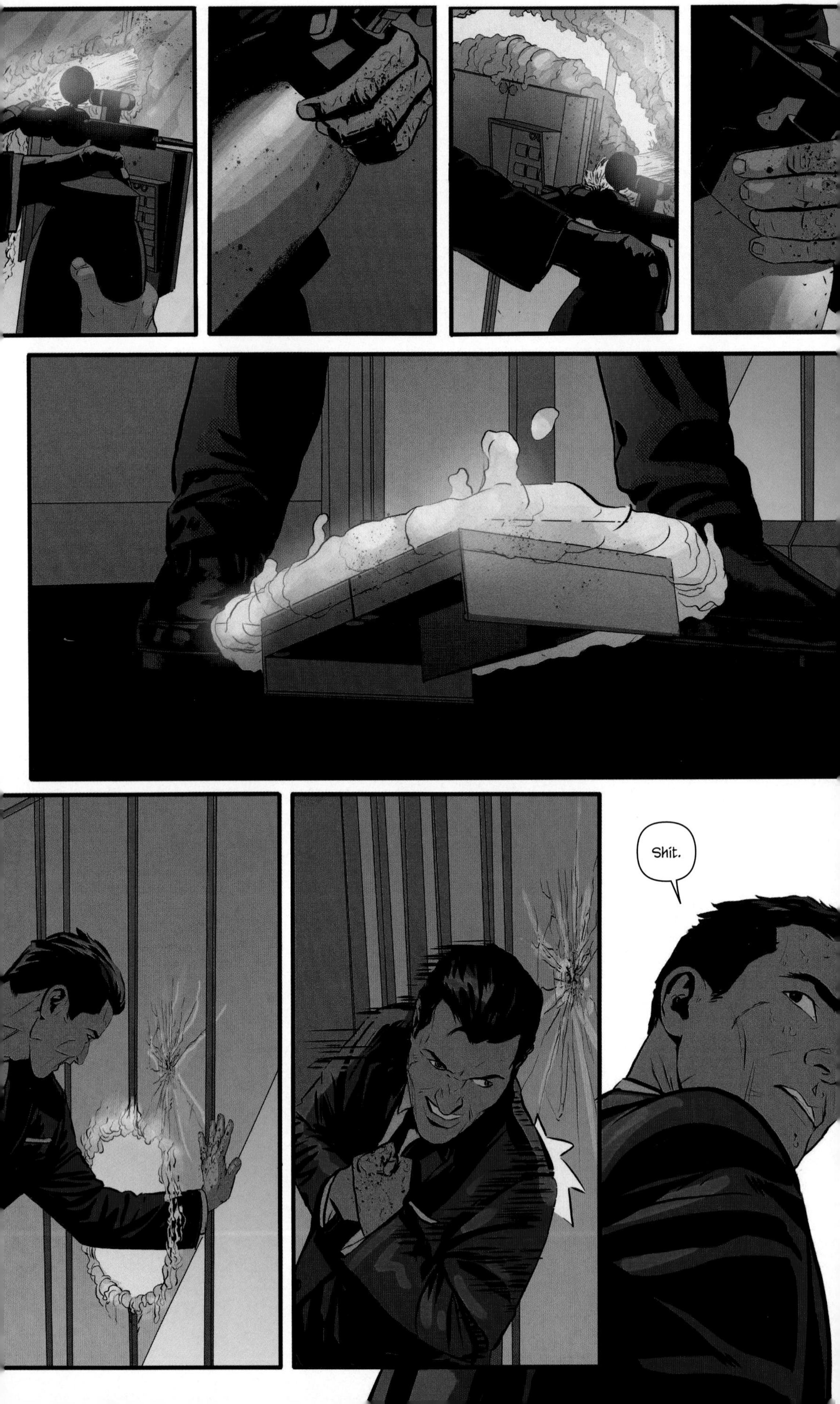
Shit.

ISSUE 005

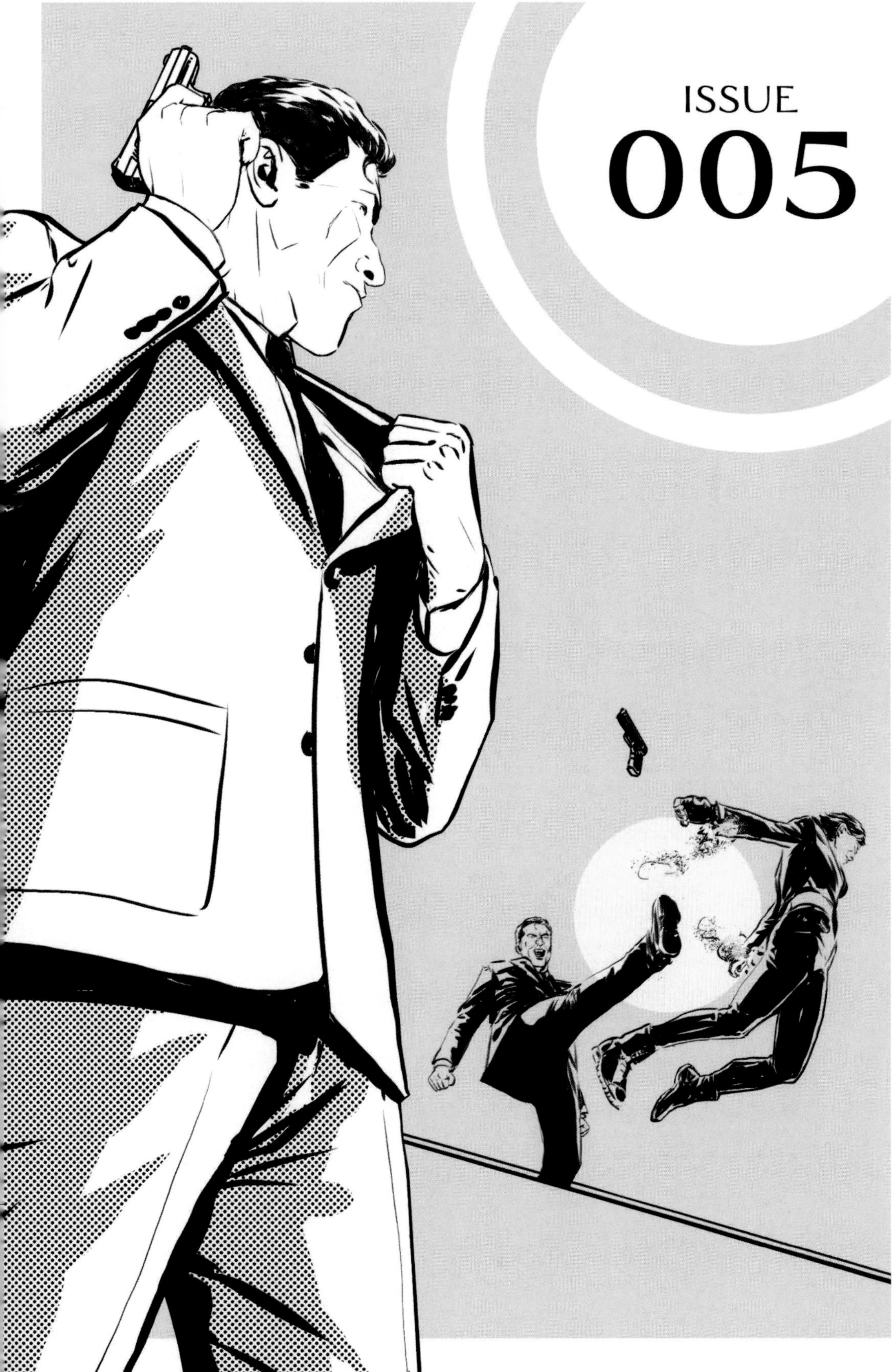

issue #5 main cover by **DOM REARDON**

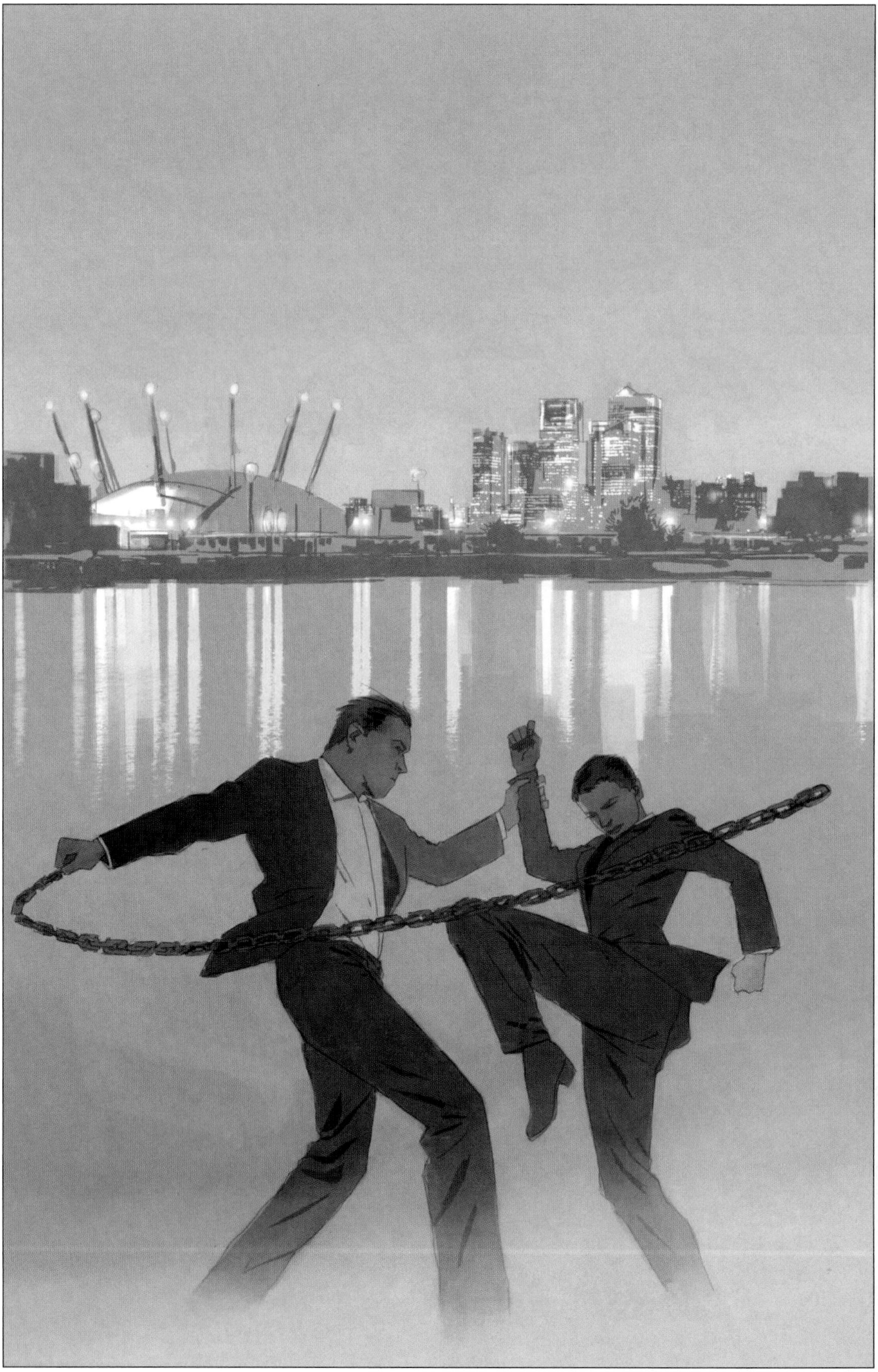

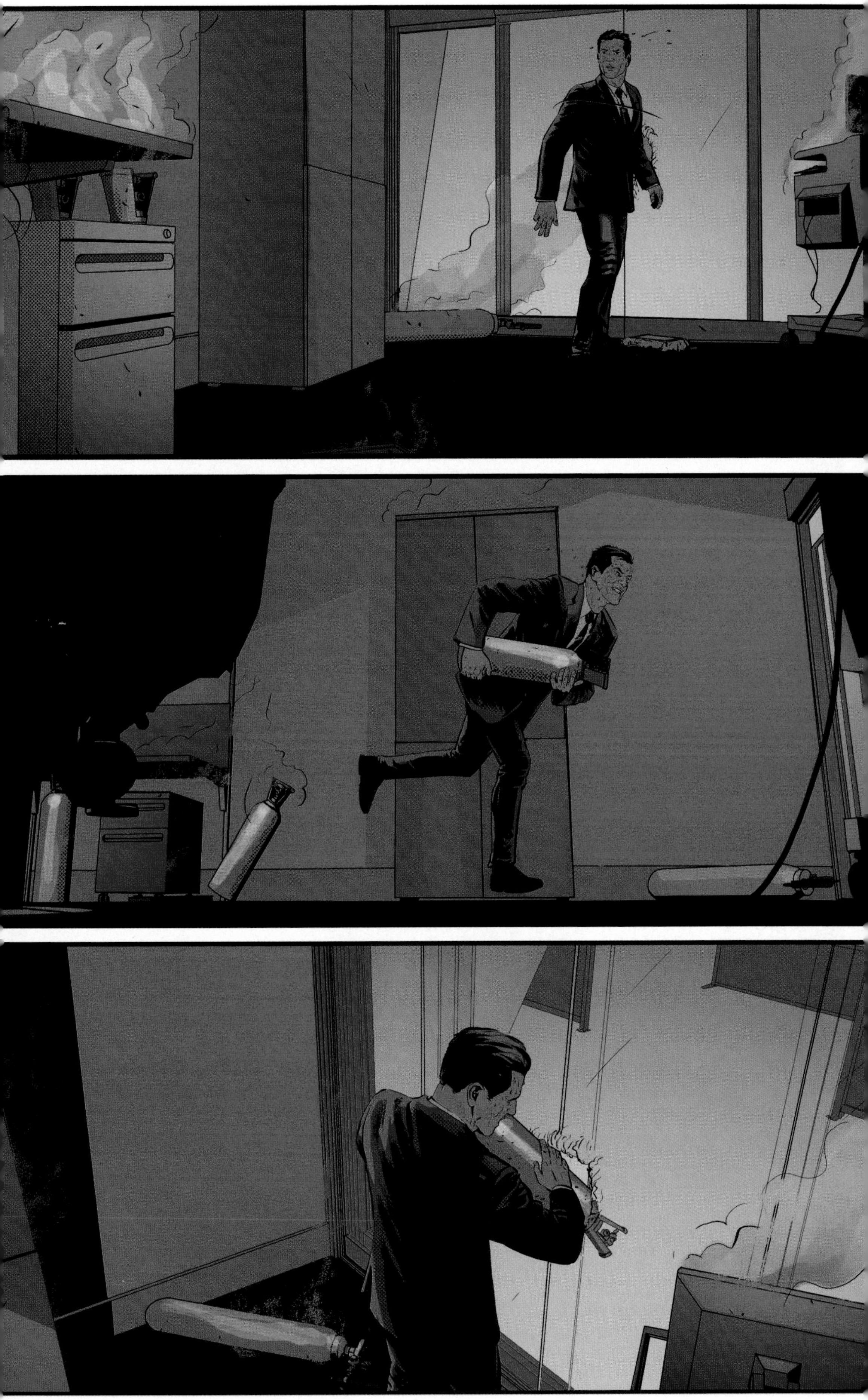

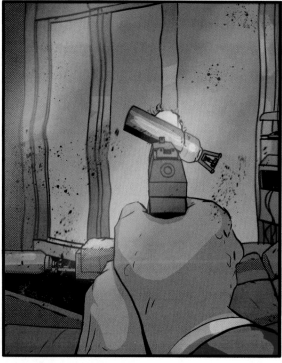

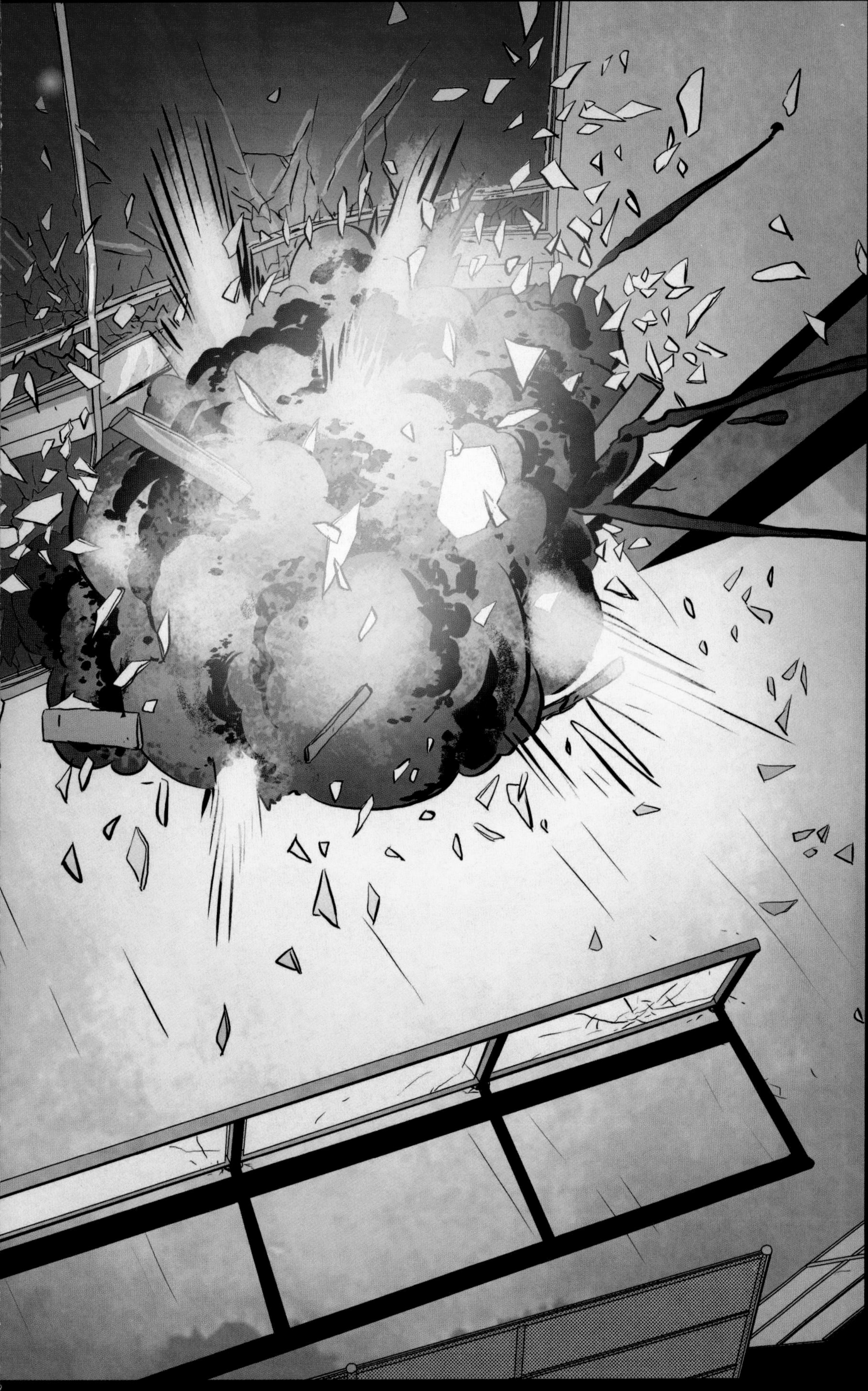

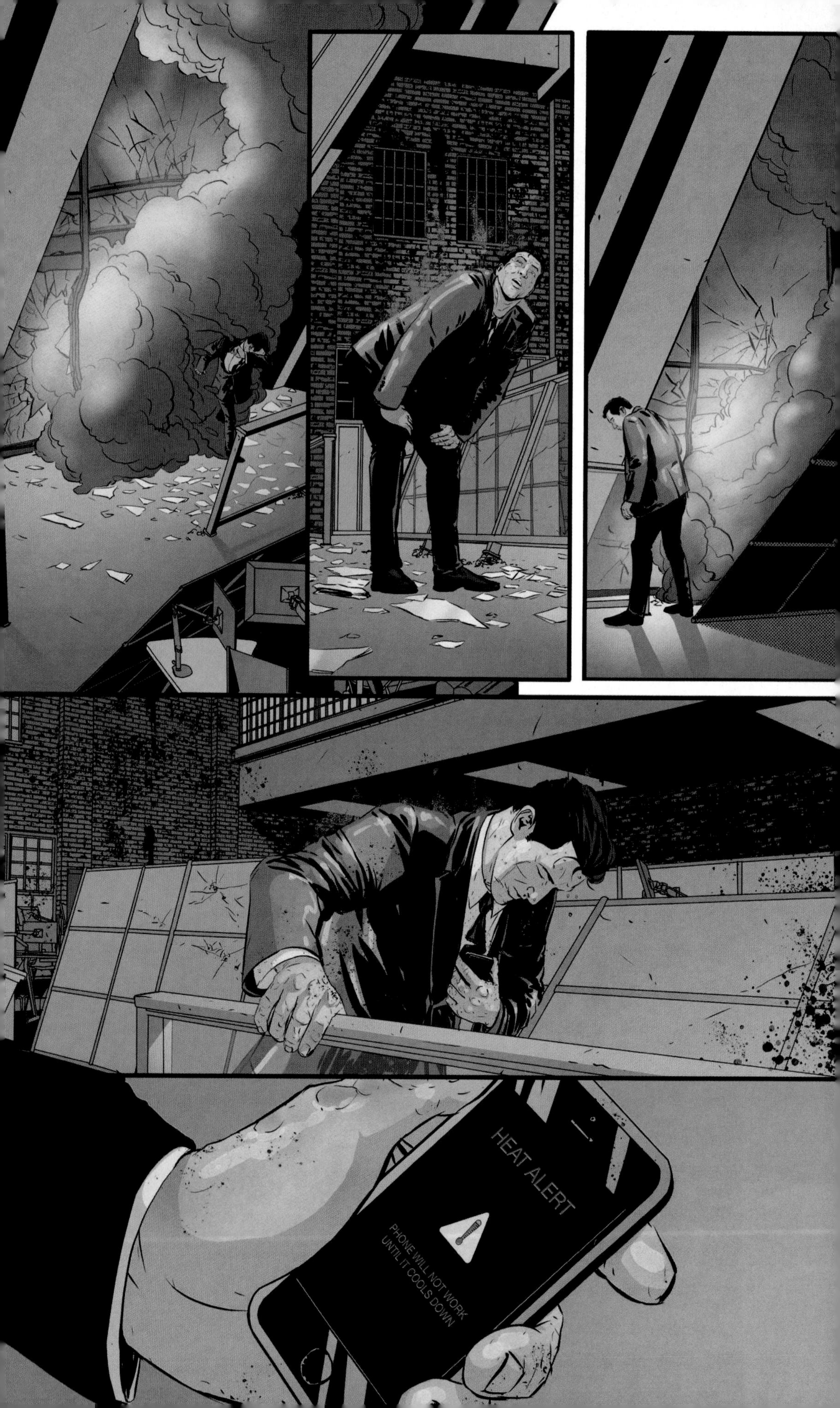
HEAT ALERT
PHONE WILL NOT WORK
UNTIL IT COOLS DOWN

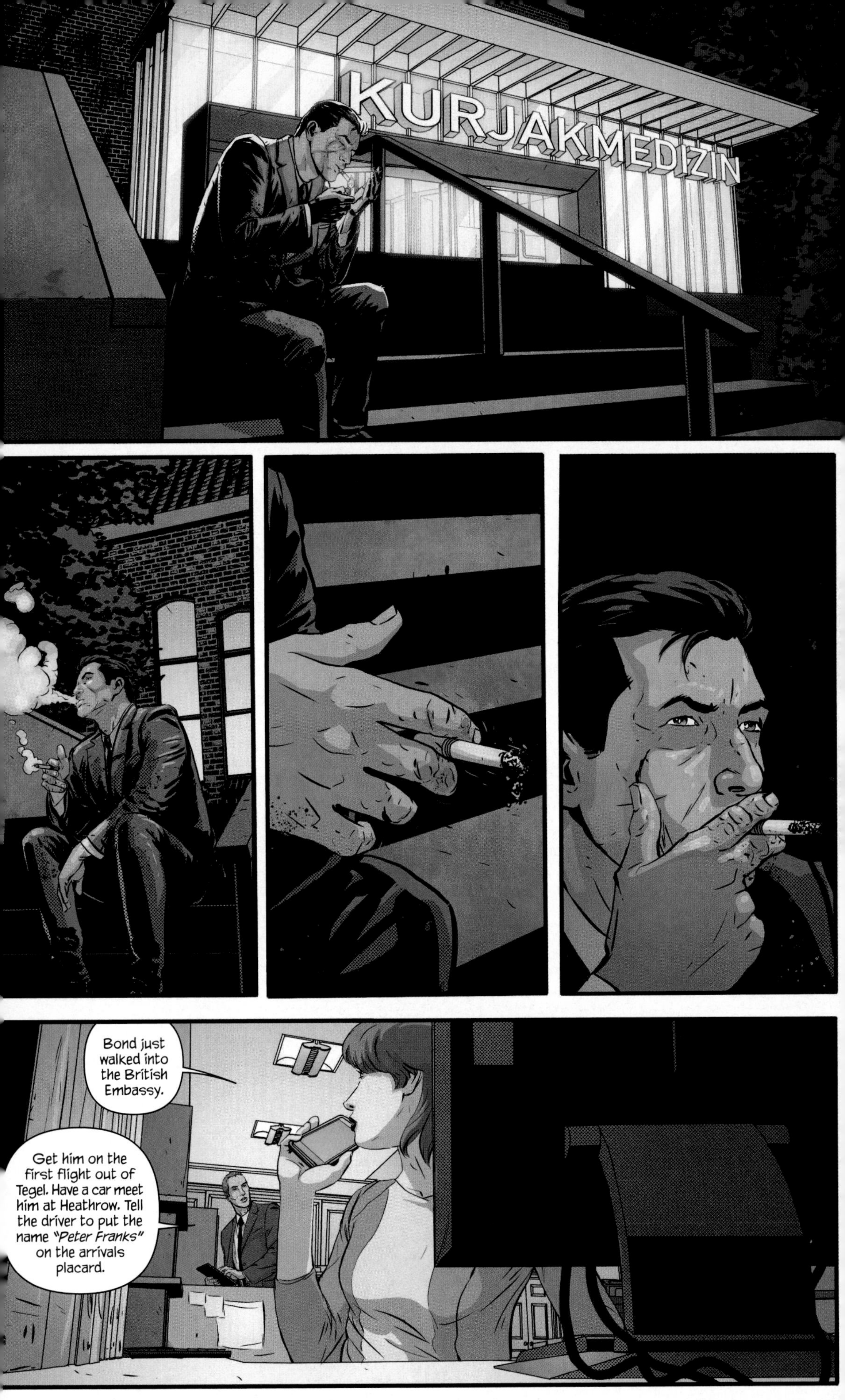
KURJAKMEDIZIN
Bond just walked into the British Embassy.
Get him on the first flight out of Tegel. Have a car meet him at Heathrow. Tell the driver to put the name *"Peter Franks"* on the arrivals placard.

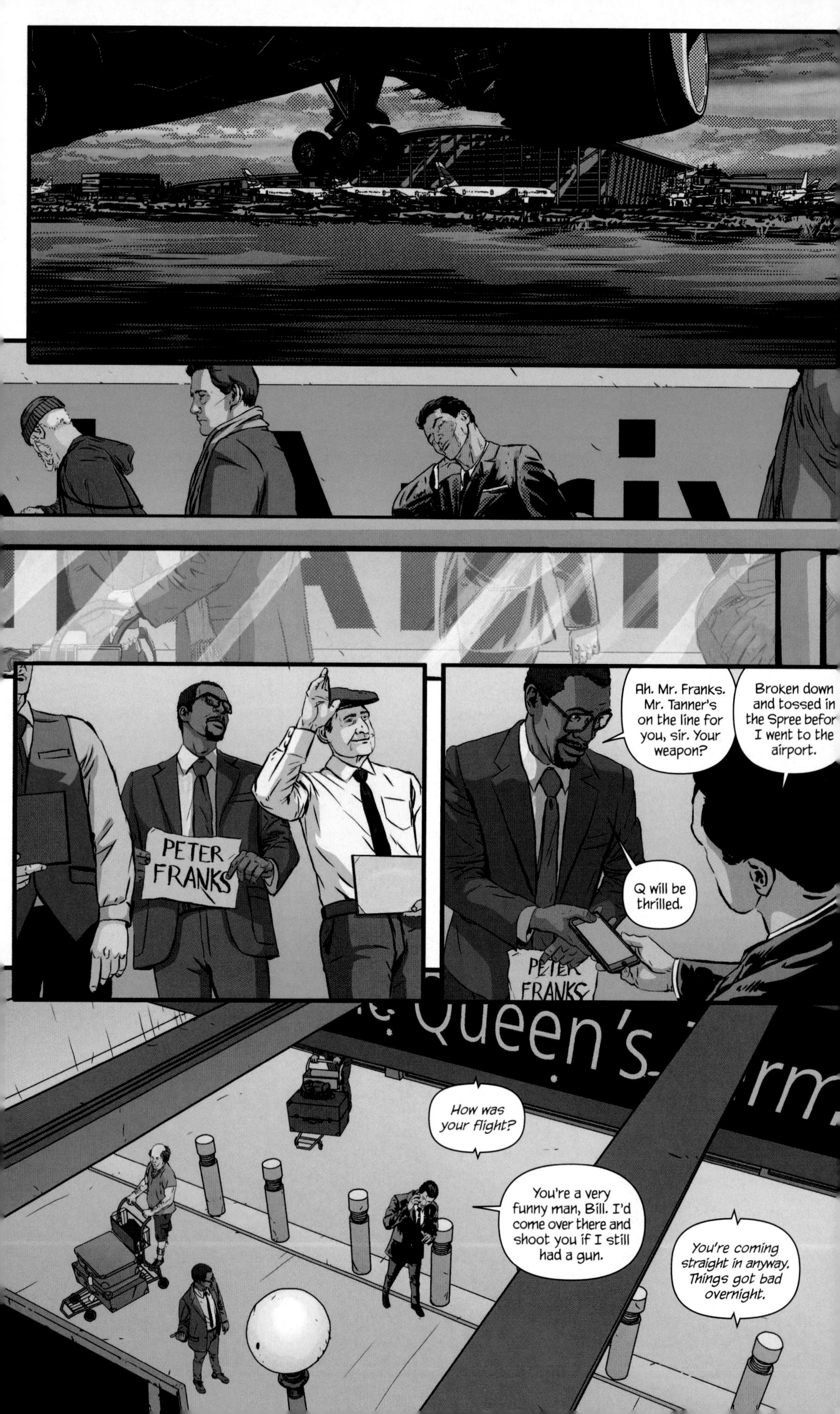
PETER FRANKS
Ah. Mr. Franks. Mr. Tanner's on the line for you, sir. Your weapon?
Broken down and tossed in the Spree befor I went to the airport.
Q will be thrilled.
Queen's
How was your flight?
You're a very funny man, Bill. I'd come over there and shoot you if I still had a gun.
You're coming straight in anyway. Things got bad overnight.

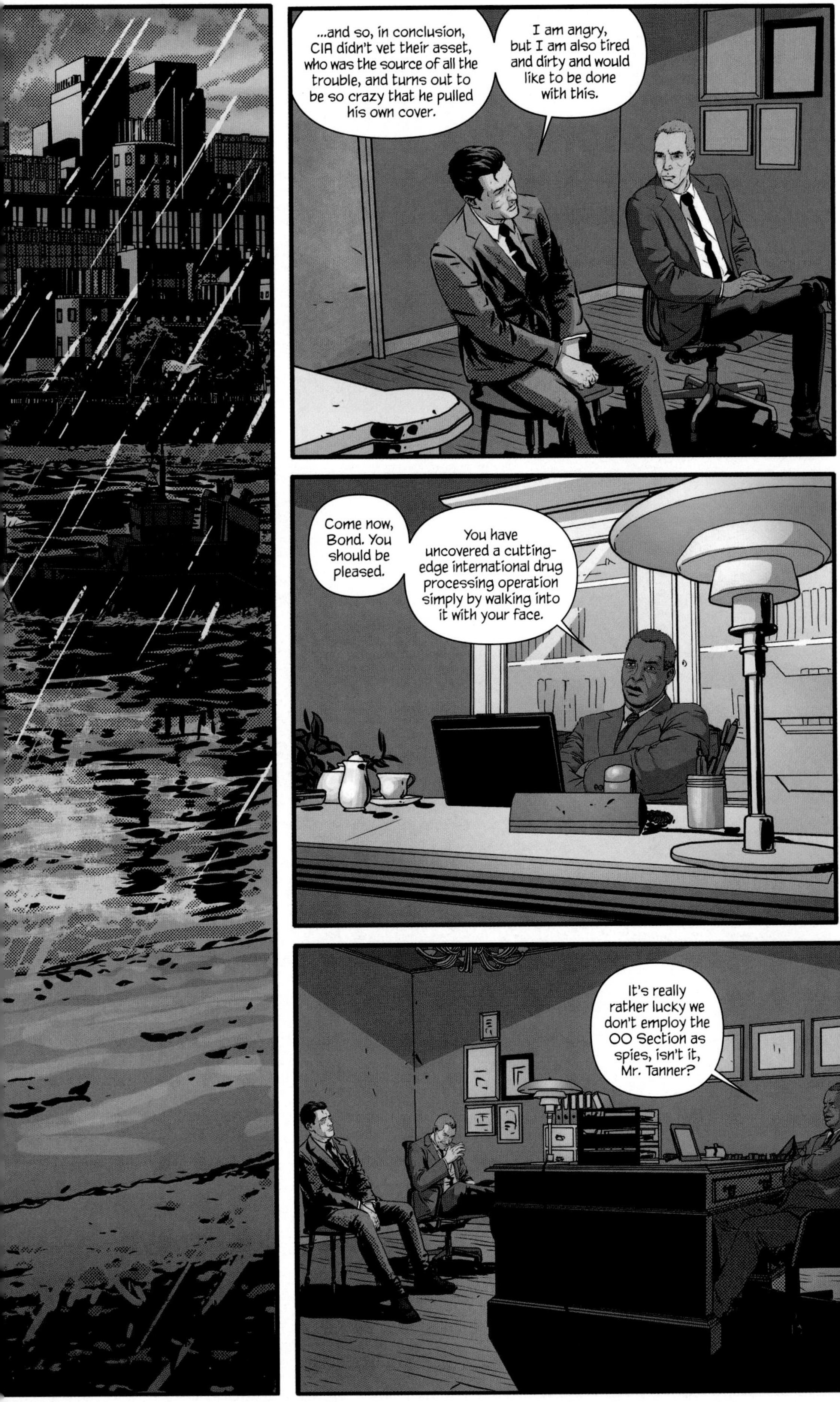
...and so, in conclusion, CIA didn't vet their asset, who was the source of all the trouble, and turns out to be so crazy that he pulled his own cover.
I am angry, but I am also tired and dirty and would like to be done with this.
Come now, Bond. You should be pleased.
You have uncovered a cutting-edge international drug processing operation simply by walking into it with your face.
It's really rather lucky we don't employ the OO Section as spies, isn't it, Mr. Tanner?

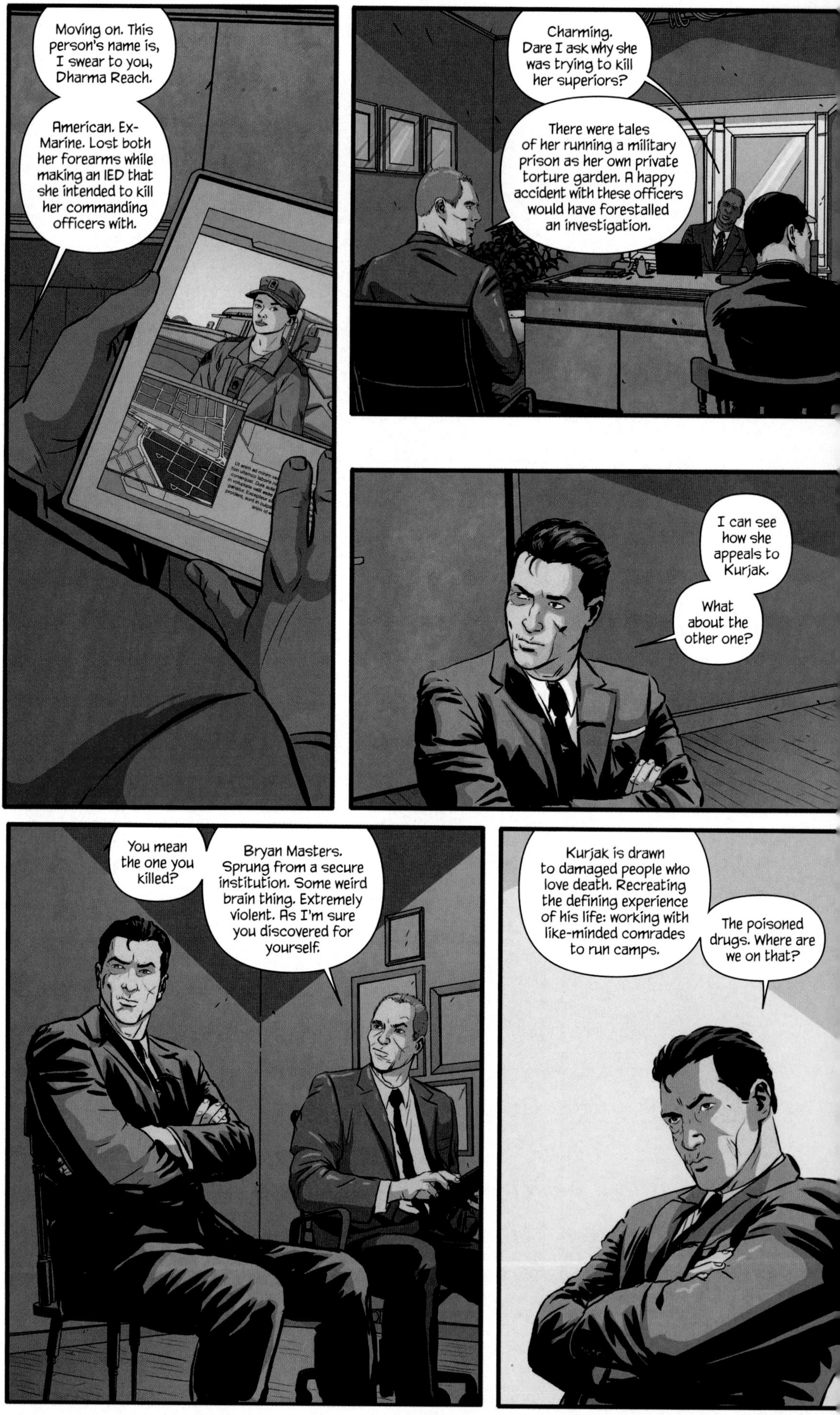
Moving on. This person's name is, I swear to you, Dharma Reach.
American. Ex-Marine. Lost both her forearms while making an IED that she intended to kill her commanding officers with.
Charming. Dare I ask why she was trying to kill her superiors?
There were tales of her running a military prison as her own private torture garden. A happy accident with these officers would have forestalled an investigation.
I can see how she appeals to Kurjak.
What about the other one?
You mean the one you killed?
Bryan Masters. Sprung from a secure institution. Some weird brain thing. Extremely violent. As I'm sure you discovered for yourself.
Kurjak is drawn to damaged people who love death. Recreating the defining experience of his life: working with like-minded comrades to run camps.
The poisoned drugs. Where are we on that?

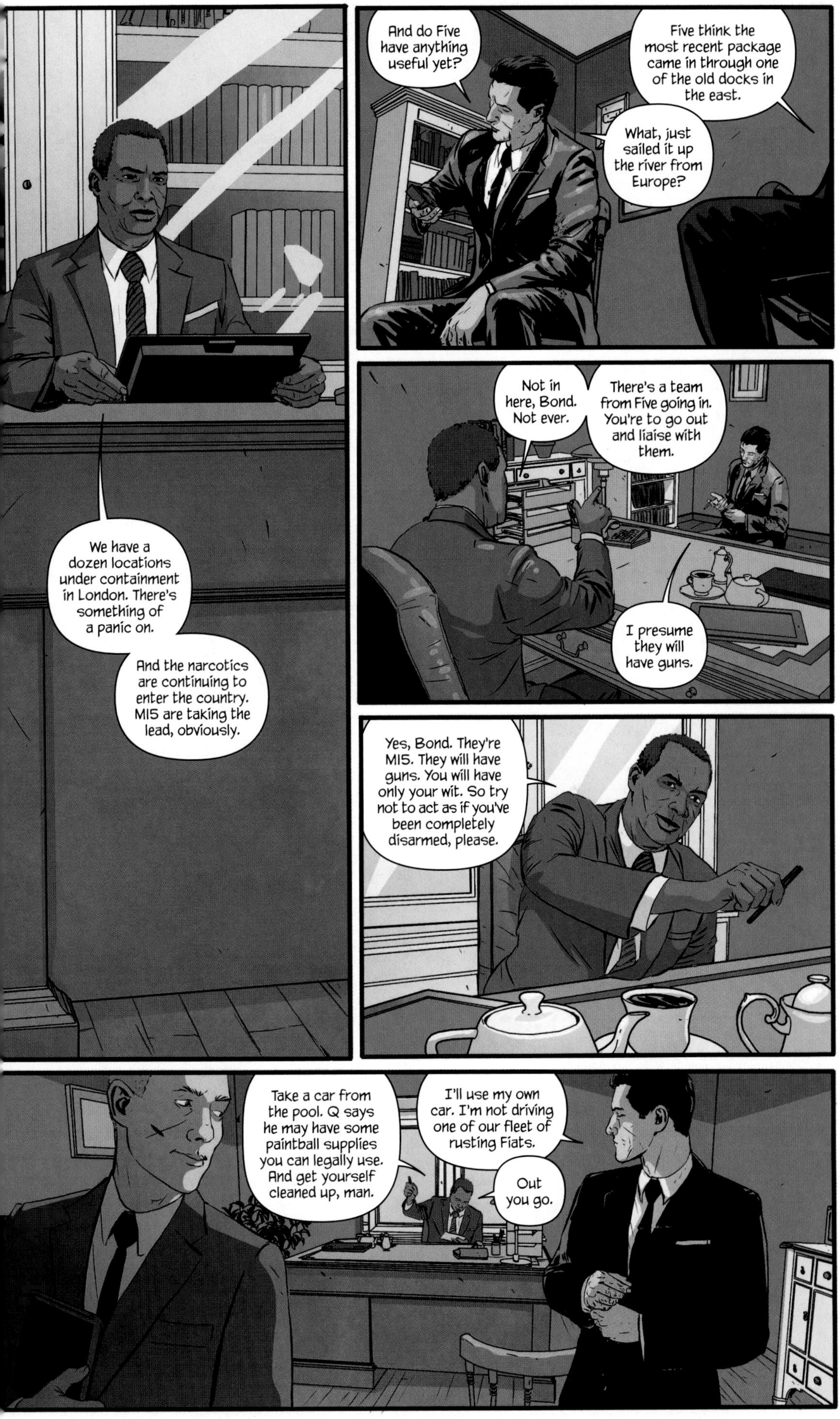
And do Five have anything useful yet?
Five think the most recent package came in through one of the old docks in the east.
What, just sailed it up the river from Europe?
We have a dozen locations under containment in London. There's something of a panic on.
And the narcotics are continuing to enter the country. MI5 are taking the lead, obviously.
Not in here, Bond. Not ever.
There's a team from Five going in. You're to go out and liaise with them.
I presume they will have guns.
Yes, Bond. They're MI5. They will have guns. You will have only your wit. So try not to act as if you've been completely disarmed, please.
Take a car from the pool. Q says he may have some paintball supplies you can legally use. And get yourself cleaned up, man.
I'll use my own car. I'm not driving one of our fleet of rusting Fiats.
Out you go.

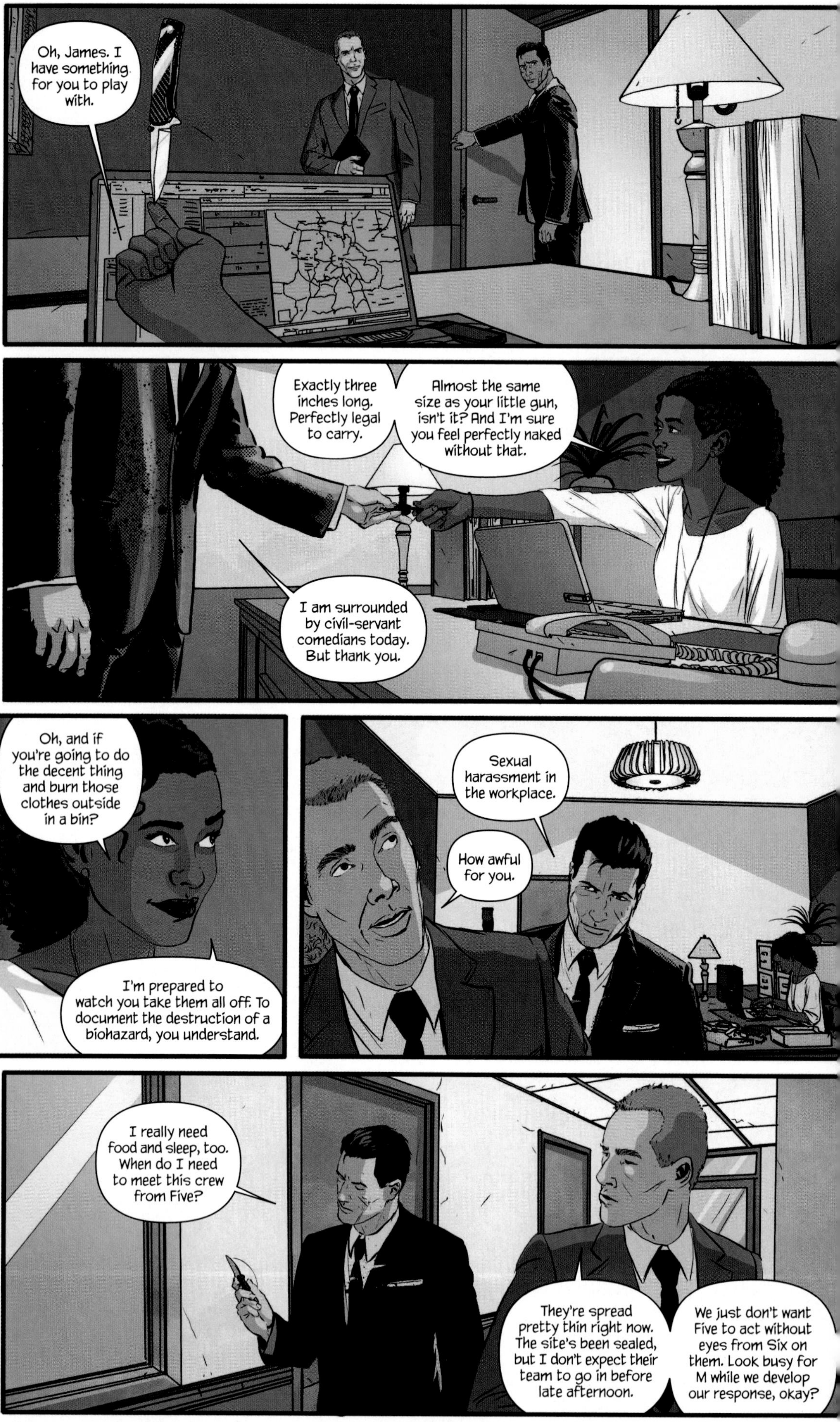
Oh, James. I have something for you to play with.
Exactly three inches long. Perfectly legal to carry.
Almost the same size as your little gun, isn't it? And I'm sure you feel perfectly naked without that.
I am surrounded by civil-servant comedians today. But thank you.
Oh, and if you're going to do the decent thing and burn those clothes outside in a bin?
I'm prepared to watch you take them all off. To document the destruction of a biohazard, you understand.
Sexual harassment in the workplace.
How awful for you.
I really need food and sleep, too. When do I need to meet this crew from Five?
They're spread pretty thin right now. The site's been sealed, but I don't expect their team to go in before late afternoon.
We just don't want Five to act without eyes from Six on them. Look busy for M while we develop our response, okay?

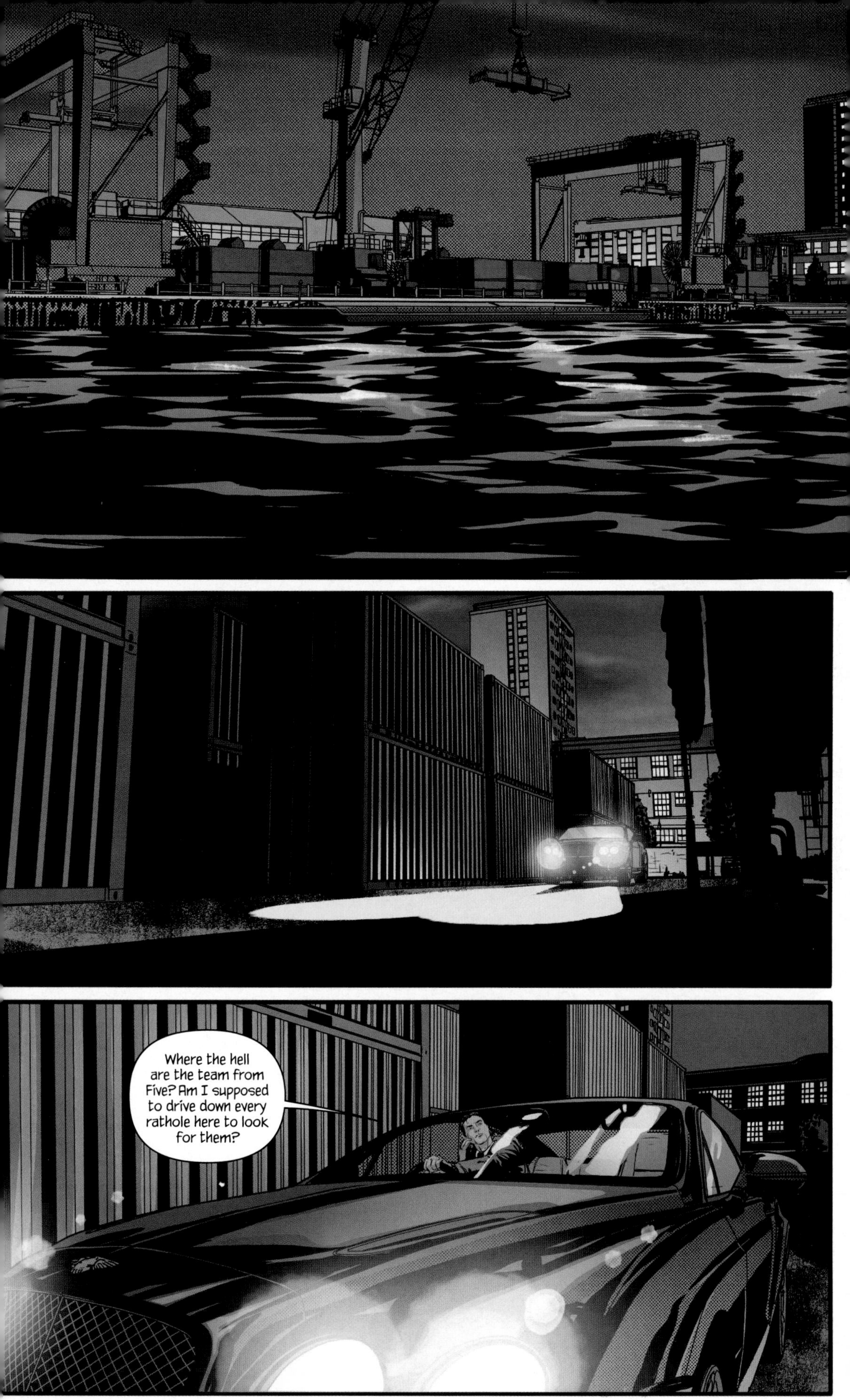
Where the hell are the team from Five? Am I supposed to drive down every rathole here to look for them?

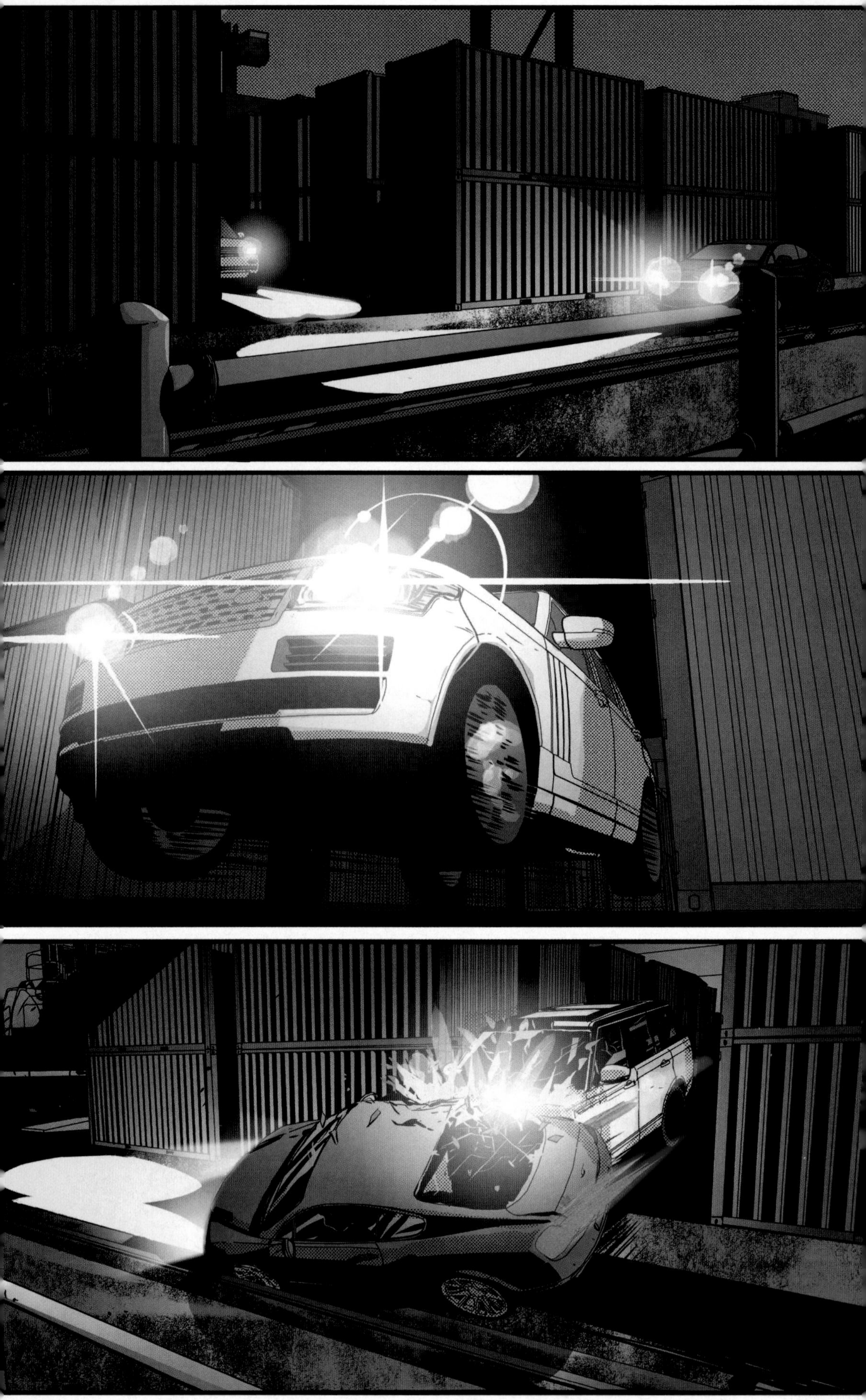

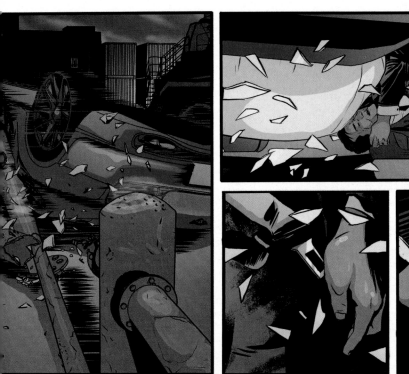
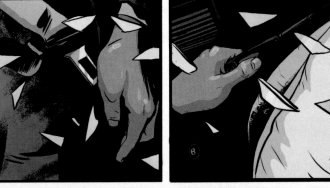

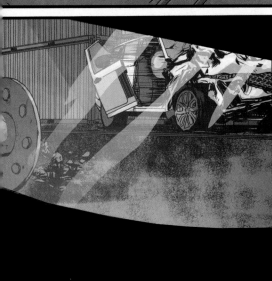
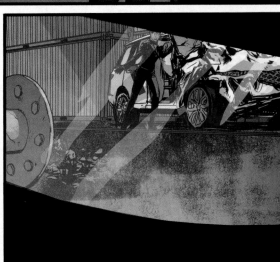

YOU KILLED HIM!

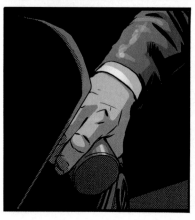

Tortured him, too.

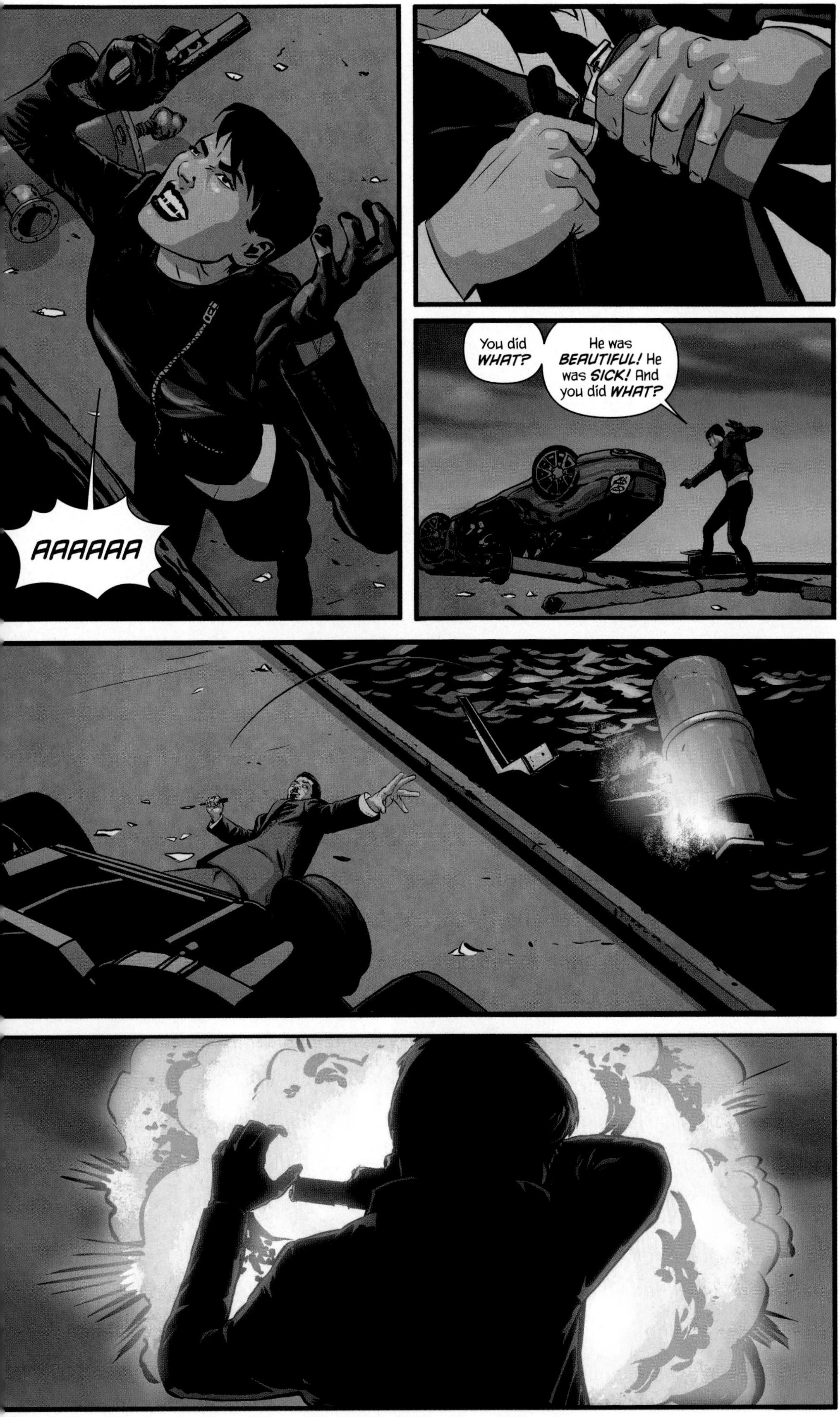
AAAAAA
You did WHAT?
He was BEAUTIFUL! He was SICK! And you did WHAT?

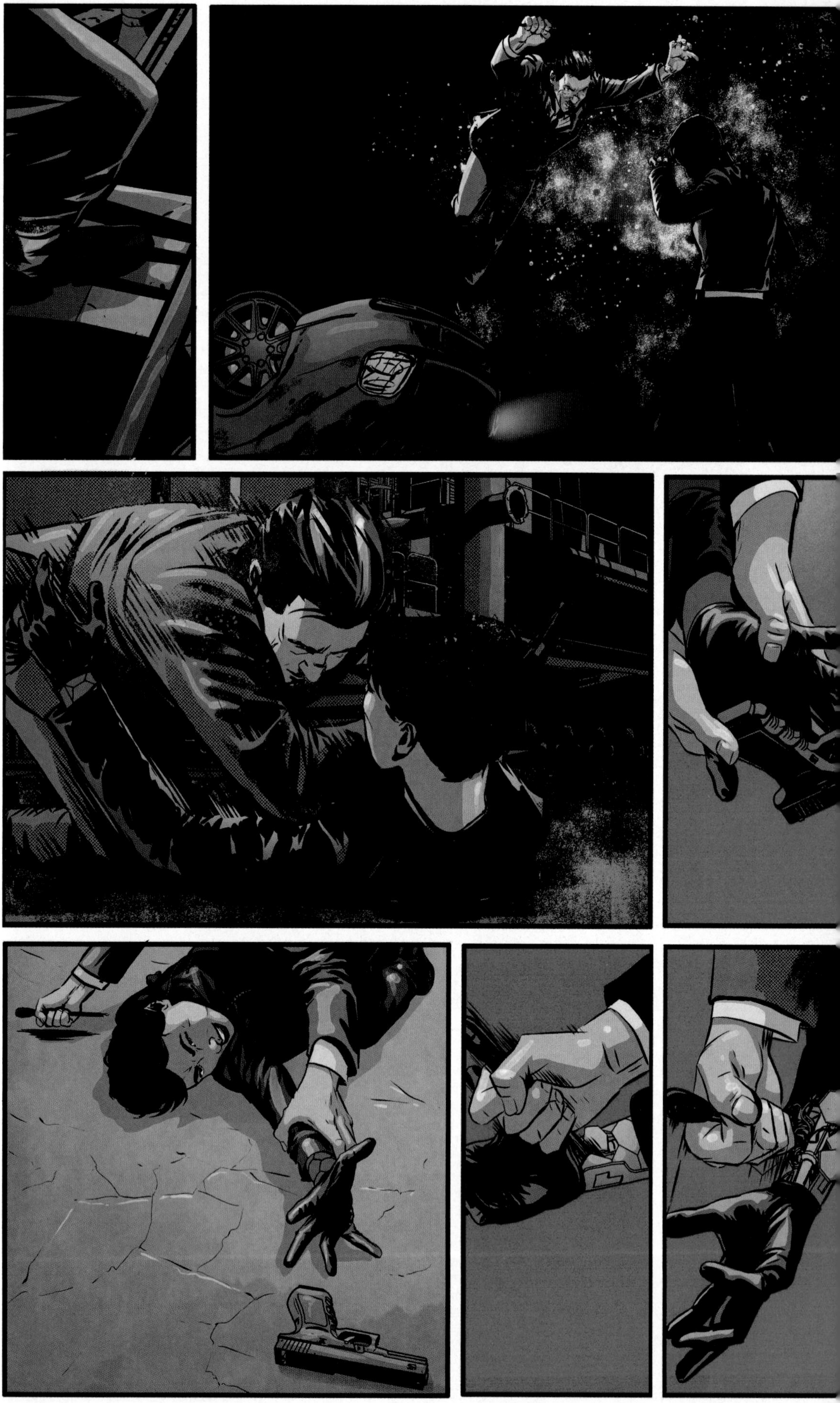

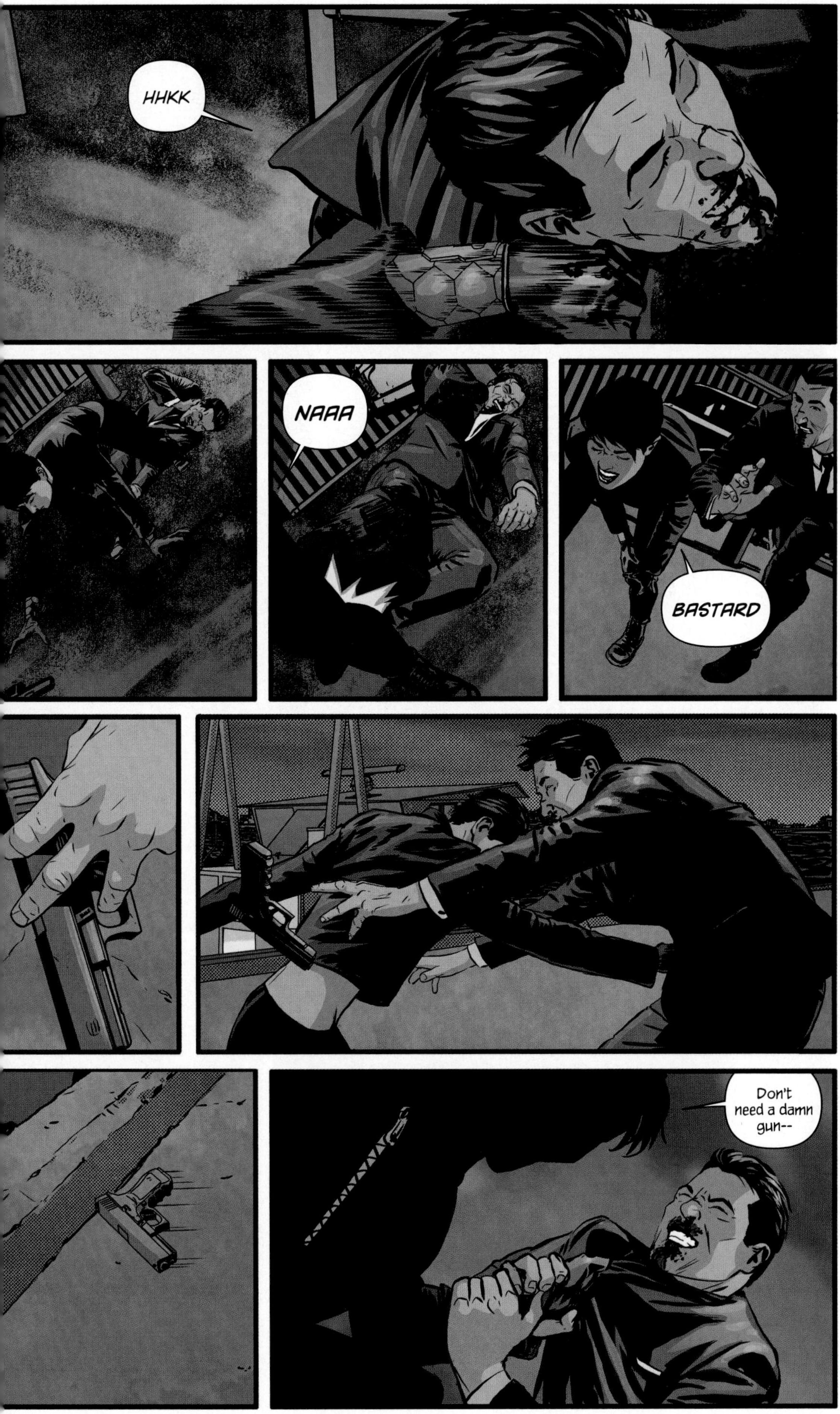
HHKK
NAAA
BASTARD
Don't need a damn gun--

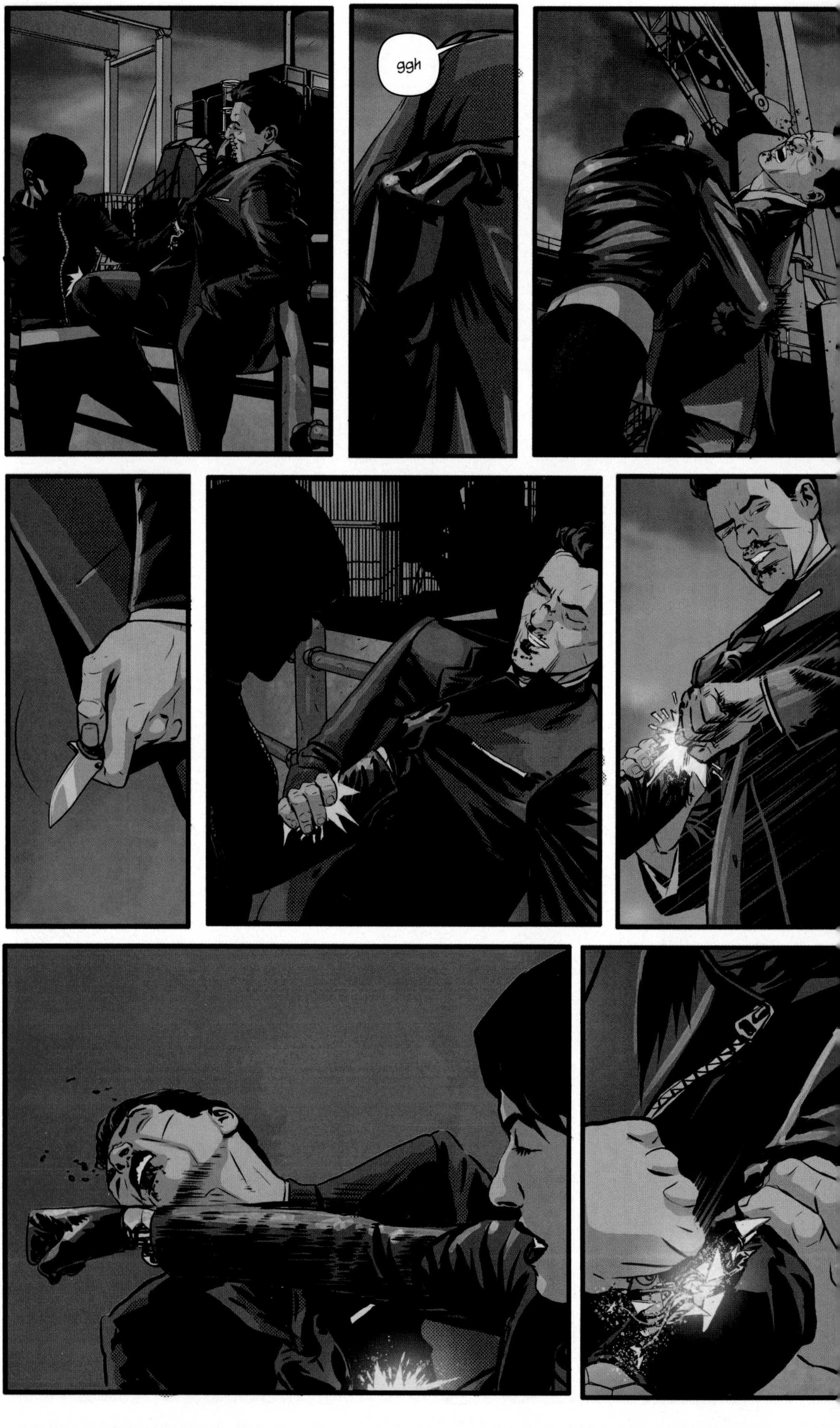
ggh

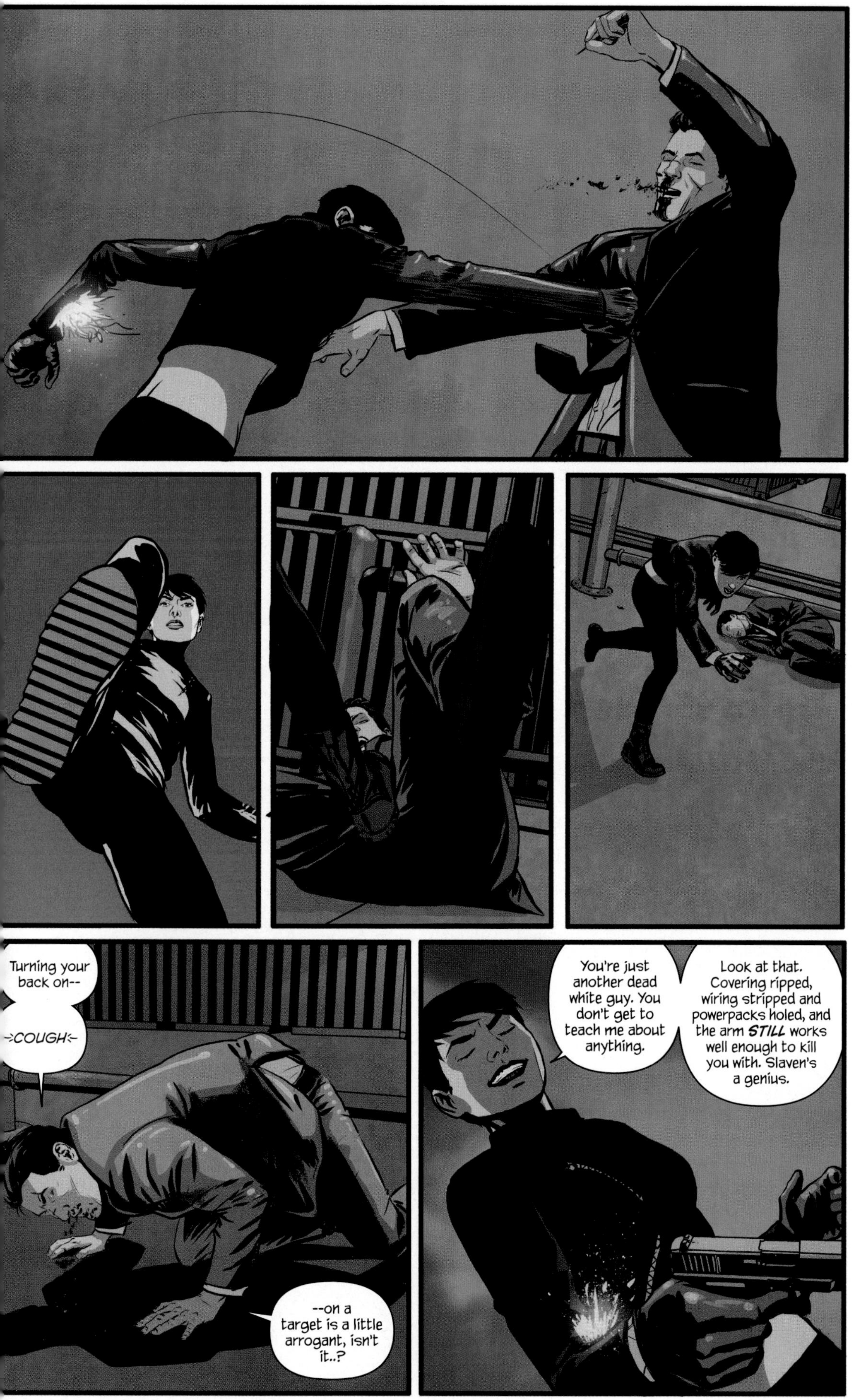
Turning your back on--
-COUGH-
--on a target is a little arrogant, isn't it..?
You're just another dead white guy. You don't get to teach me about anything.
Look at that. Covering ripped, wiring stripped and powerpacks holed, and the arm STILL works well enough to kill you with. Slaven's a genius.

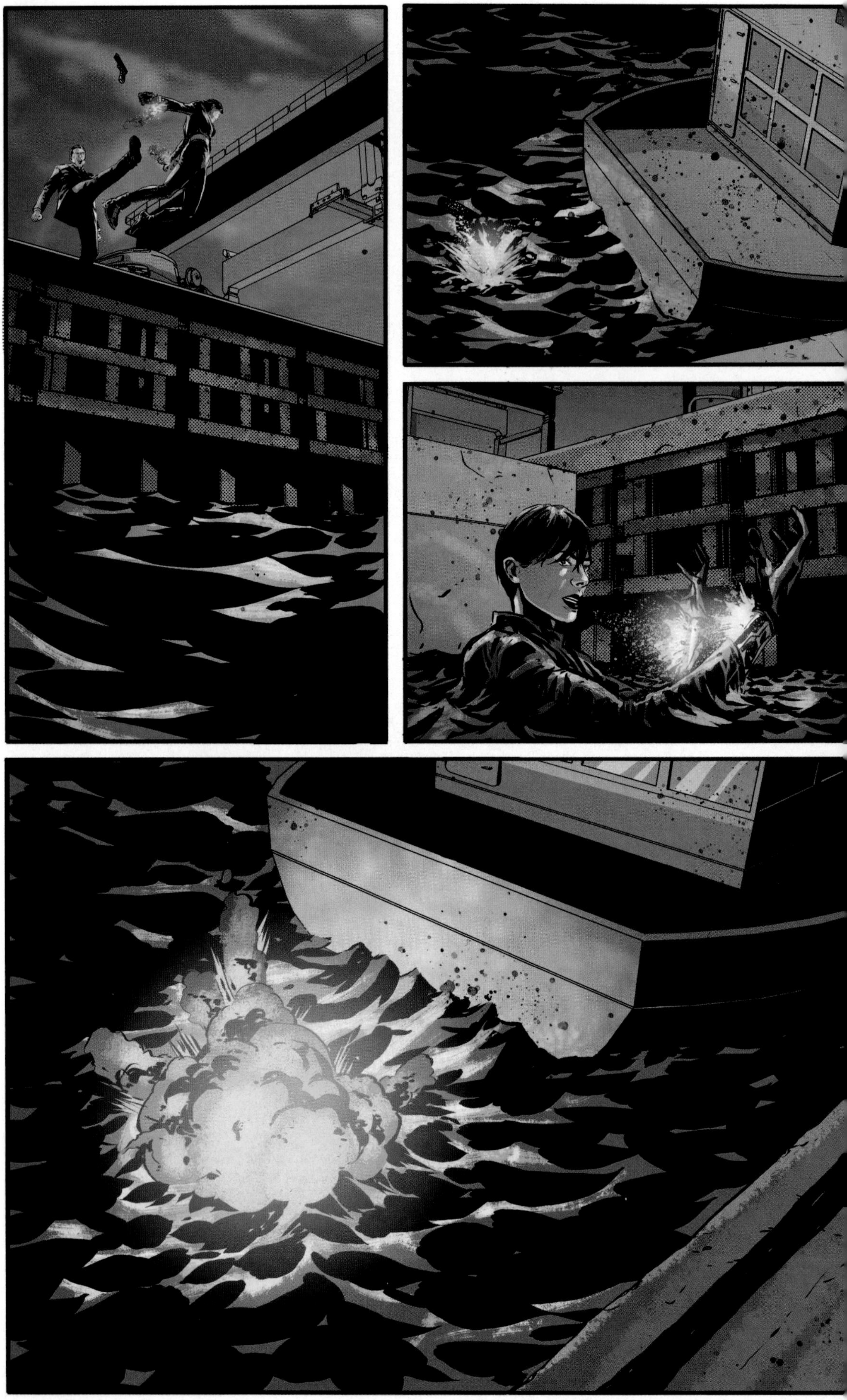

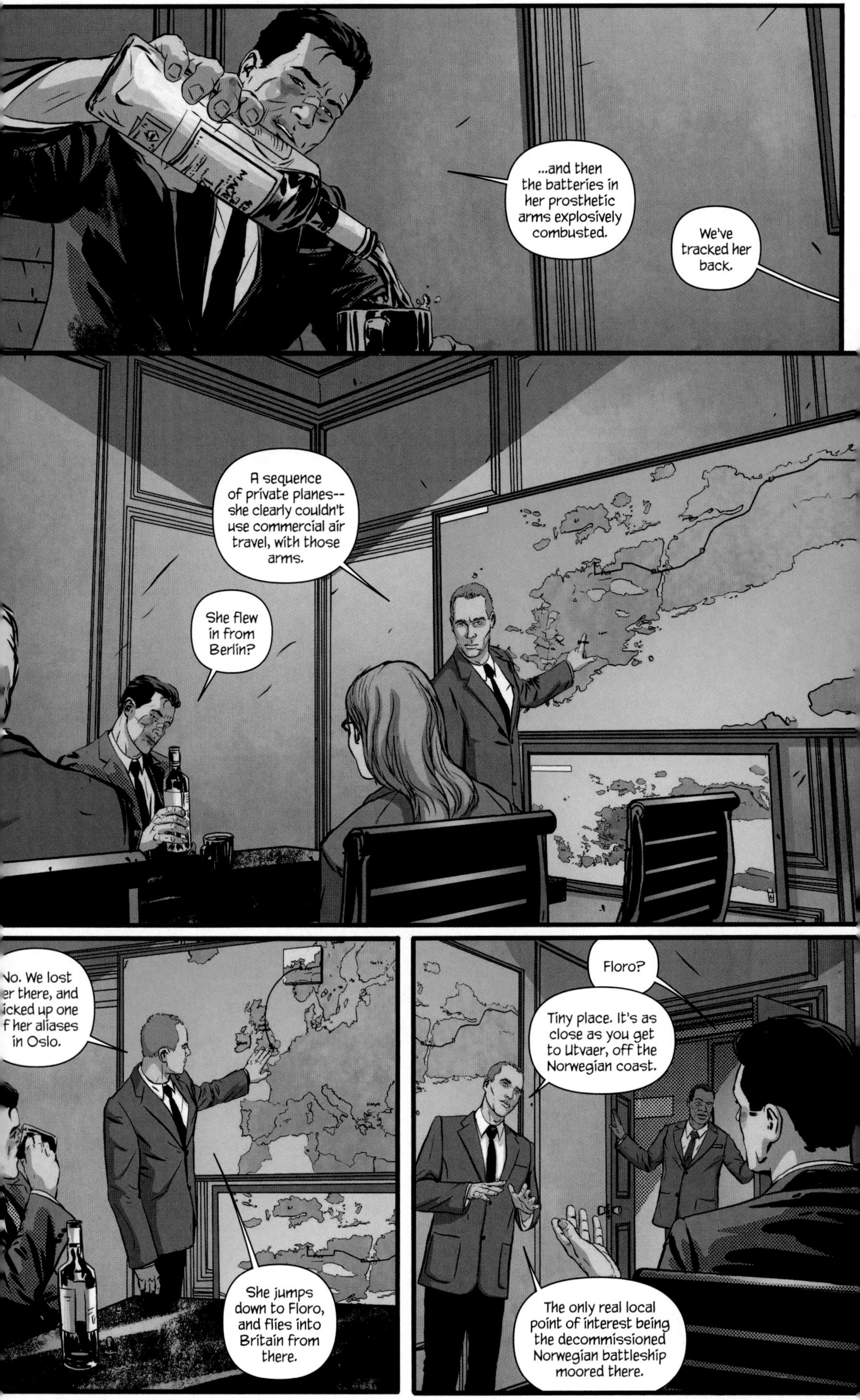
...and then the batteries in her prosthetic arms explosively combusted.
We've tracked her back.
A sequence of private planes--she clearly couldn't use commercial air travel, with those arms.
She flew in from Berlin?
No. We lost her there, and picked up one of her aliases in Oslo.
She jumps down to Floro, and flies into Britain from there.
Floro?
Tiny place. It's as close as you get to Utvaer, off the Norwegian coast.
The only real local point of interest being the decommissioned Norwegian battleship moored there.

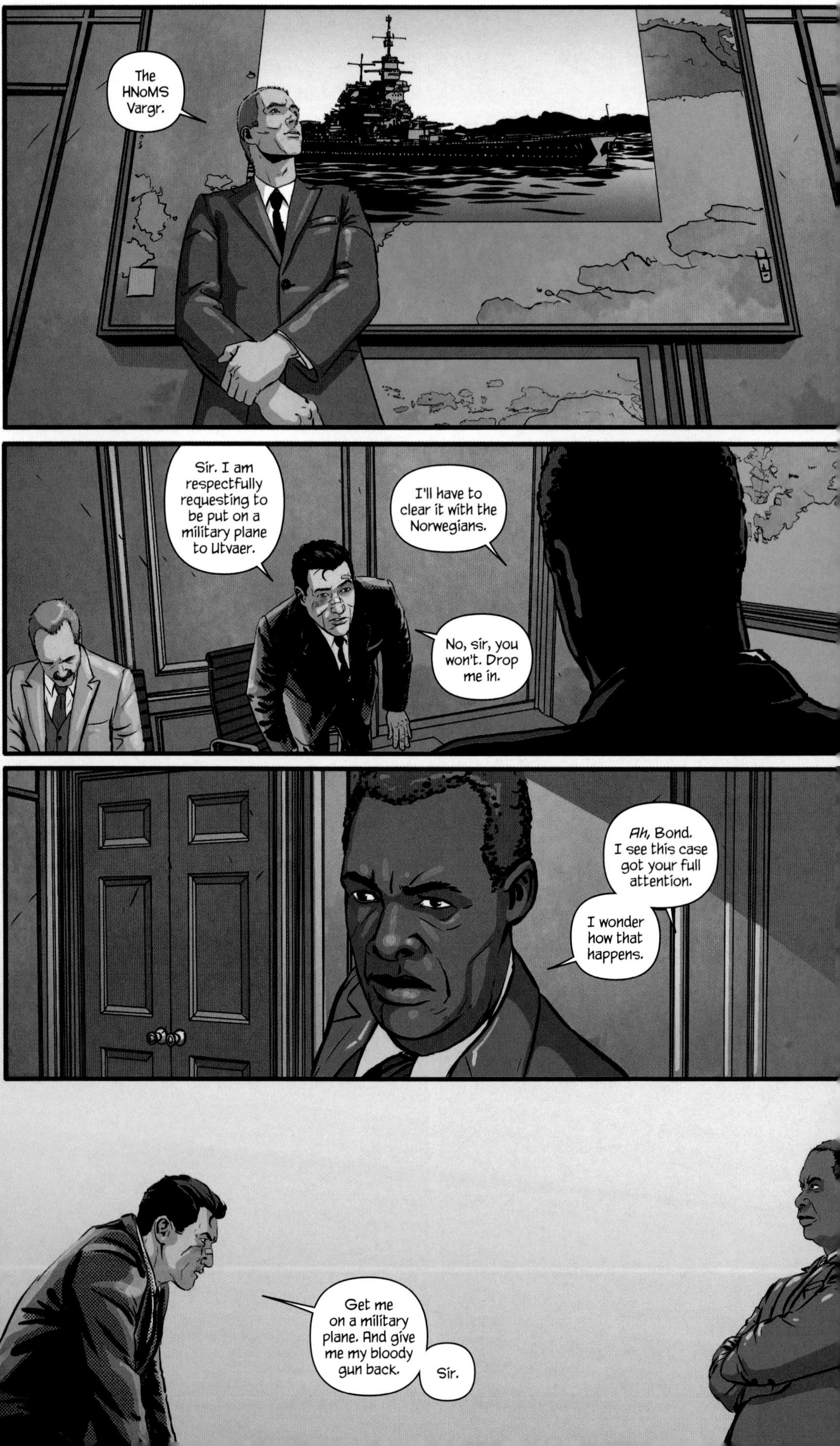
The HNoMS Vargr.
Sir. I am respectfully requesting to be put on a military plane to Utvaer.
I'll have to clear it with the Norwegians.
No, sir, you won't. Drop me in.
Ah, Bond. I see this case got your full attention.
I wonder how that happens.
Get me on a military plane. And give me my bloody gun back.
Sir.

ISSUE 006

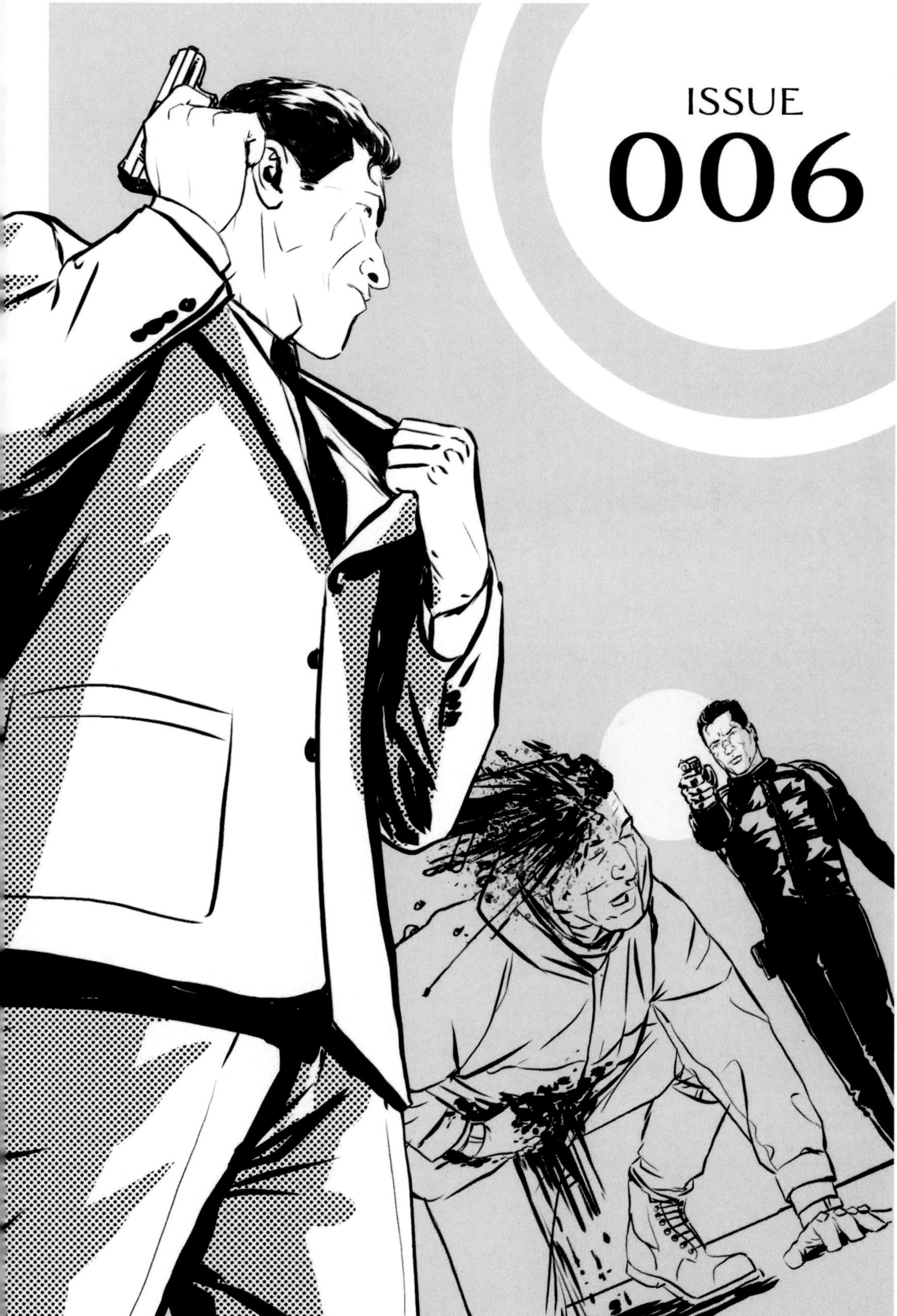

issue #6 main cover by **DOM REARDON**

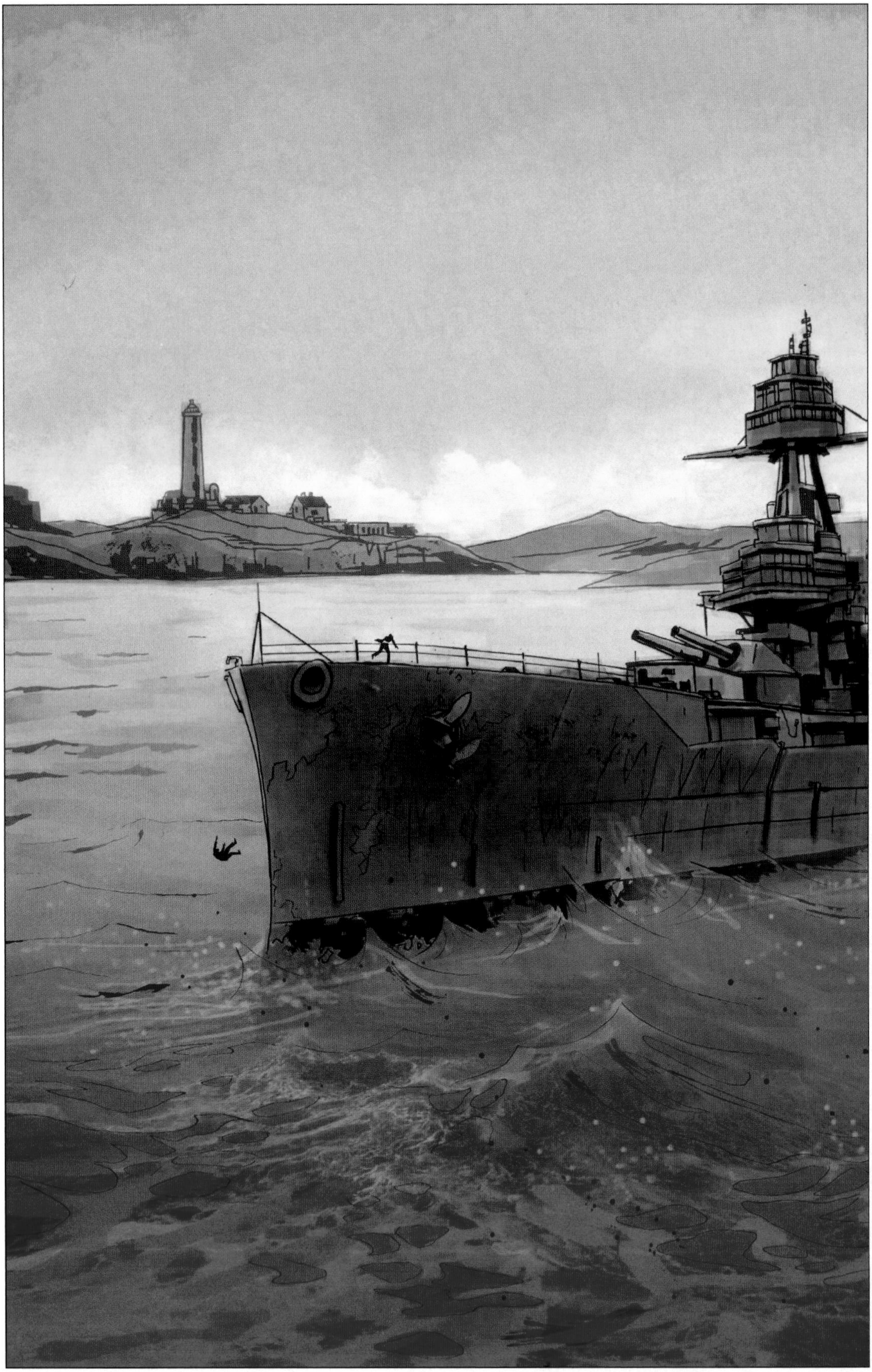

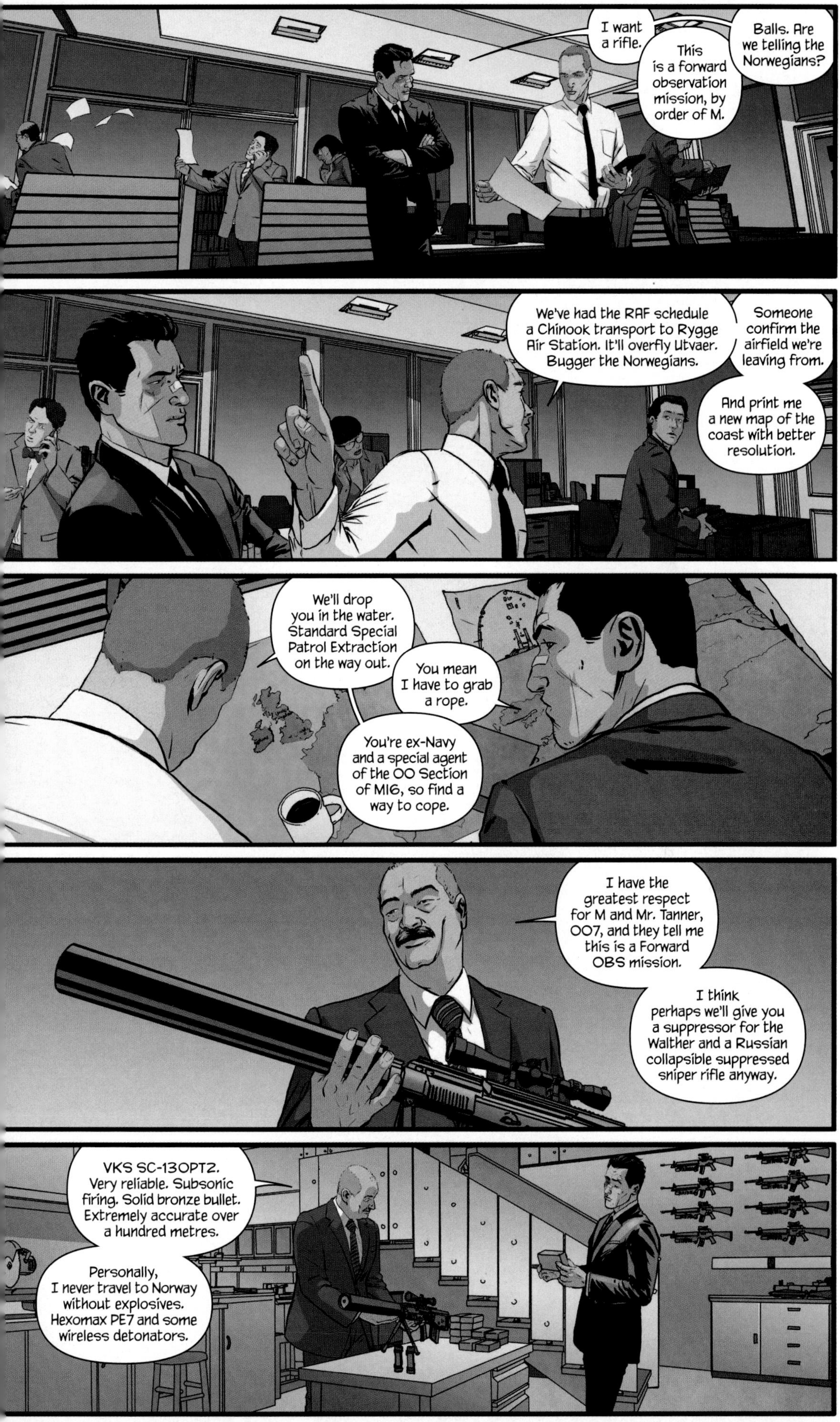
I want a rifle.
This is a forward observation mission, by order of M.
Balls. Are we telling the Norwegians?
We've had the RAF schedule a Chinook transport to Rygge Air Station. It'll overfly Utvaer. Bugger the Norwegians.
Someone confirm the airfield we're leaving from.
And print me a new map of the coast with better resolution.
We'll drop you in the water. Standard Special Patrol Extraction on the way out.
You mean I have to grab a rope.
You're ex-Navy and a special agent of the 00 Section of MI6, so find a way to cope.
I have the greatest respect for M and Mr. Tanner, 007, and they tell me this is a Forward OBS mission.
I think perhaps we'll give you a suppressor for the Walther and a Russian collapsible suppressed sniper rifle anyway.
VKS SC-130PT2. Very reliable. Subsonic firing. Solid bronze bullet. Extremely accurate over a hundred metres.
Personally, I never travel to Norway without explosives. Hexomax PE7 and some wireless detonators.

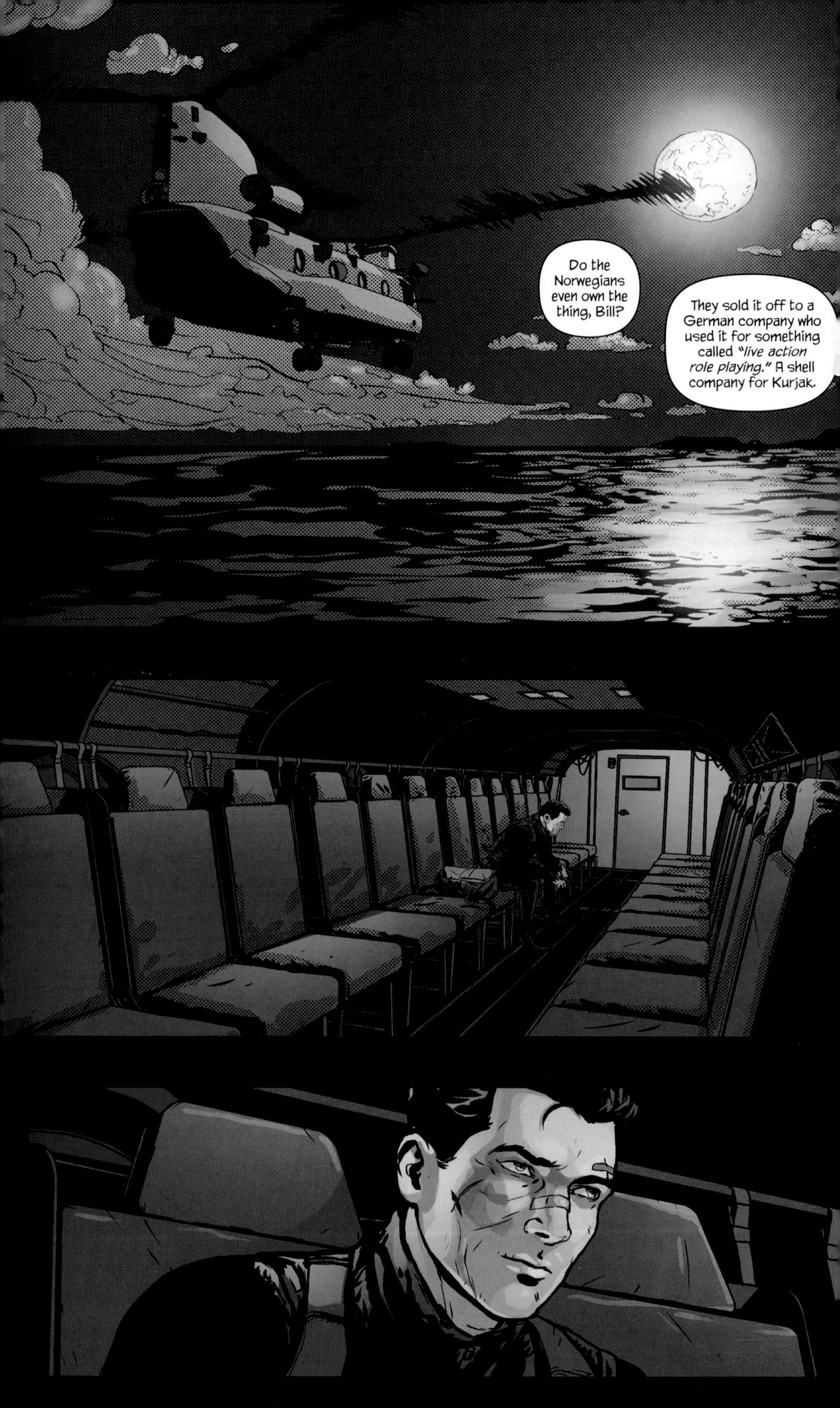
Do the Norwegians even own the thing, Bill?
They sold it off to a German company who used it for something called "live action role playing." A shell company for Kurjak.

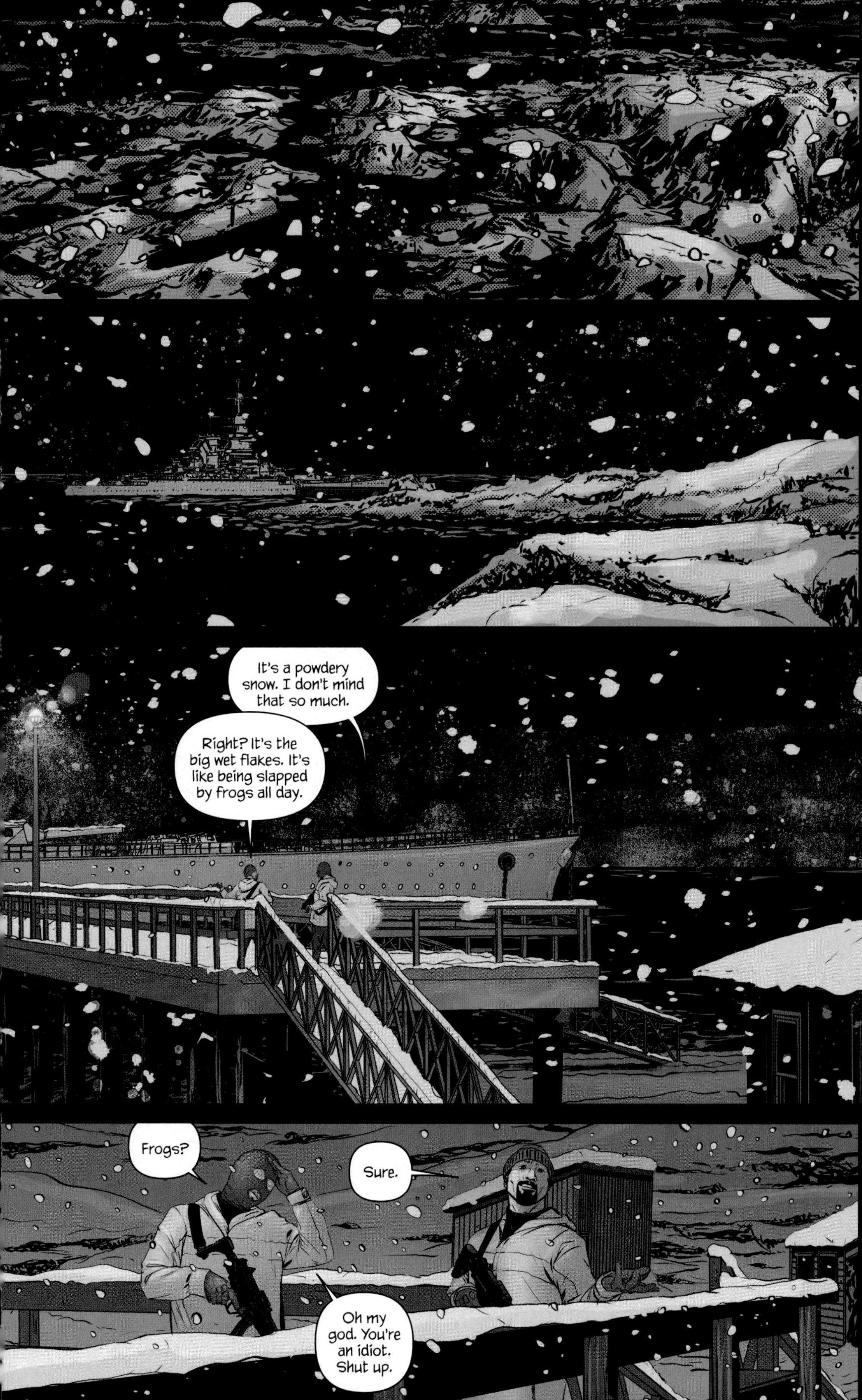
It's a powdery snow. I don't mind that so much.
Right? It's the big wet flakes. It's like being slapped by frogs all day.
Frogs?
Sure.
Oh my god. You're an idiot. Shut up.

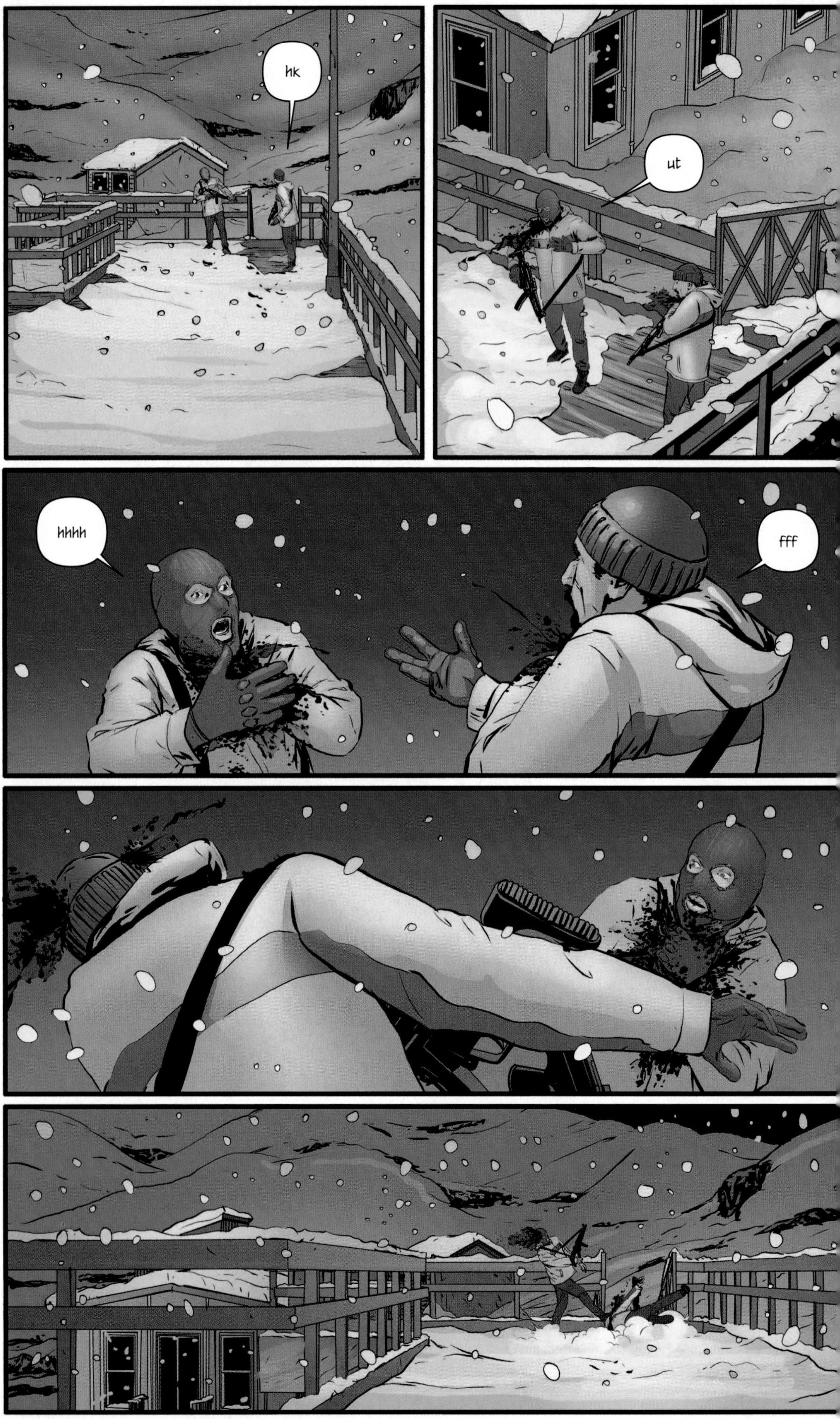
hk
ut
hhhh
fff

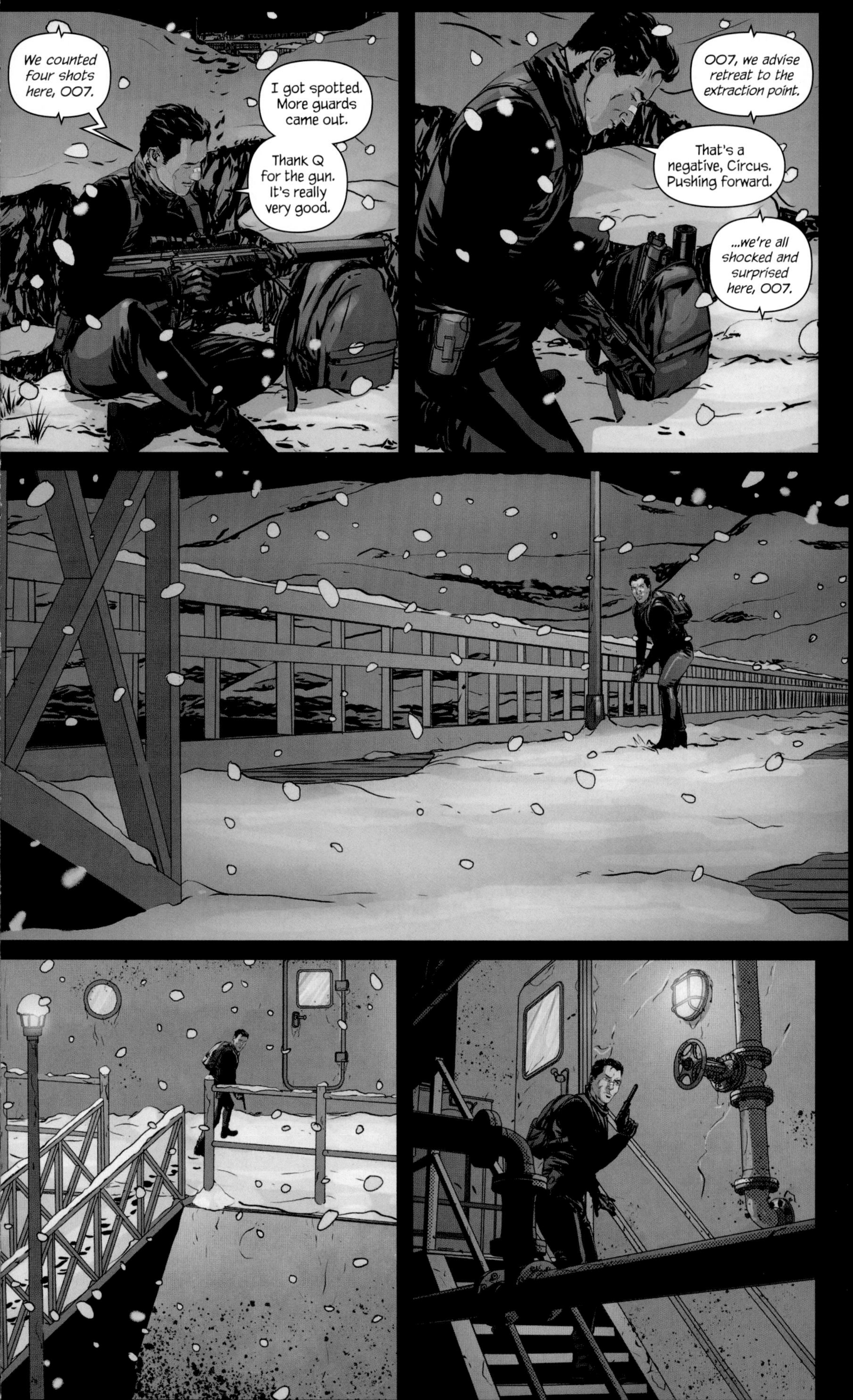
We counted four shots here, 007.
I got spotted. More guards came out.
Thank Q for the gun. It's really very good.
007, we advise retreat to the extraction point.
That's a negative, Circus. Pushing forward.
...we're all shocked and surprised here, 007.

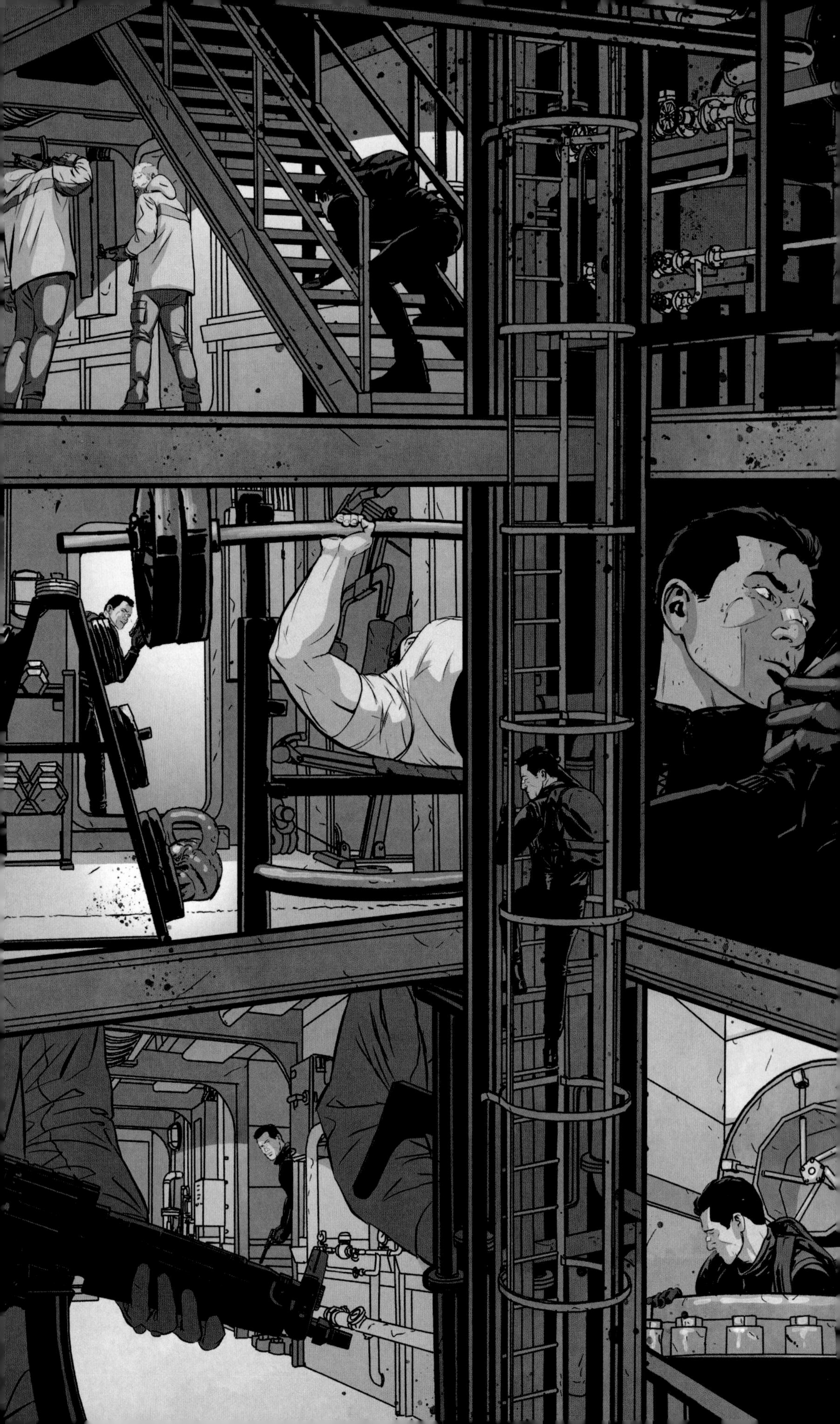

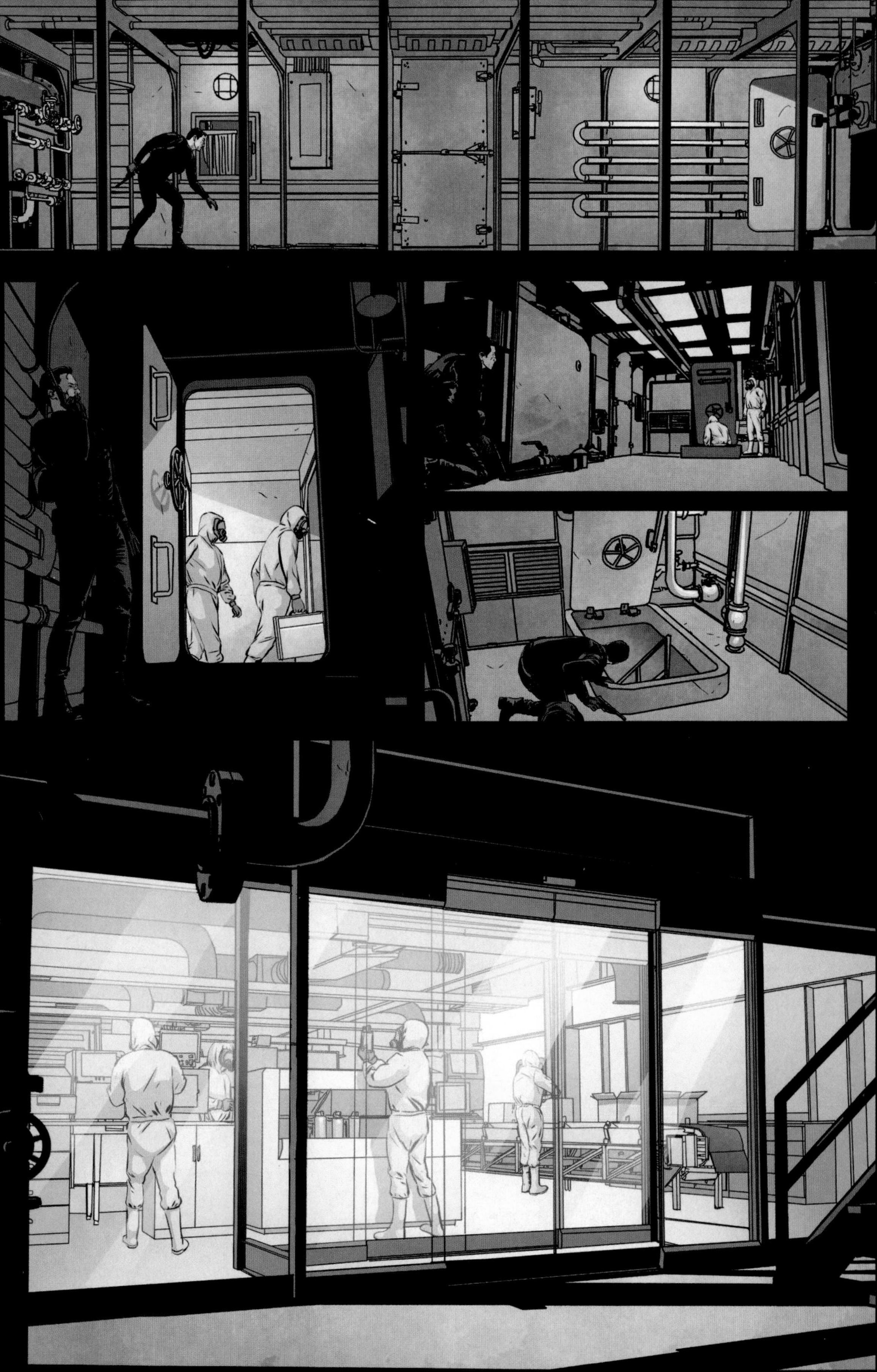

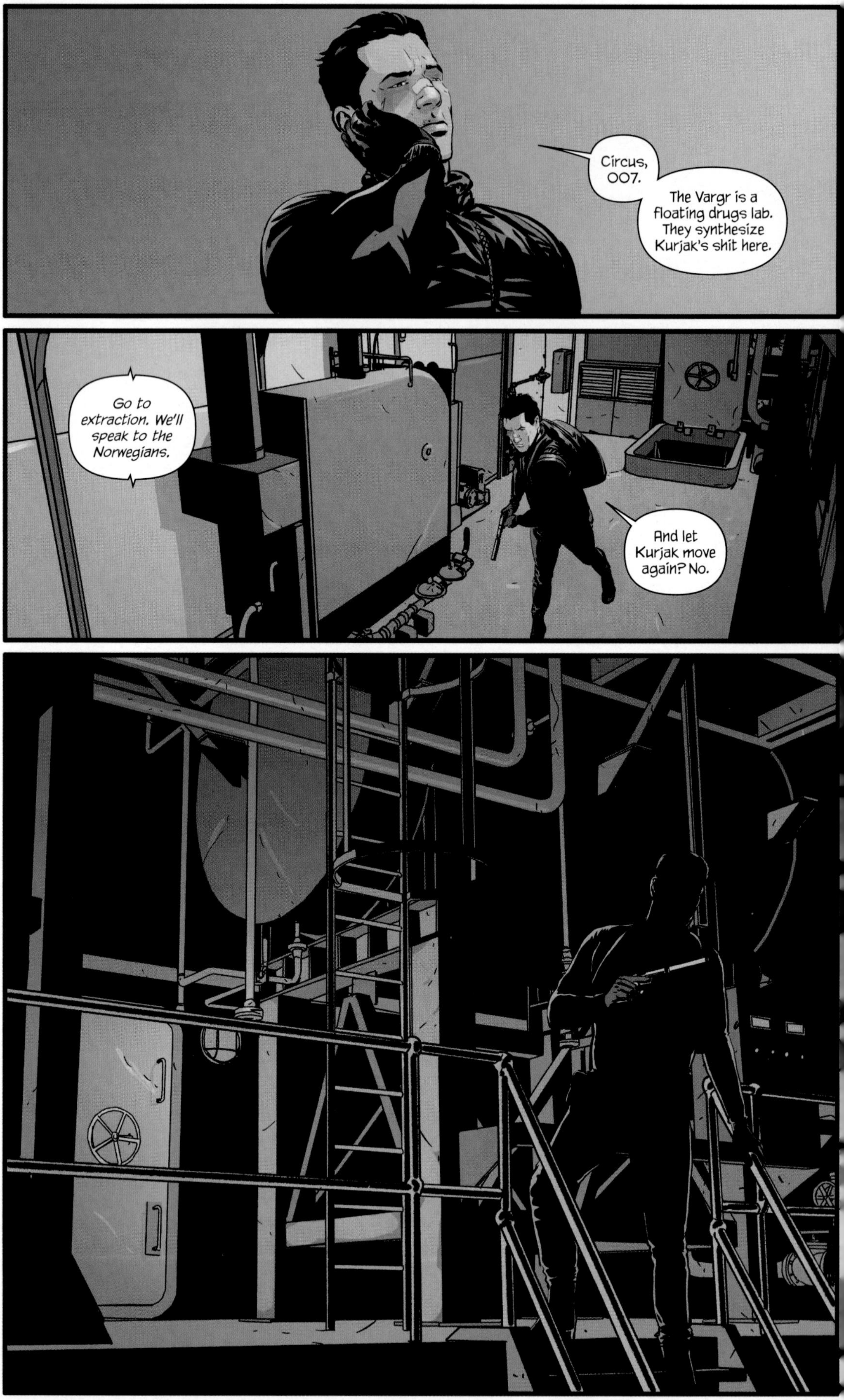
Circus, 007.
The Vargr is a floating drugs lab. They synthesize Kurjak's shit here.
Go to extraction. We'll speak to the Norwegians.
And let Kurjak move again? No.

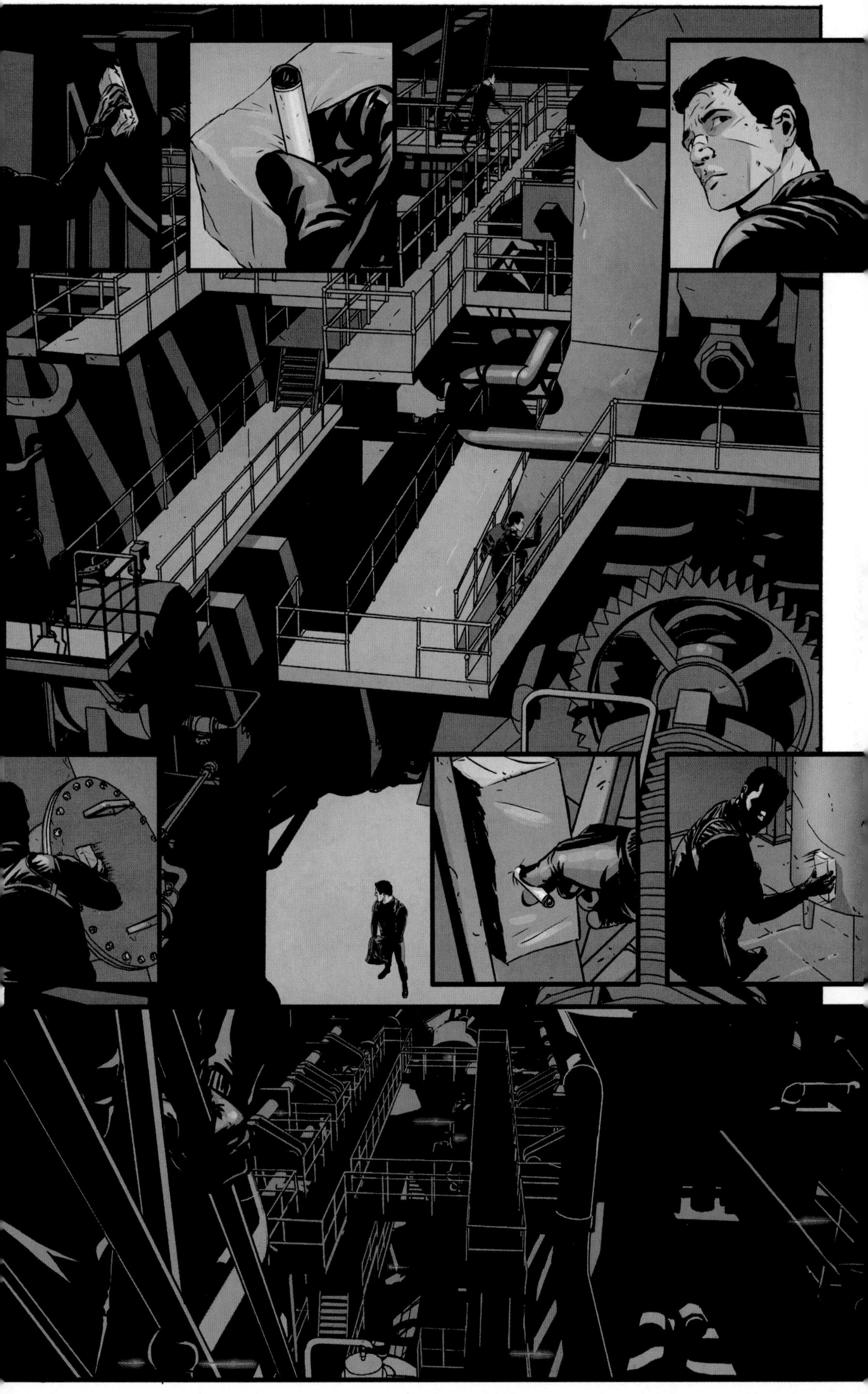

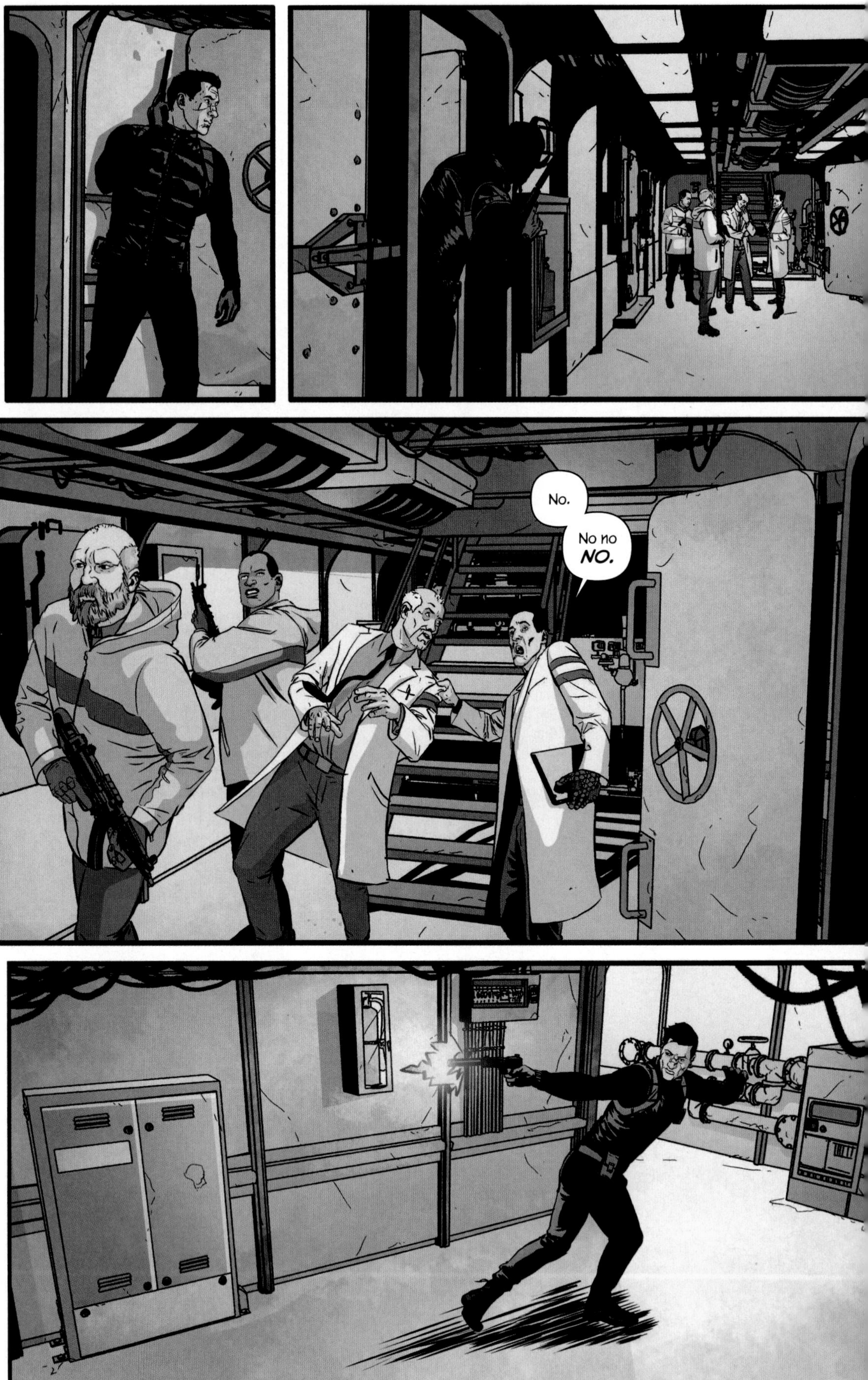
No.
No no NO.

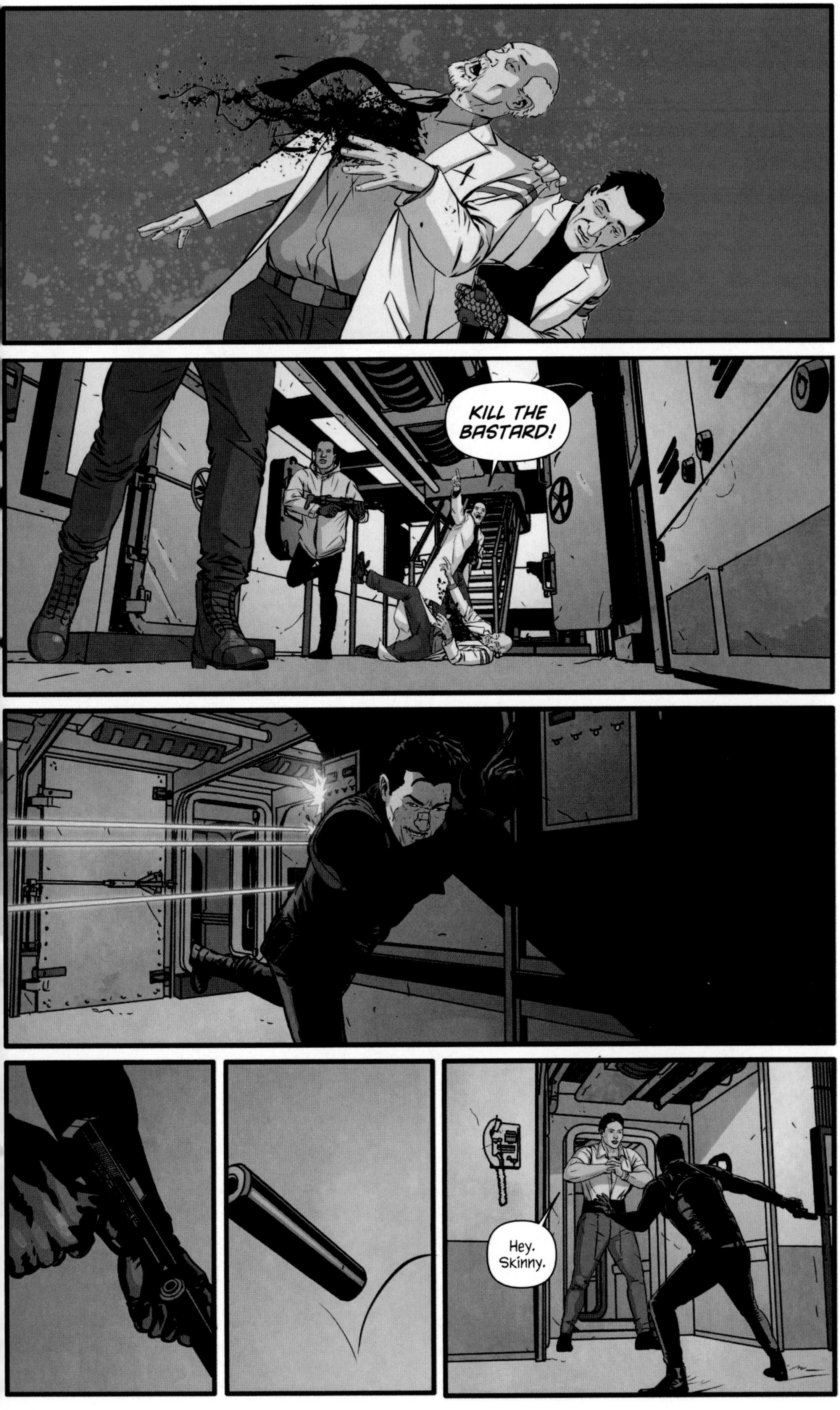
KILL THE BASTARD!
Hey. Skinny.

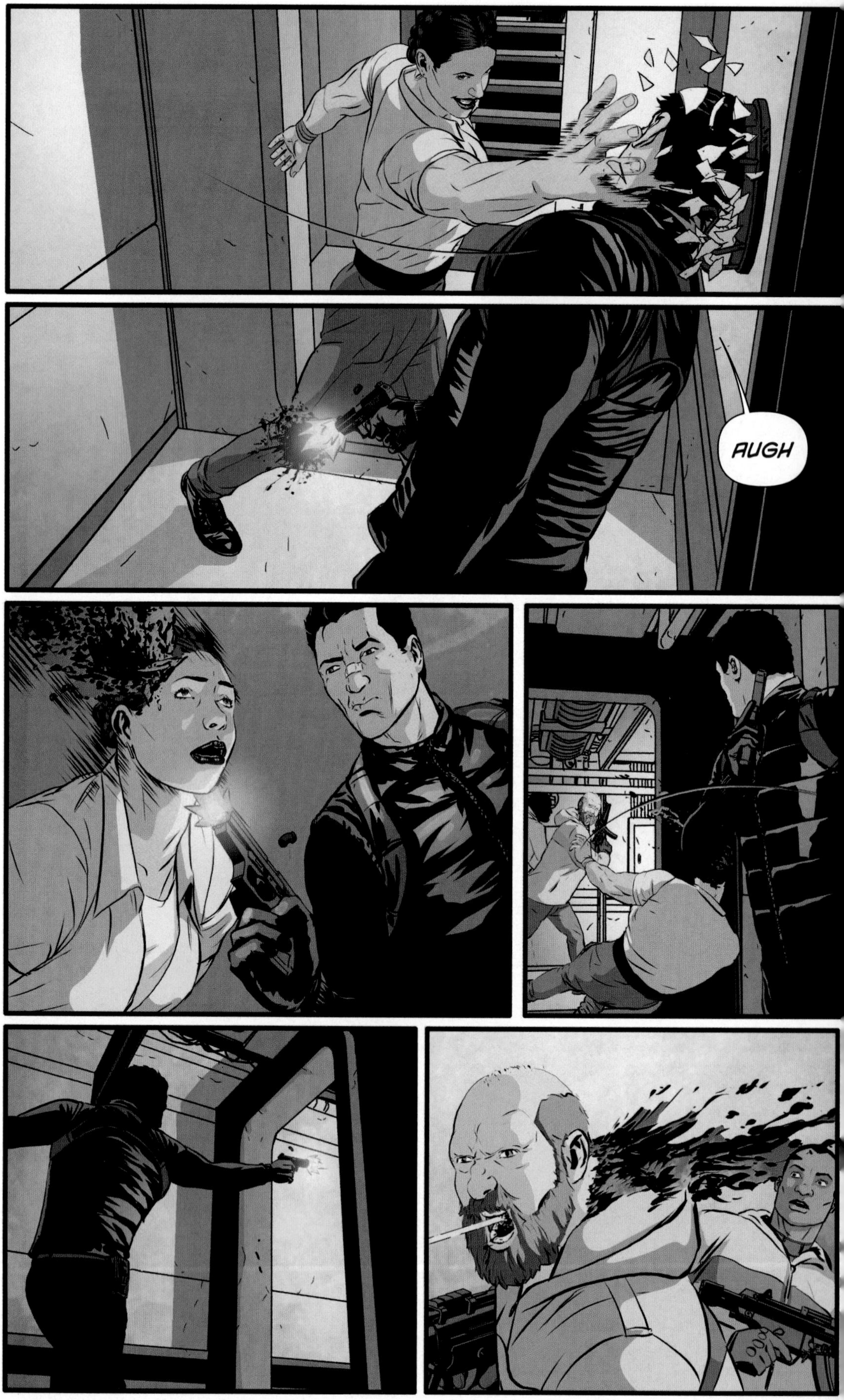
AUGH

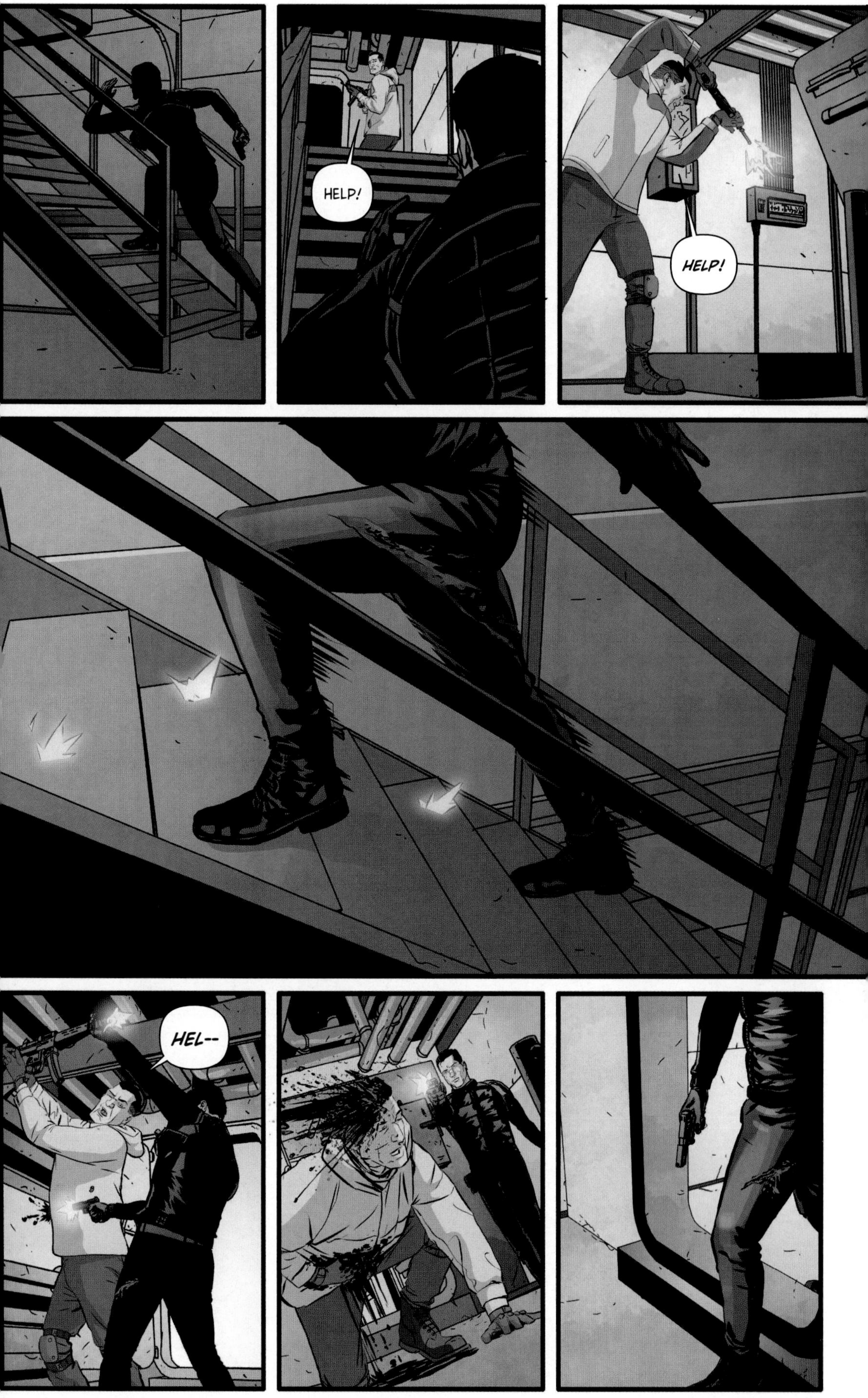
HELP!
HELP!
HEL--

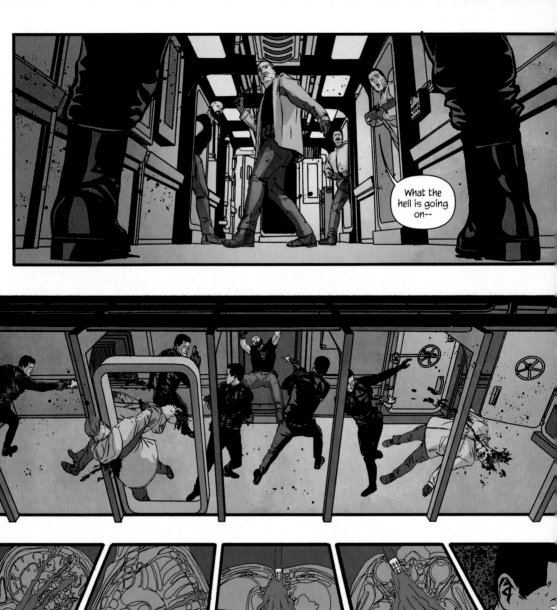

What the hell is going on--

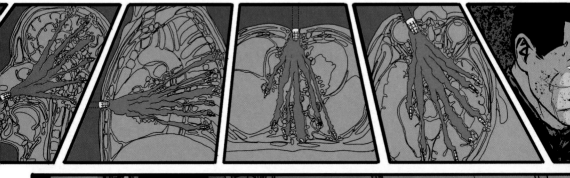

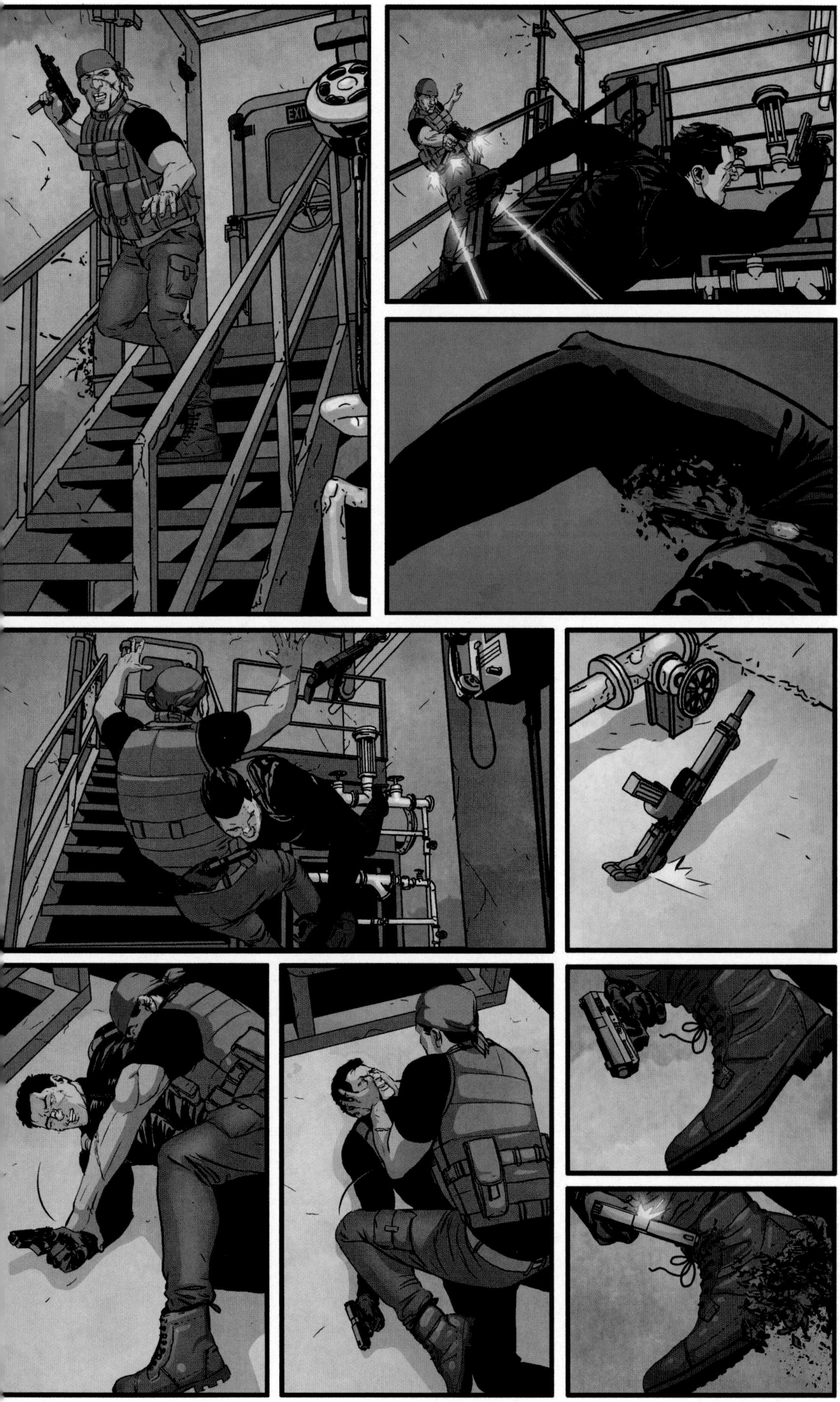
EXIT

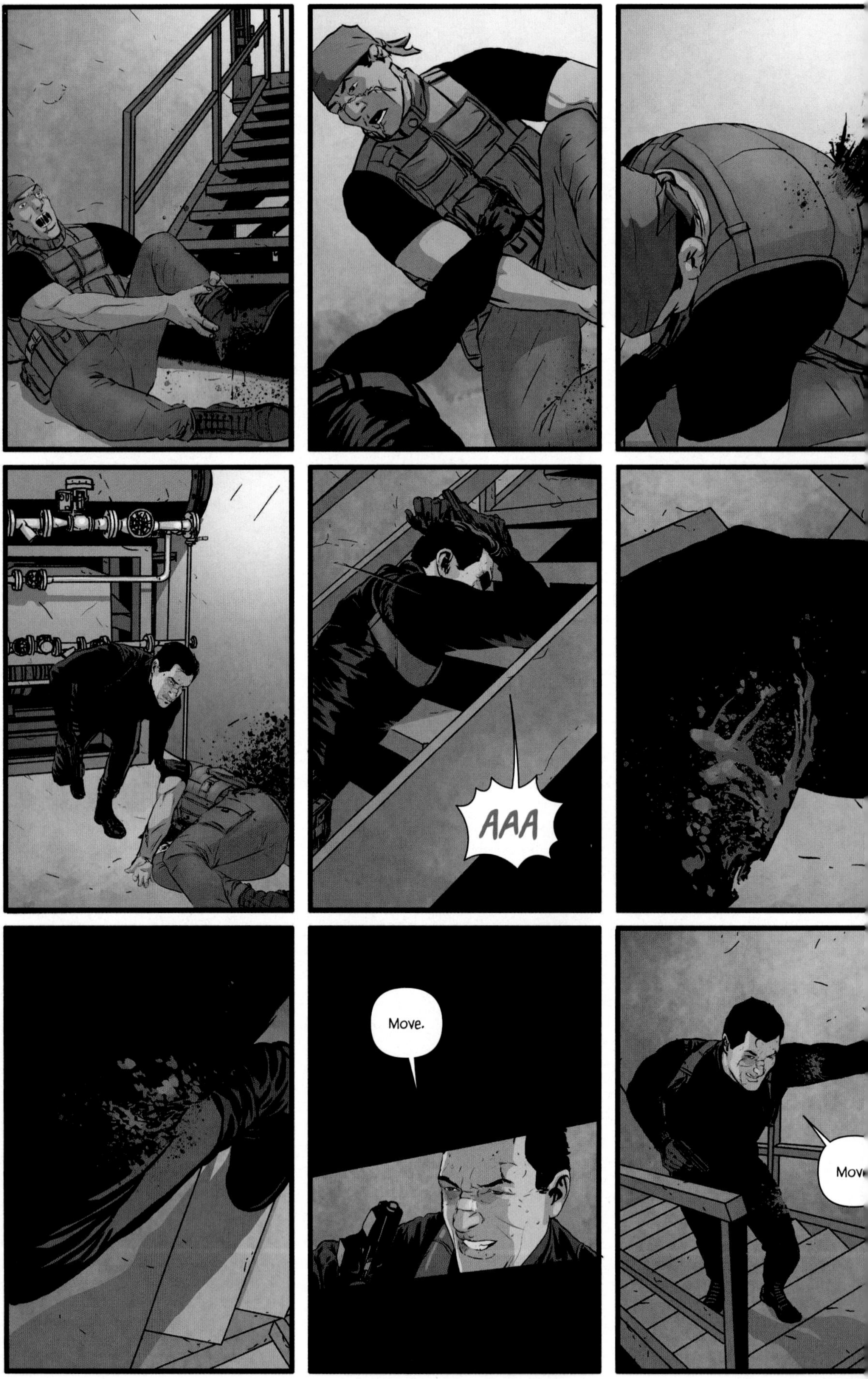
AAA
Move.
Mov

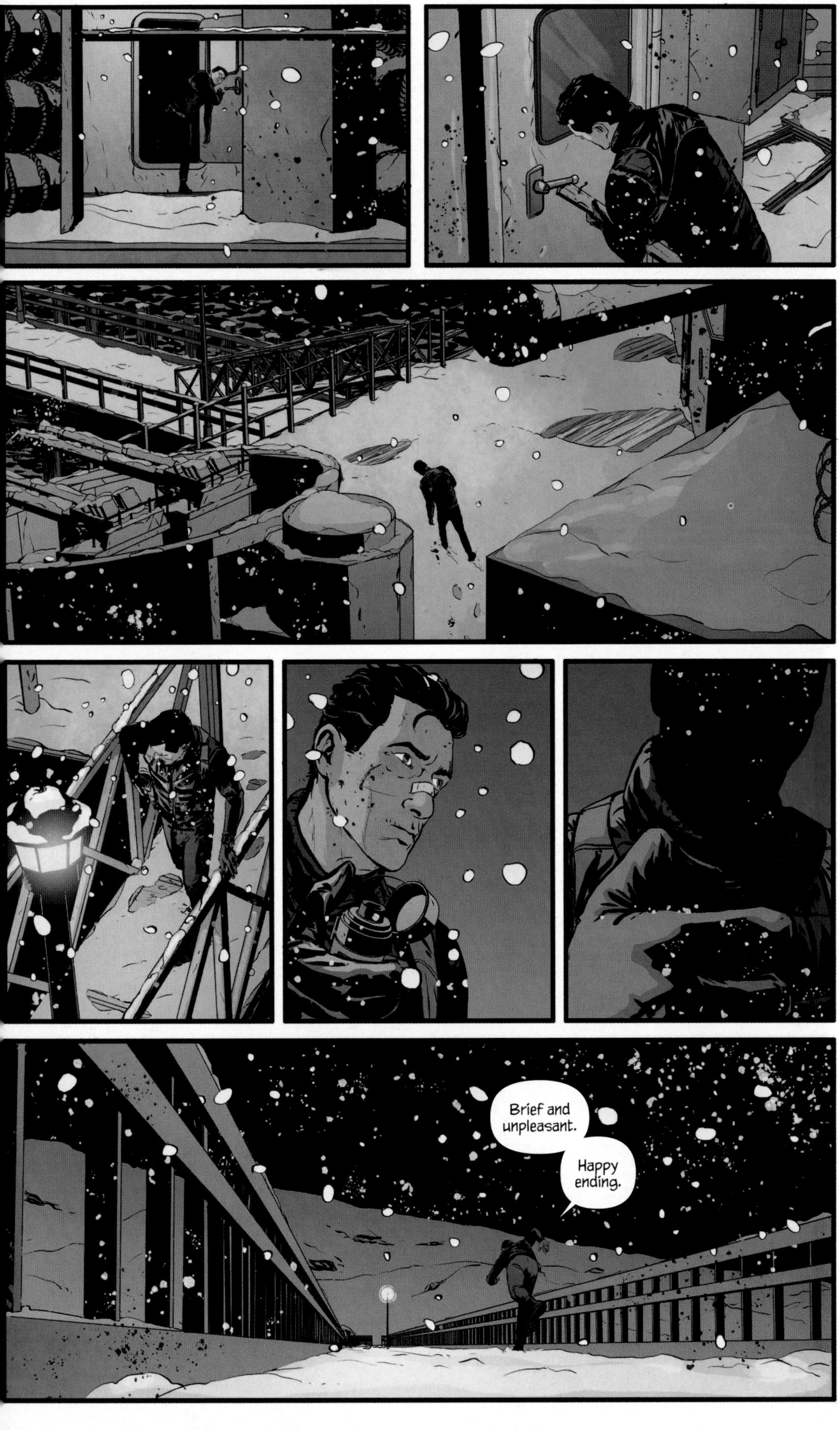
Brief and unpleasant.
Happy ending.

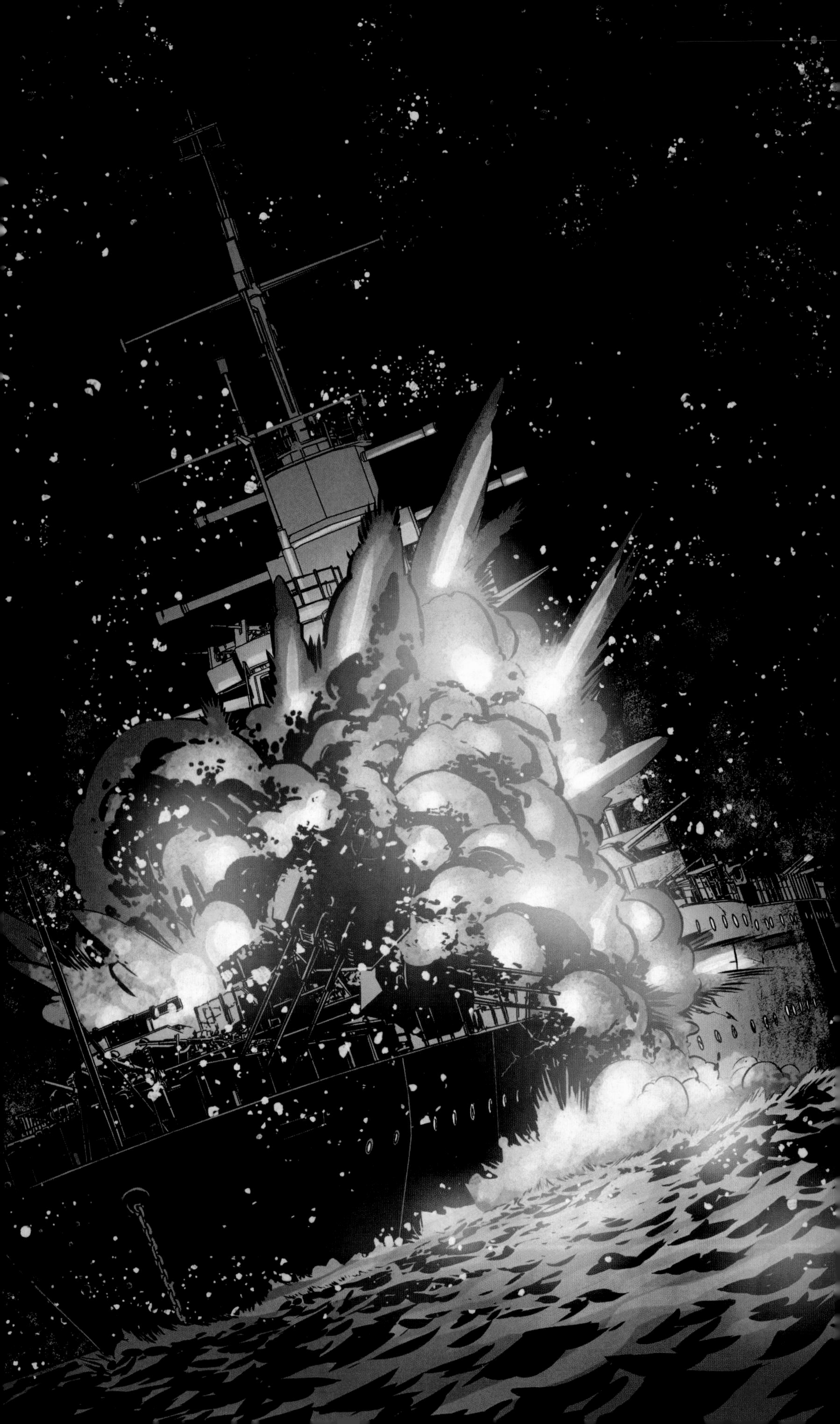

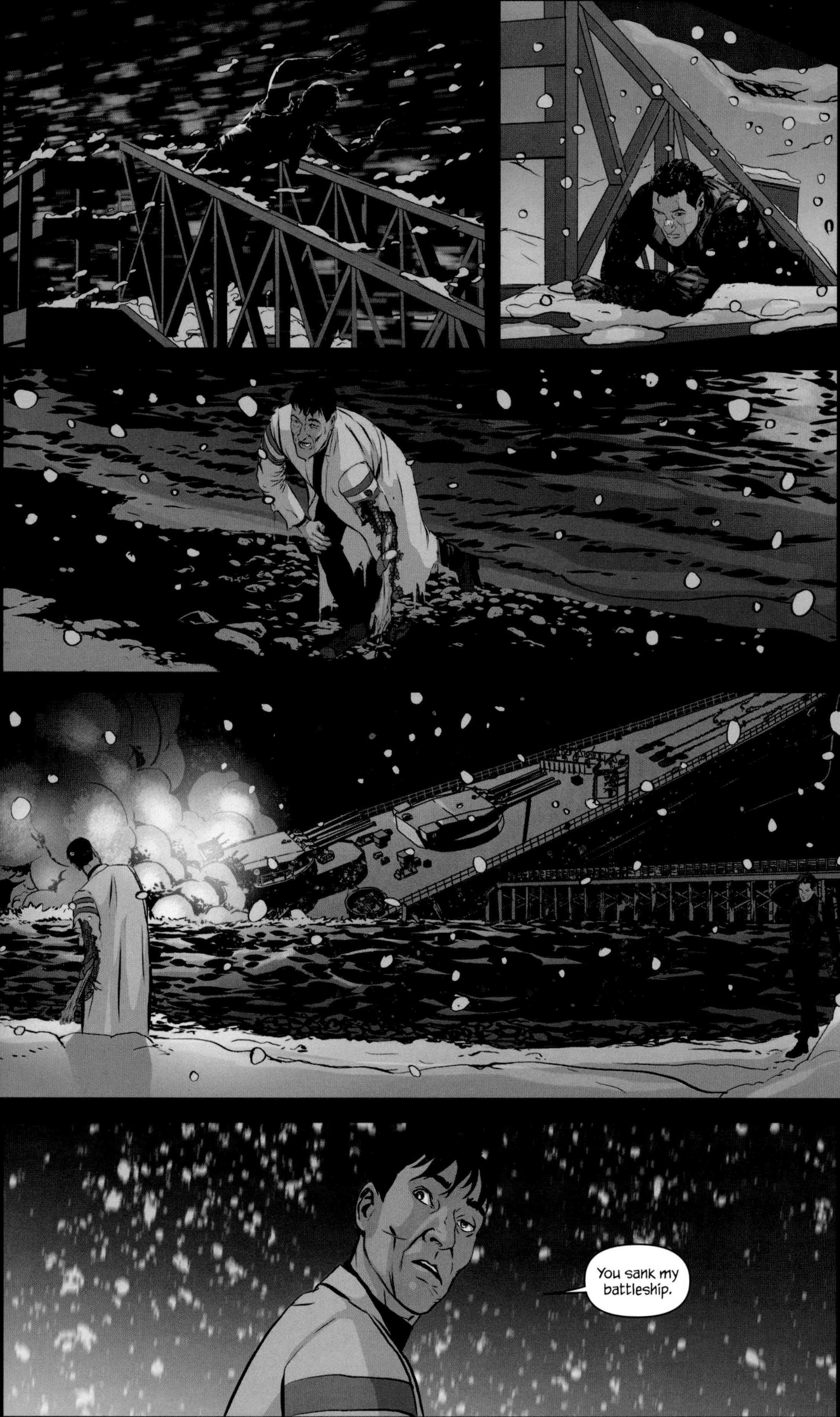
You sank my battleship.

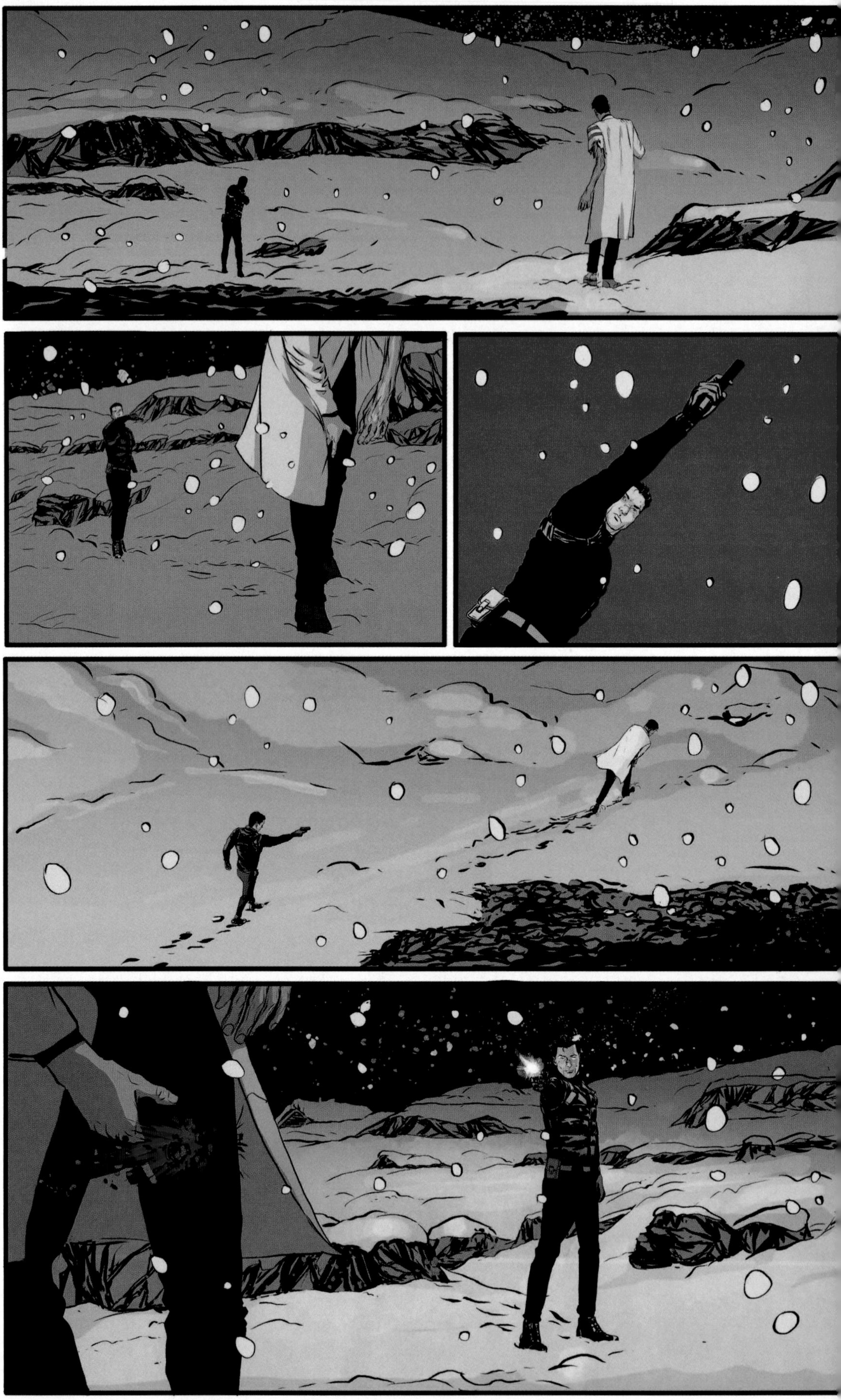

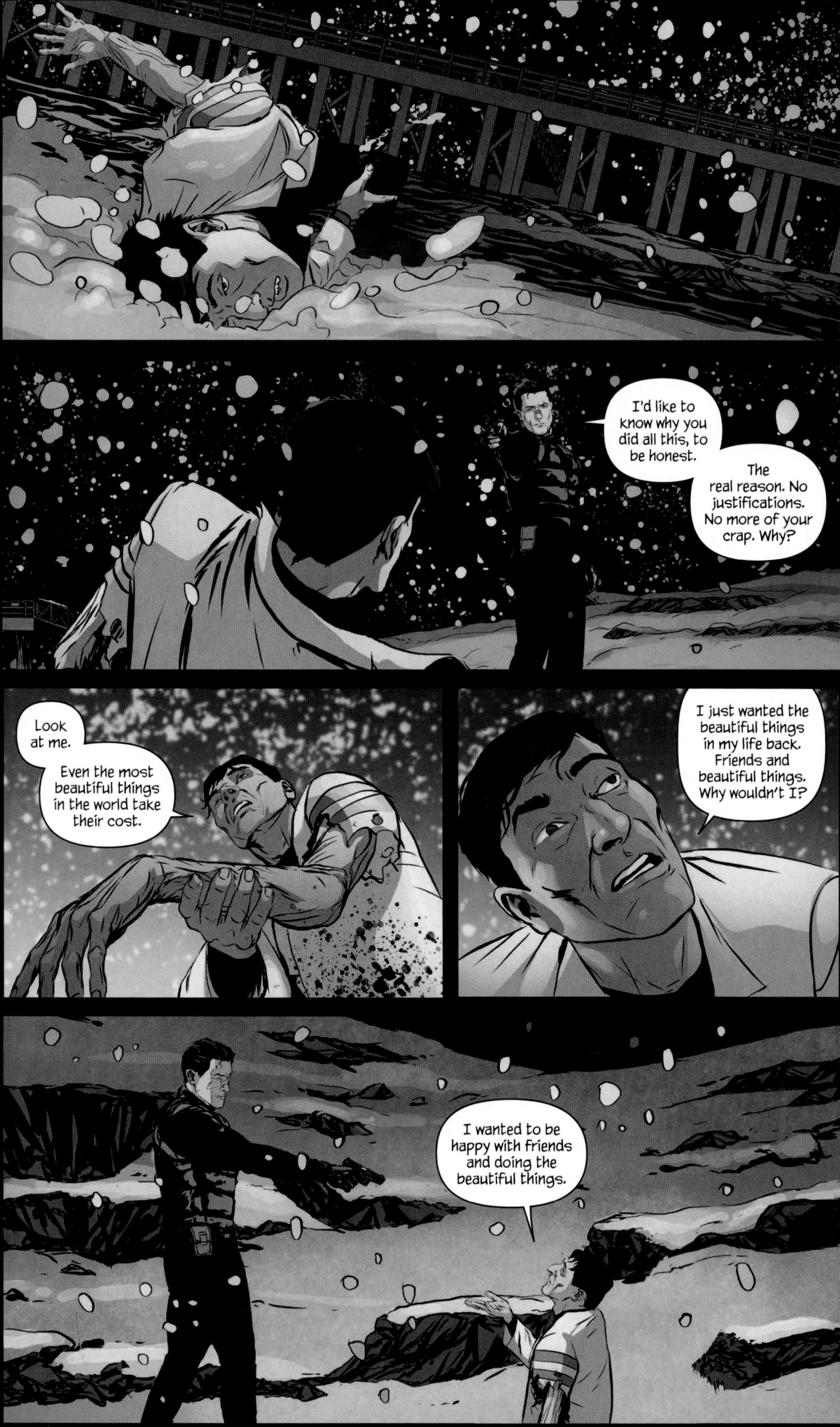
I'd like to know why you did all this, to be honest.
The real reason. No justifications. No more of your crap. Why?
Look at me.
Even the most beautiful things in the world take their cost.
I just wanted the beautiful things in my life back. Friends and beautiful things. Why wouldn't I?
I wanted to be happy with friends and doing the beautiful things.

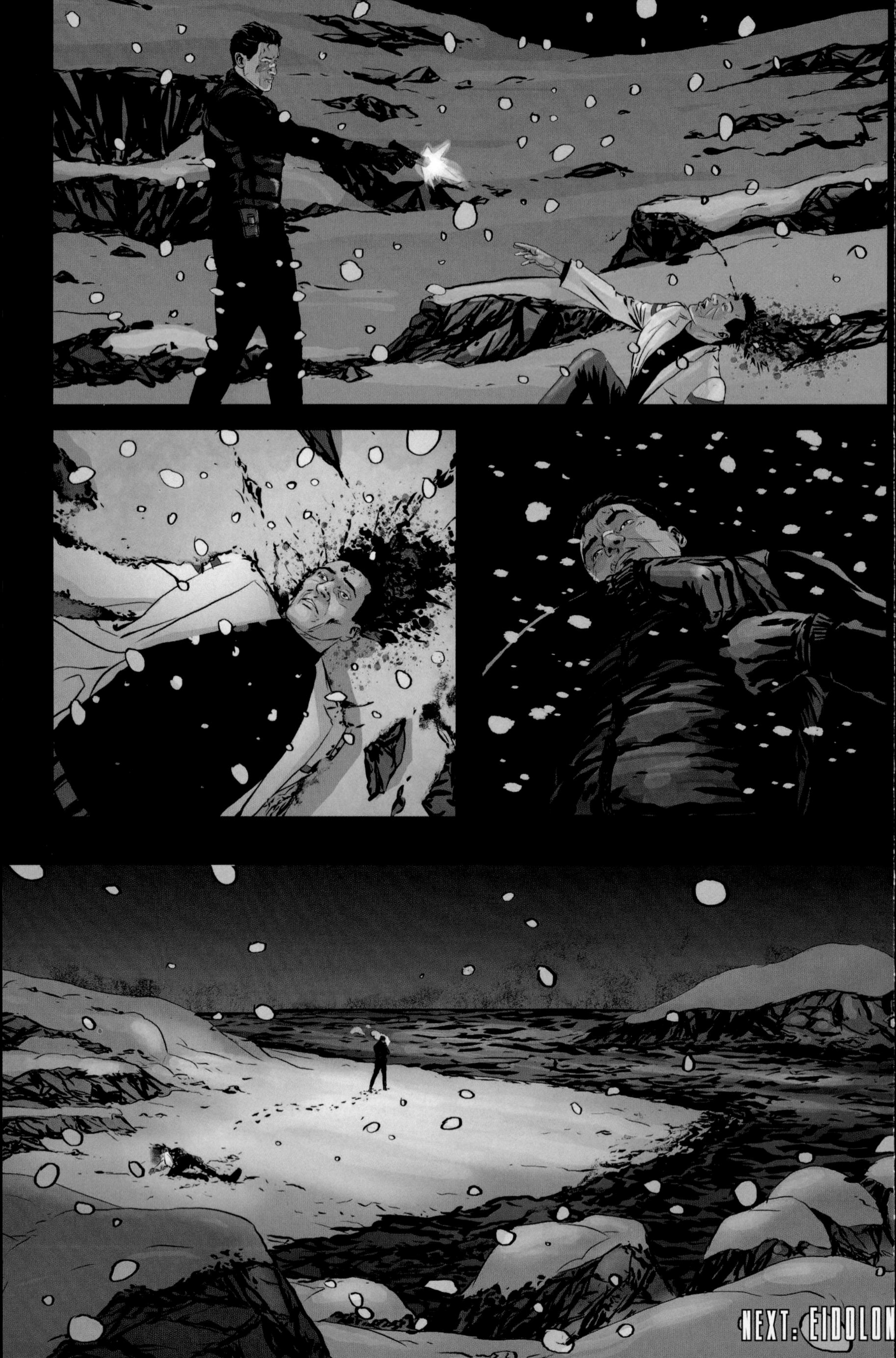
NEXT: EIDOLON

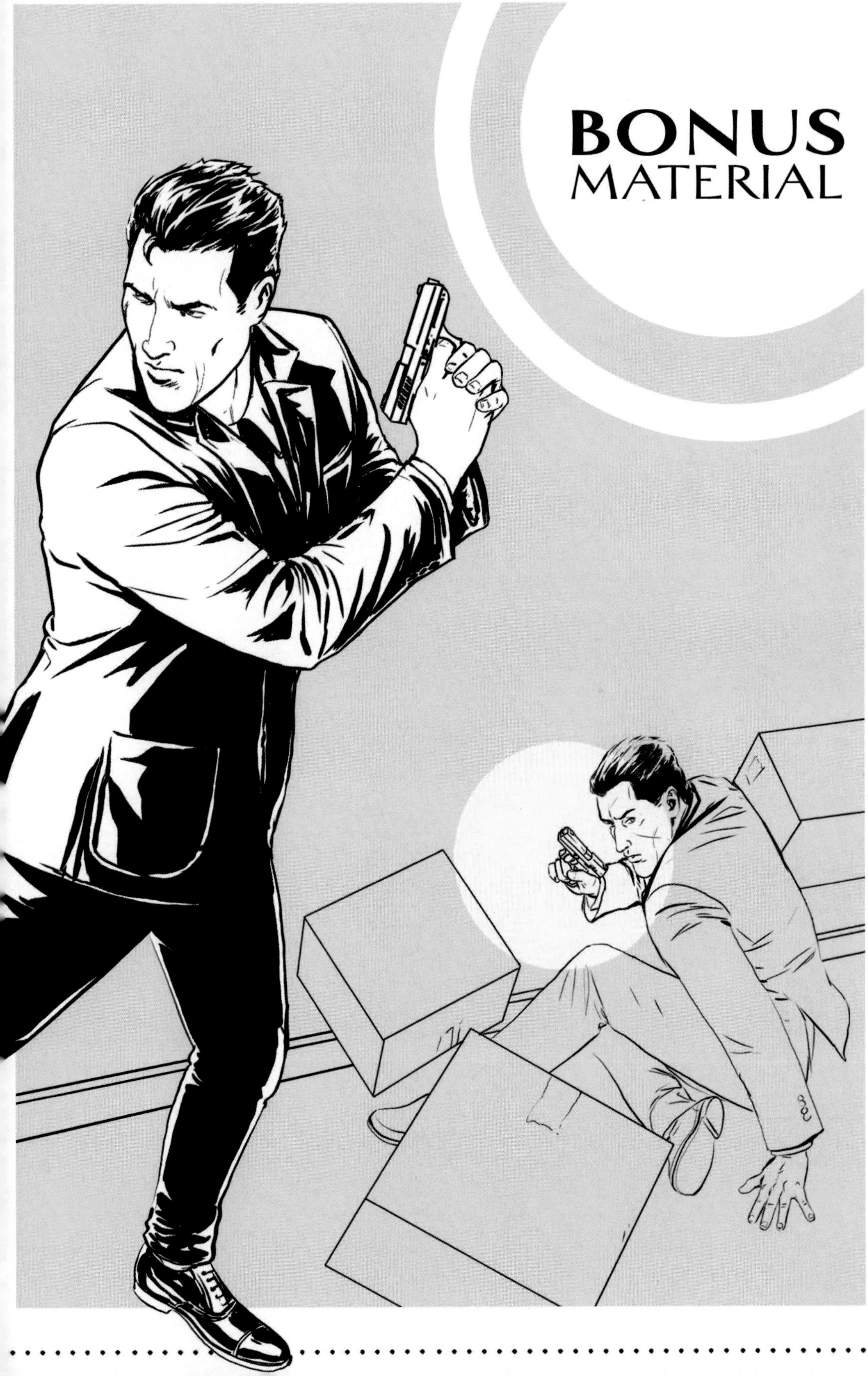
BONUS
MATERIAL

issue #1 alternate cover by **GLENN FABRY**

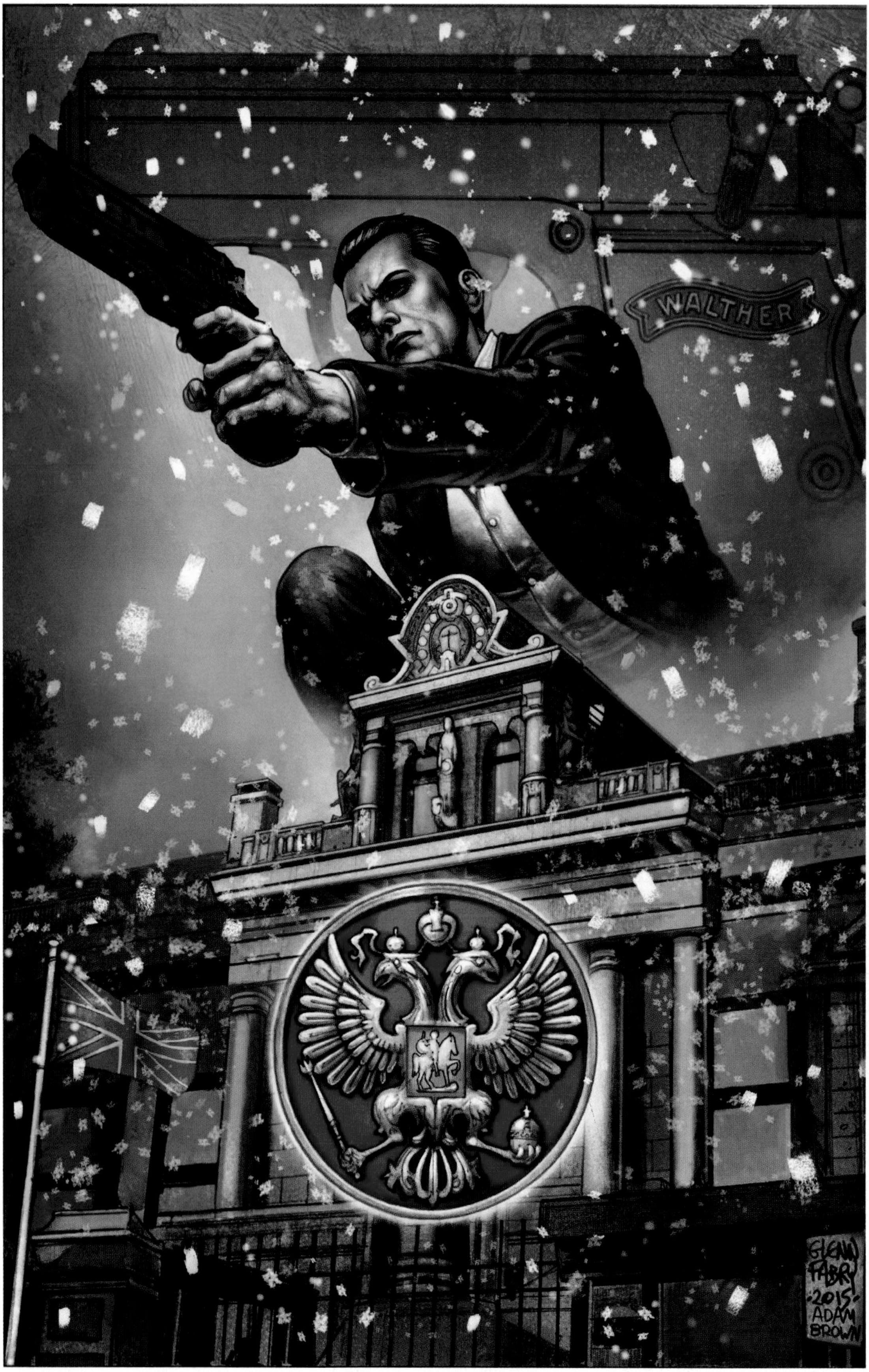
WALTHER
GLENN FABRY -2015- ADAM BROWN

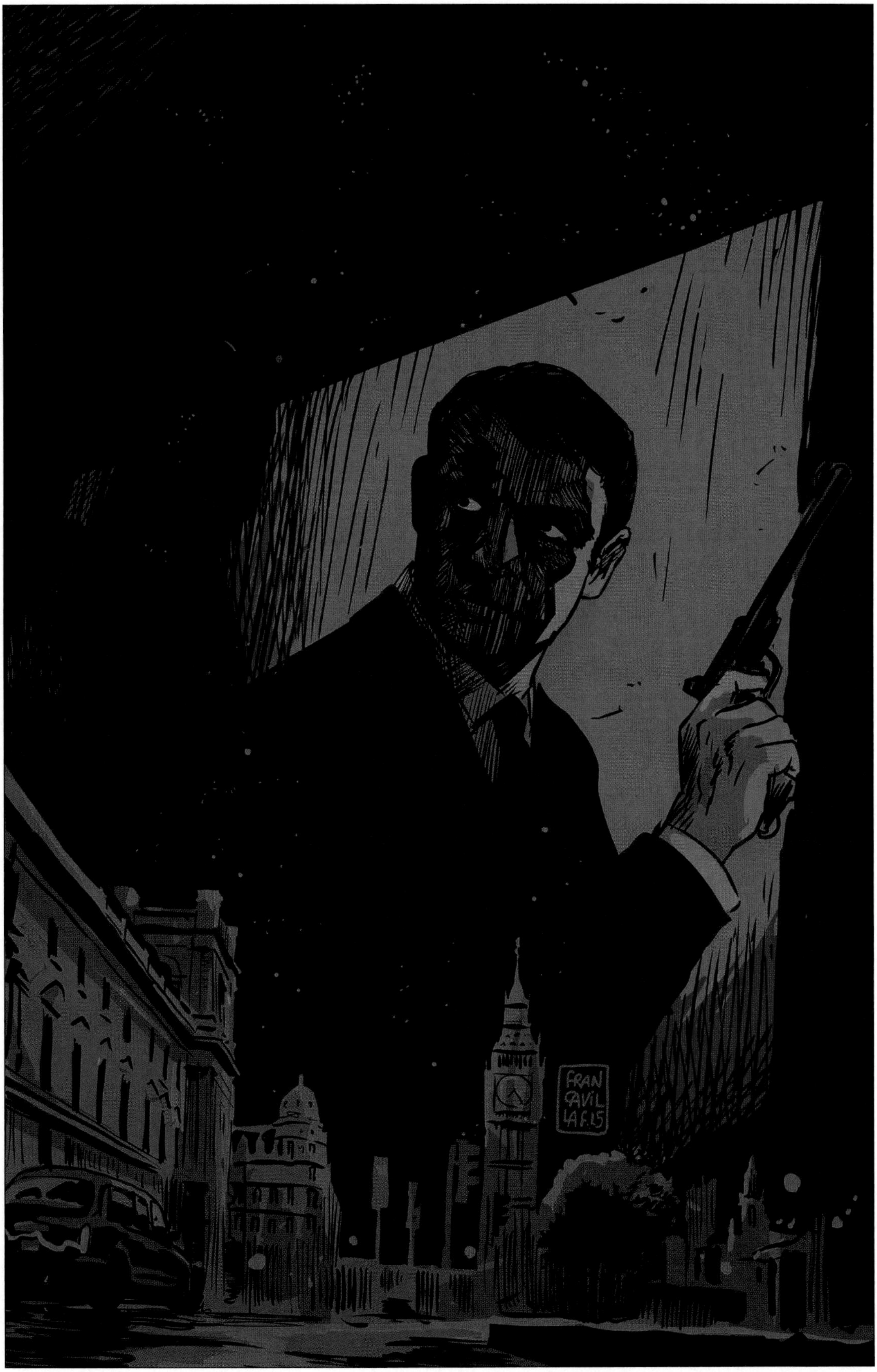
FRAN
CAVIL
LA F.15

issue #1 alternate cover by **GABRIEL HARDMAN**

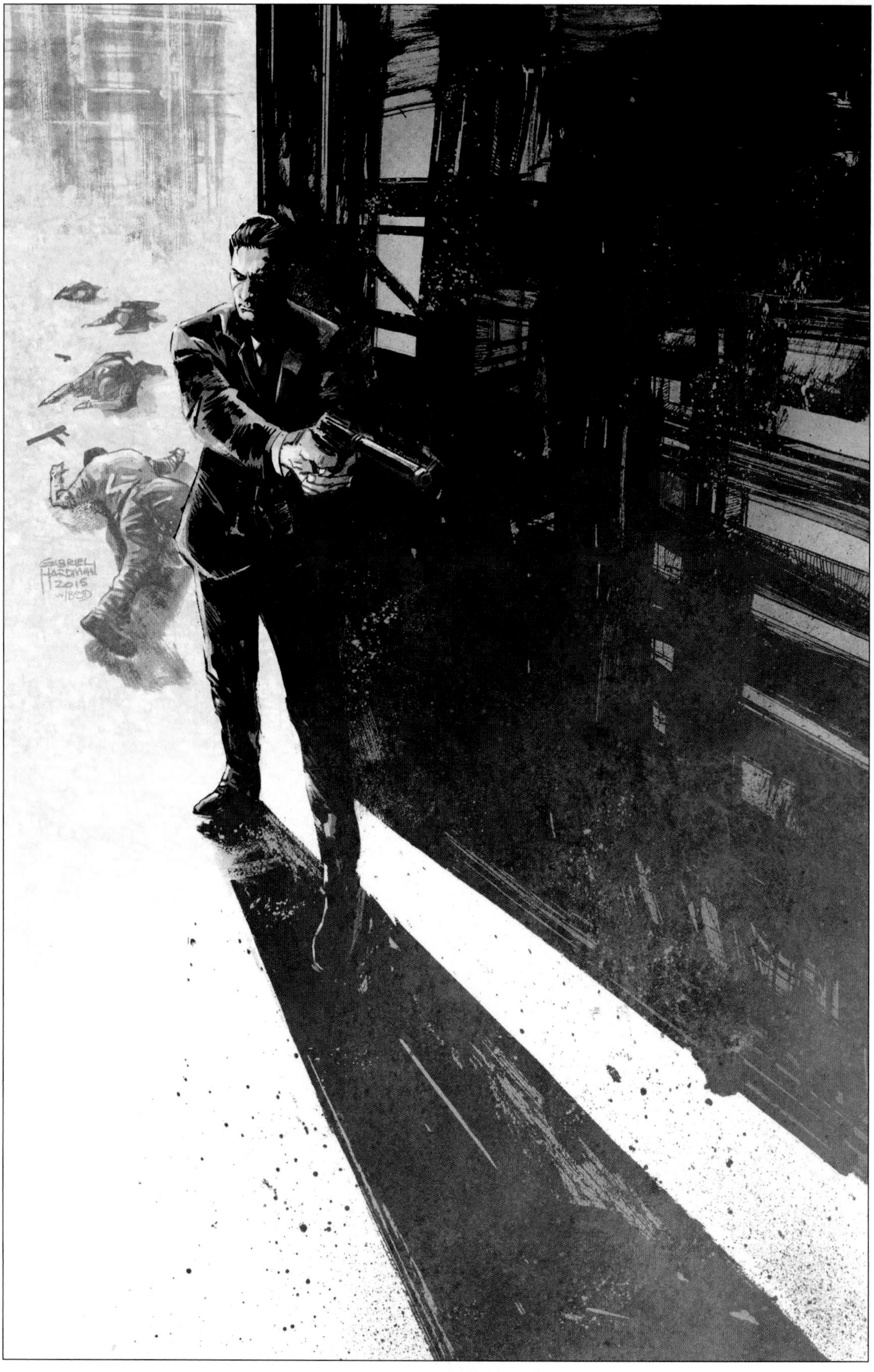
GABRIEL HARDMAN 2015 w/BOND

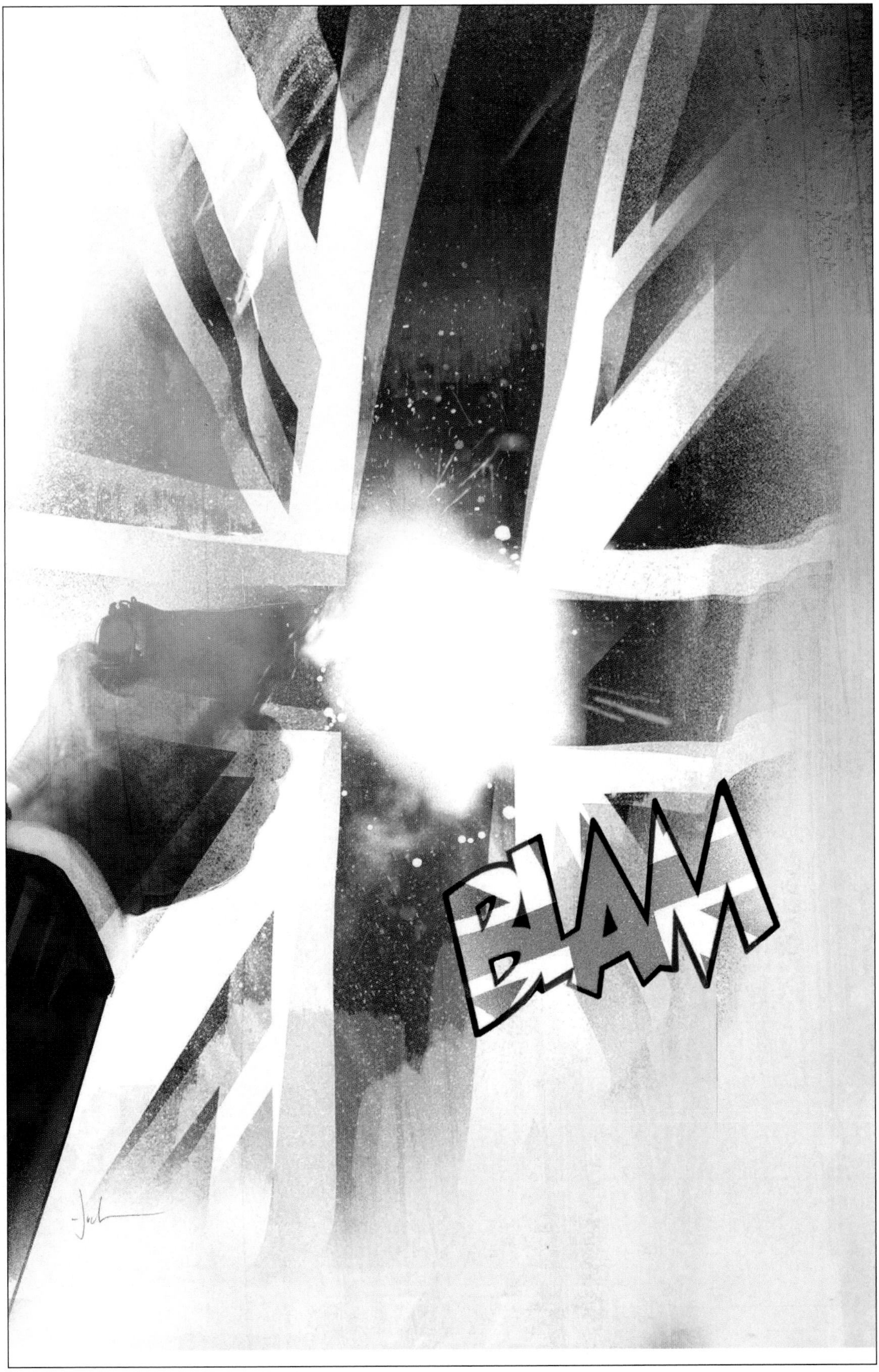
BLAM

issue #1 alternate cover by **STEPHEN MOONEY**

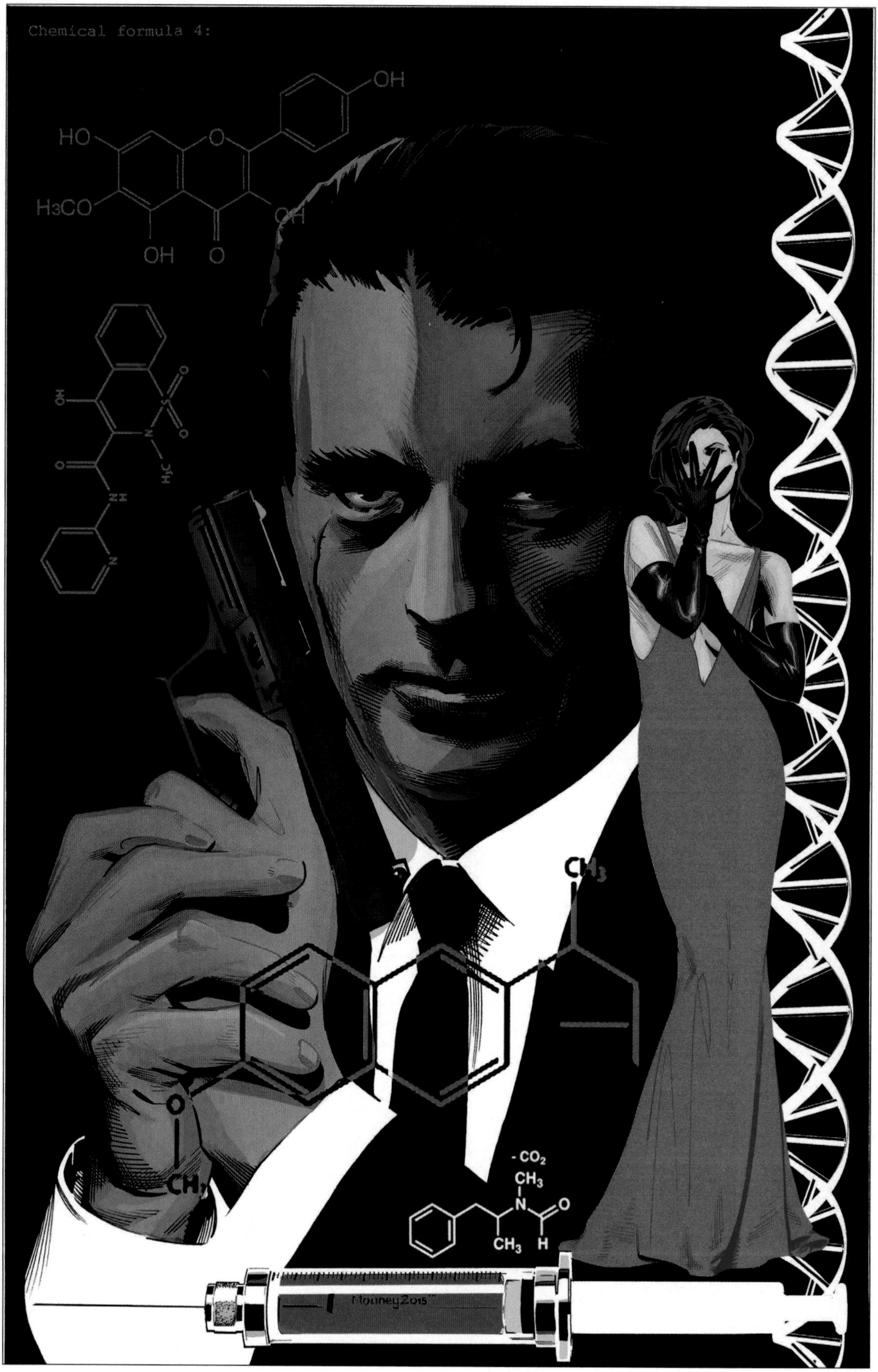
Chemical formula 4:
OH
HO
H3CO
OH
OH
O
CH3
- CO2
CH3
N
O
CH3
H
Mooney2015

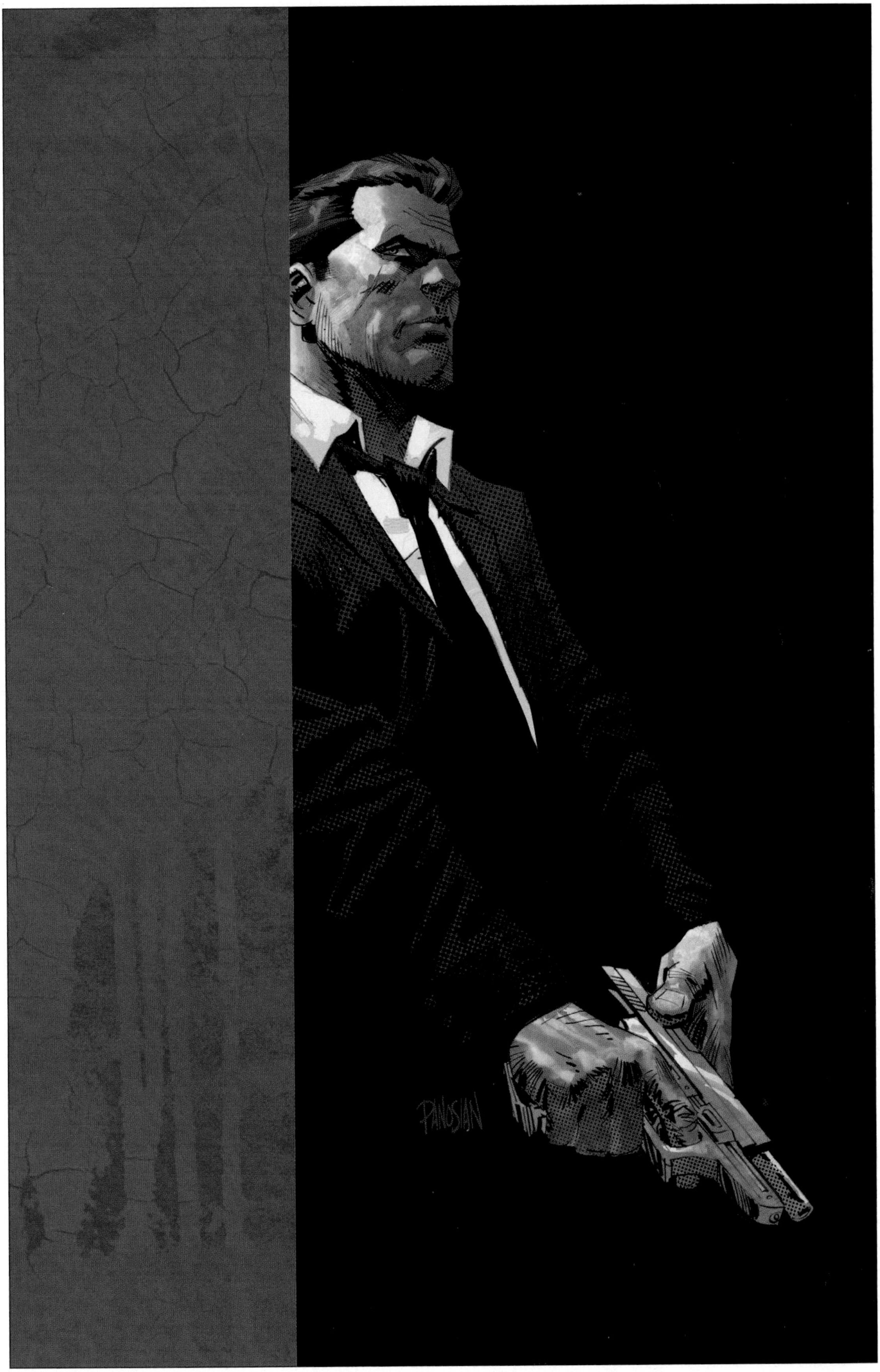
PANOSIAN

issue #1 retailer shared exclusive cover by **JASON MASTERS**

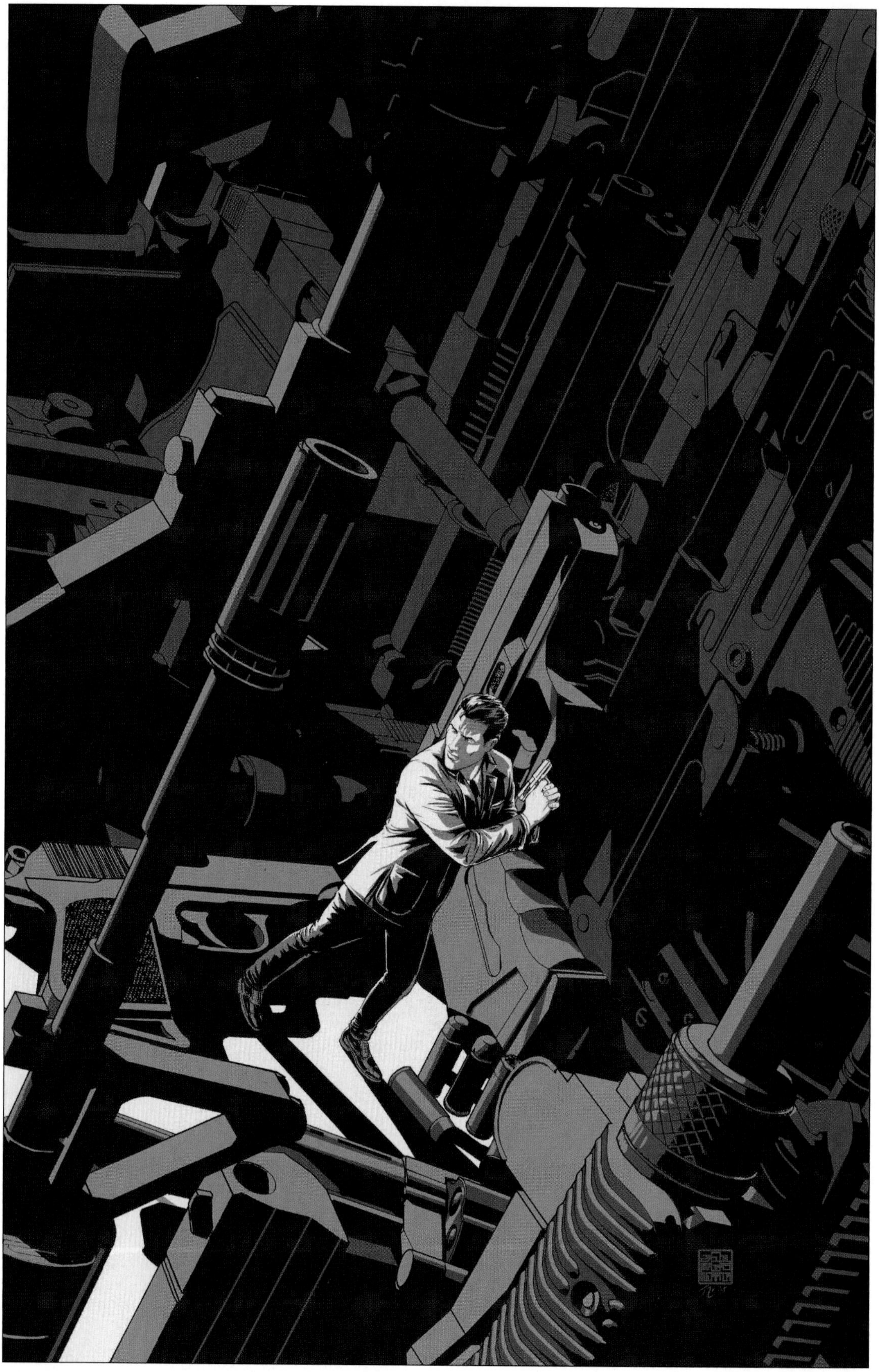

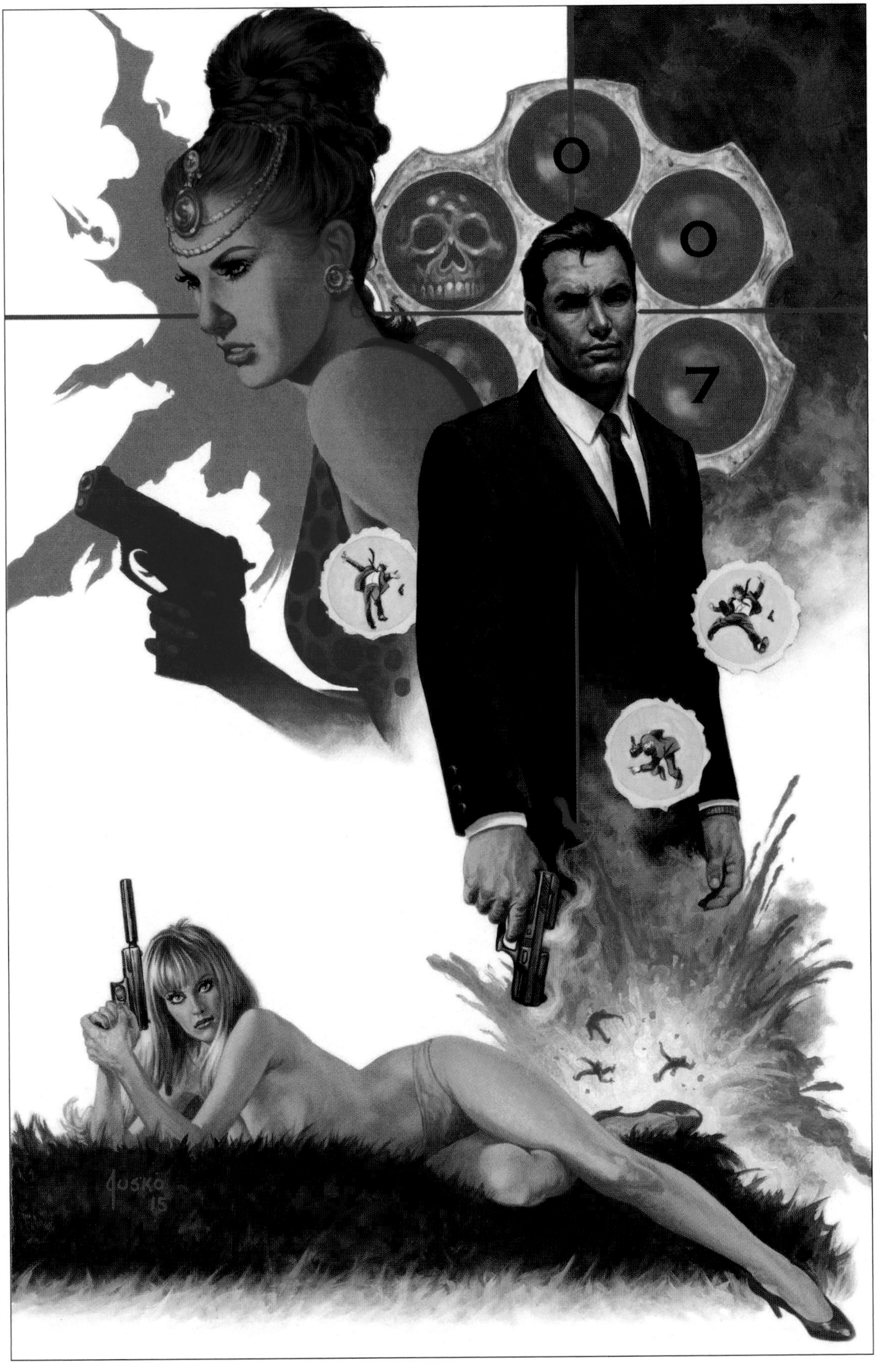
O
O
7
JUSKO
15

issue #1 Black Cat Comics exclusive cover by **AARON CAMPBELL**

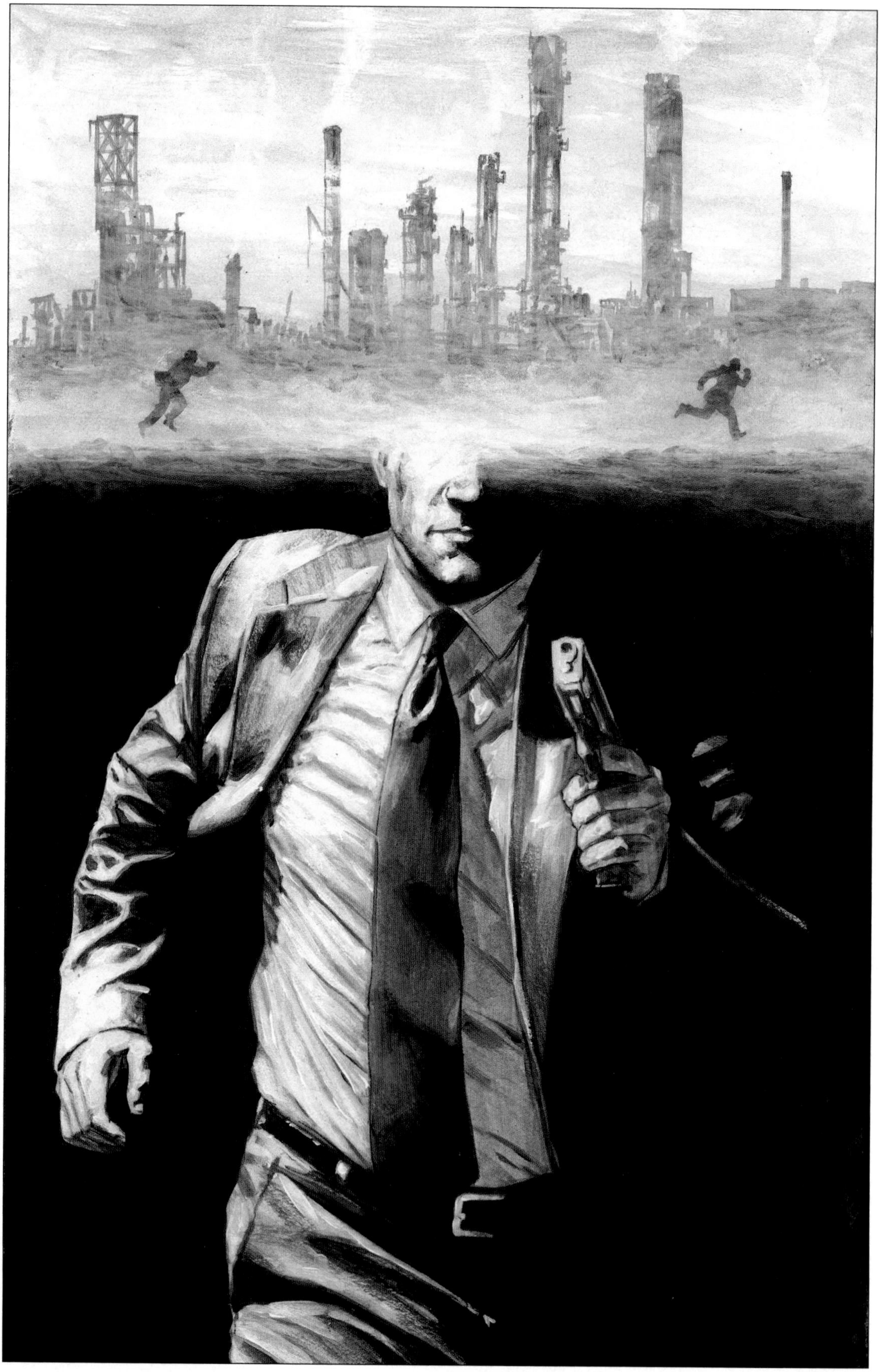

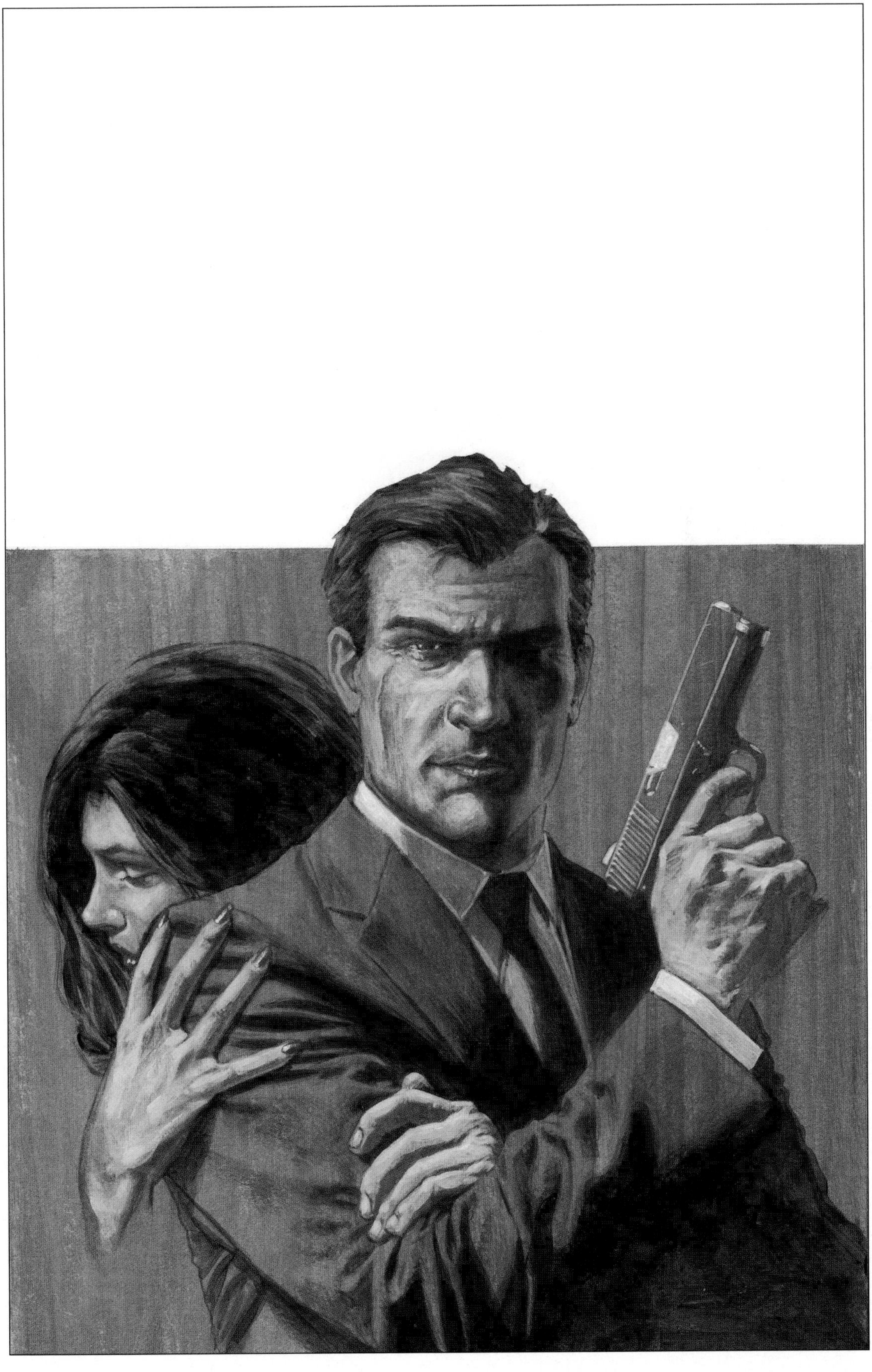

issue #1 Fried Pie exclusive cover by **FRANCESCO FRANCAVILLA**

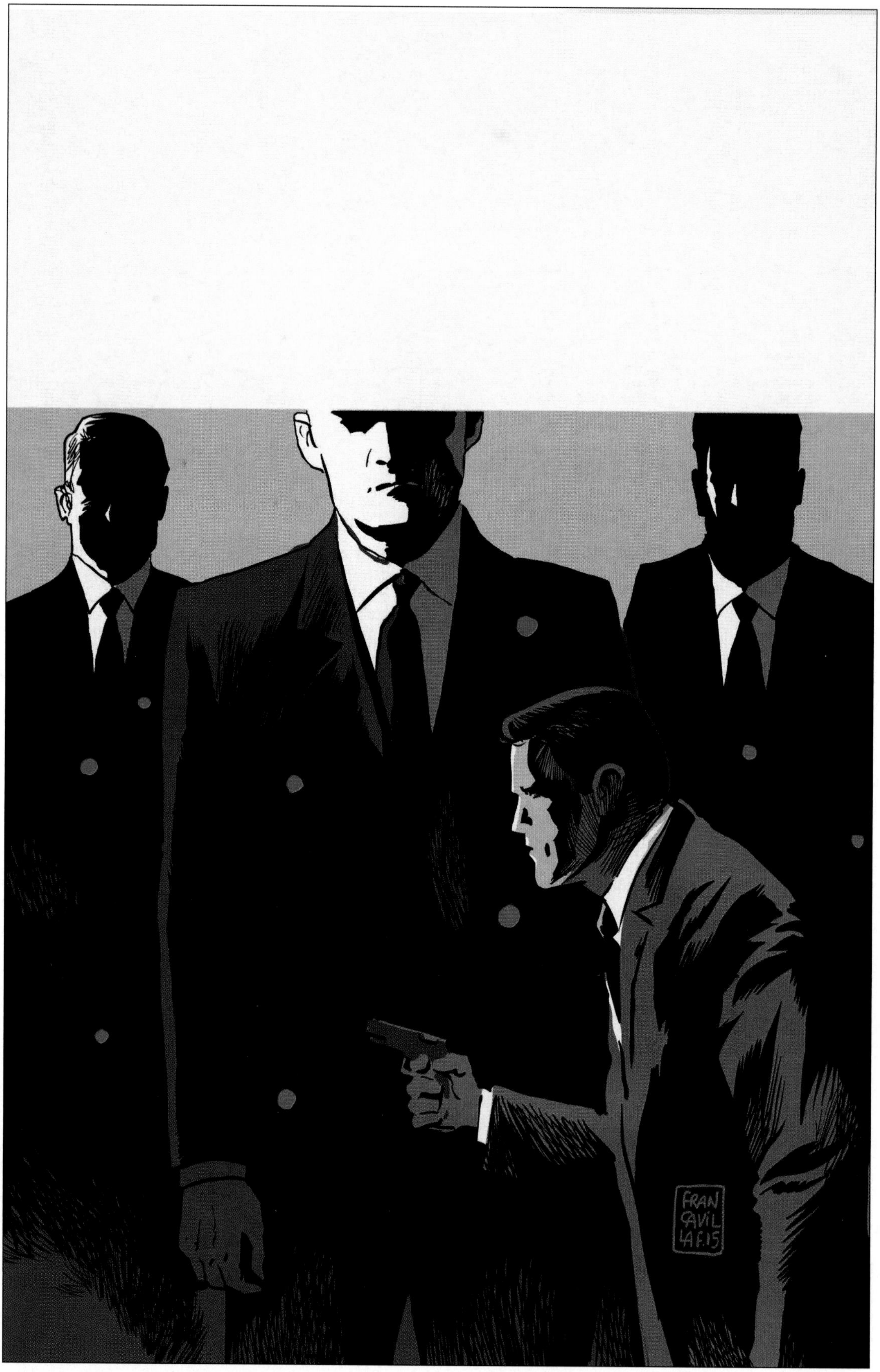

FRAN
CAVIL
LA F.15

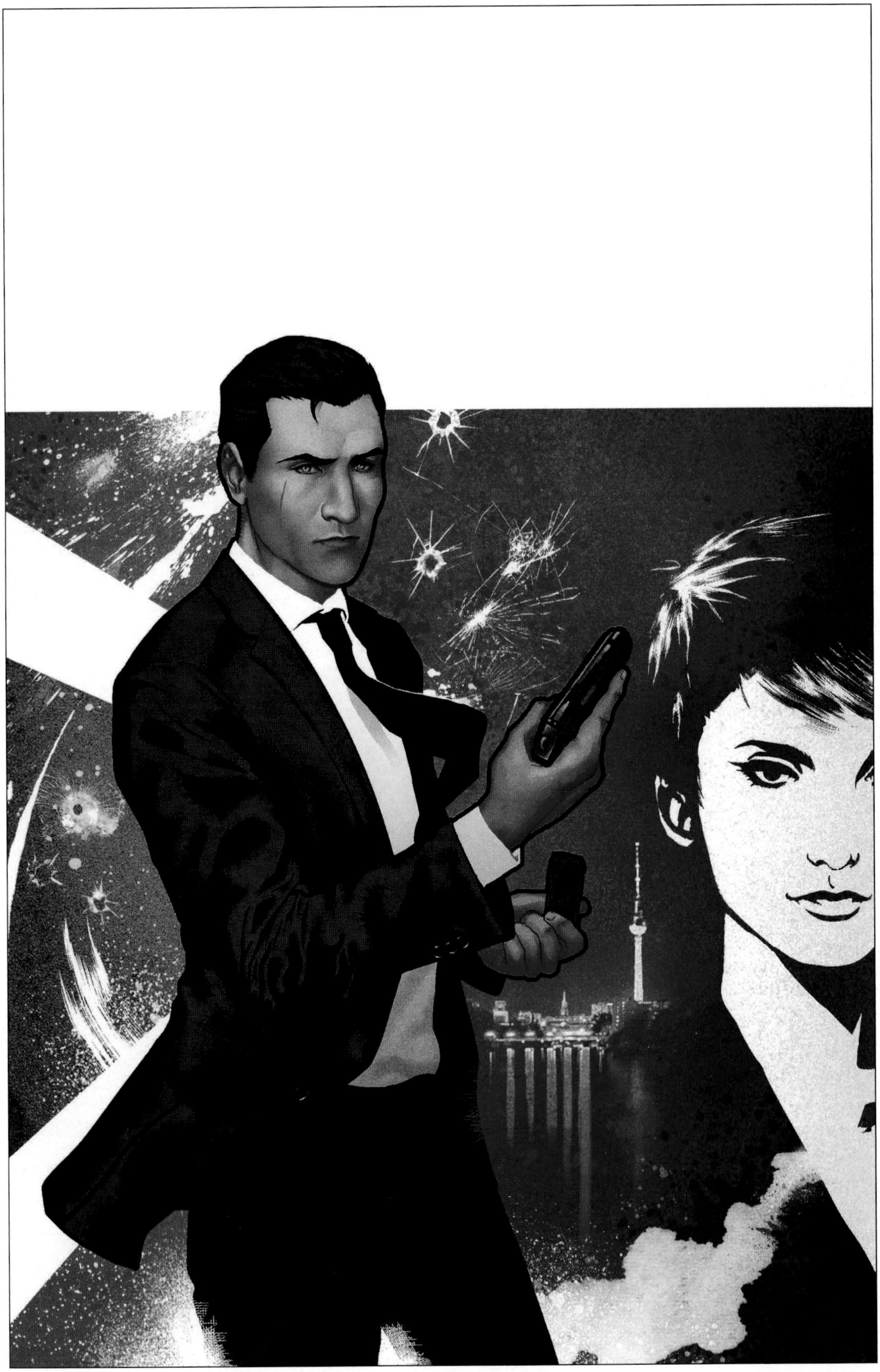

issue #1 Madness Comics exclusive cover by **AARON CAMPBELL**

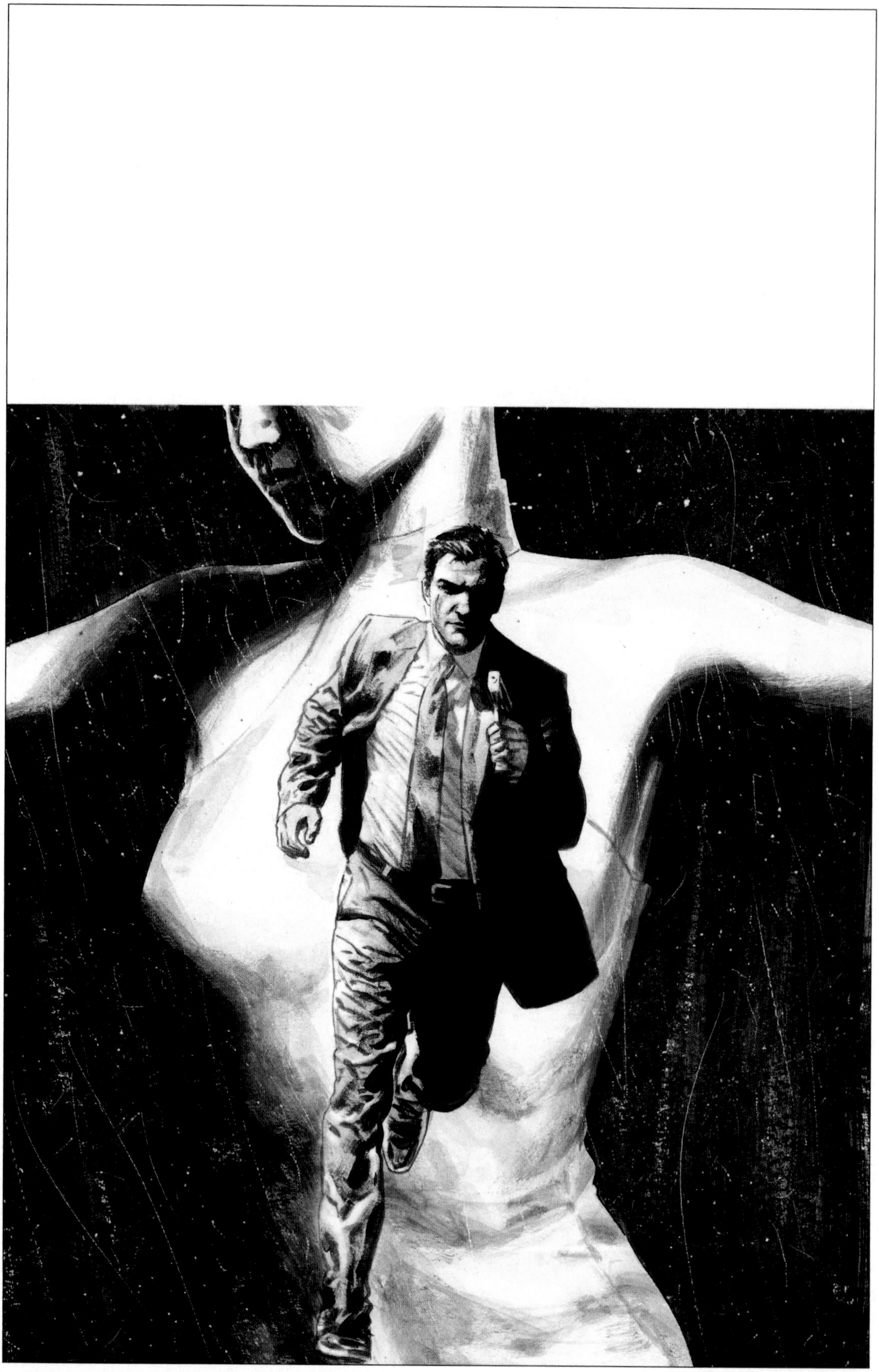

issue #1 Maximum Comics exclusive cover by **DENNIS CALERO**

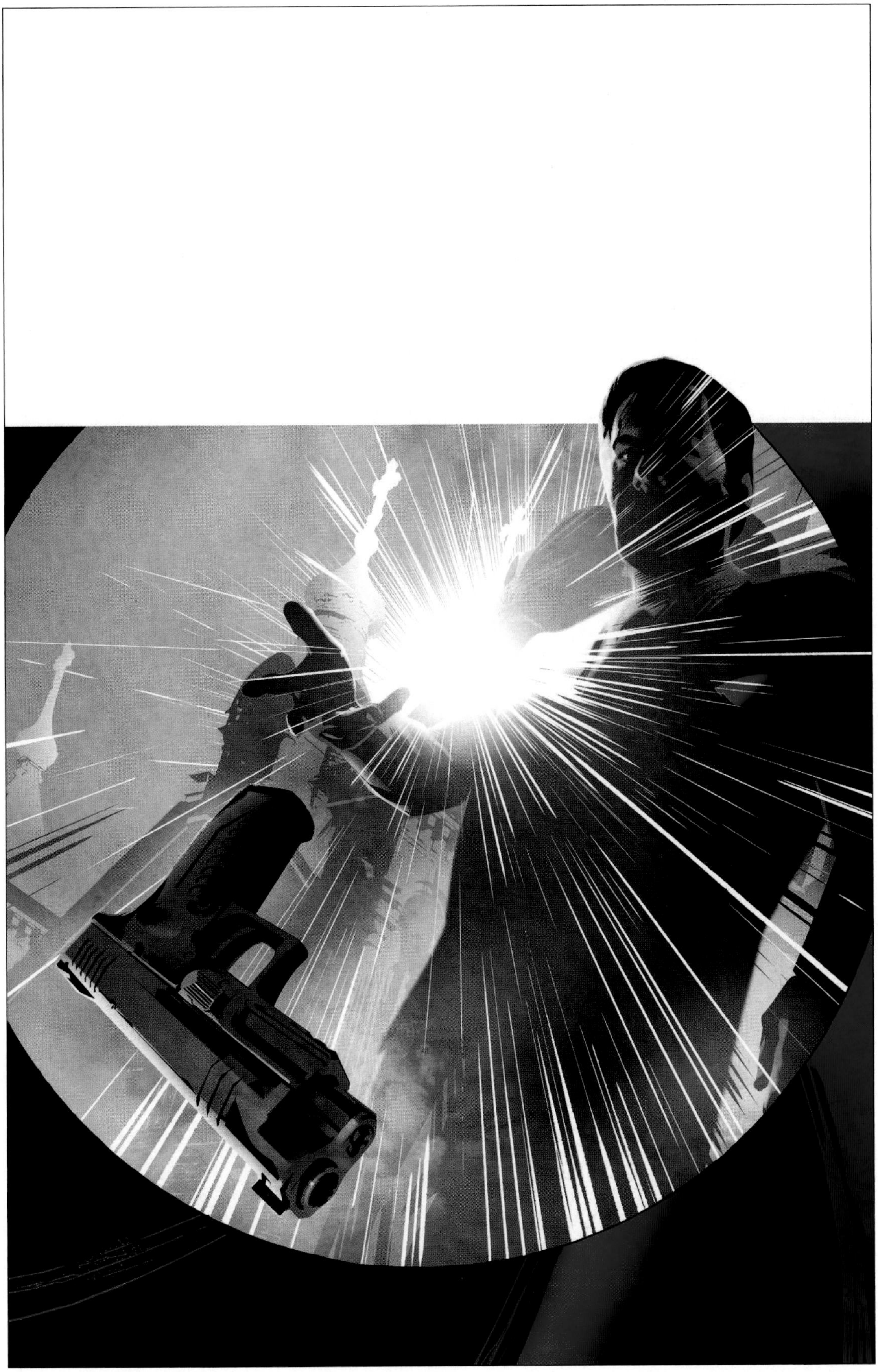

issue #1 Midtown Comics exclusive cover by **ROBERT HACK**

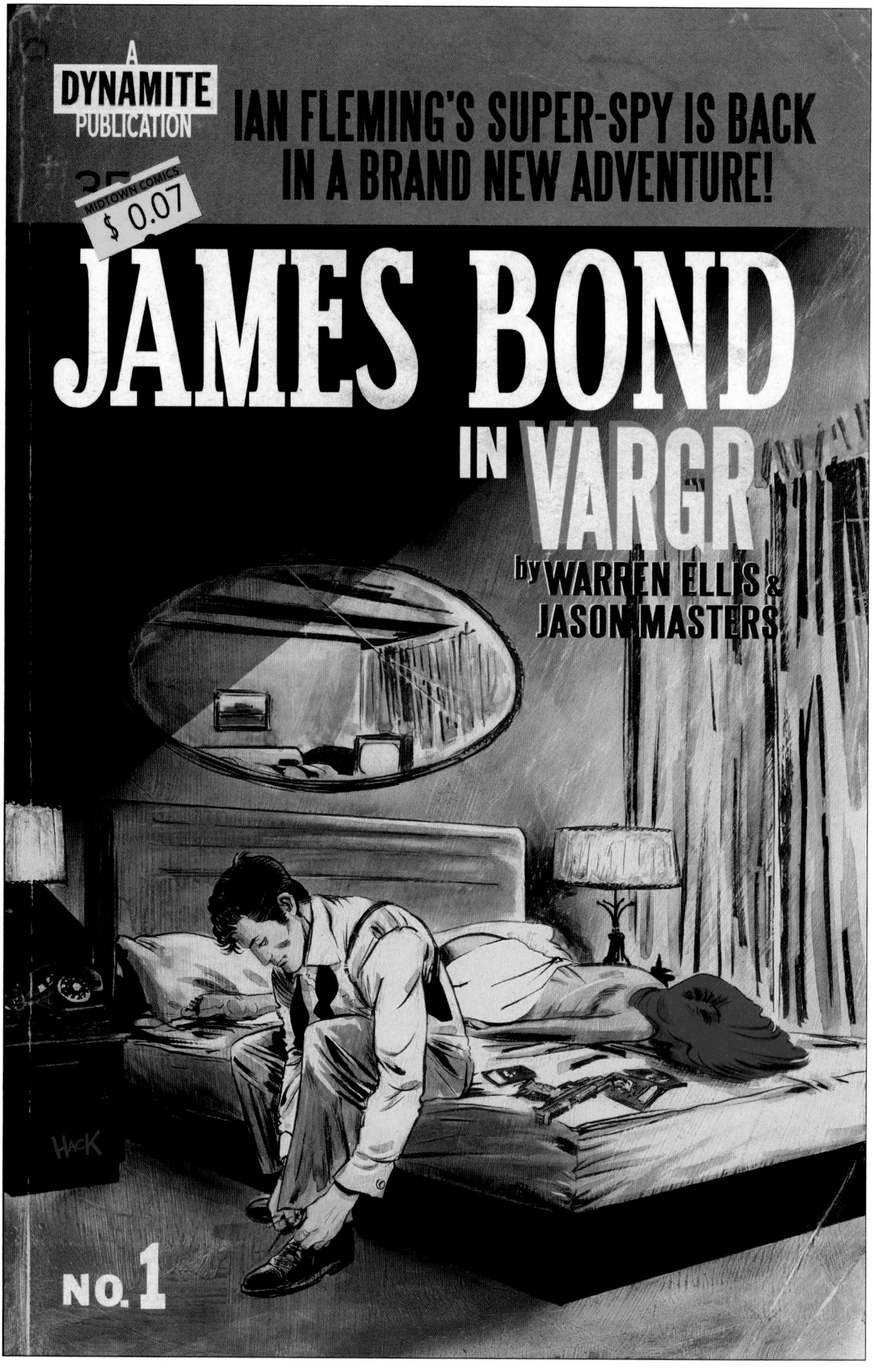

A
DYNAMITE
PUBLICATION
IAN FLEMING'S SUPER-SPY IS BACK
IN A BRAND NEW ADVENTURE!
MIDTOWN COMICS
$ 0.07
JAMES BOND
IN VARGR
by WARREN ELLIS &
JASON MASTERS
HACK
NO. 1

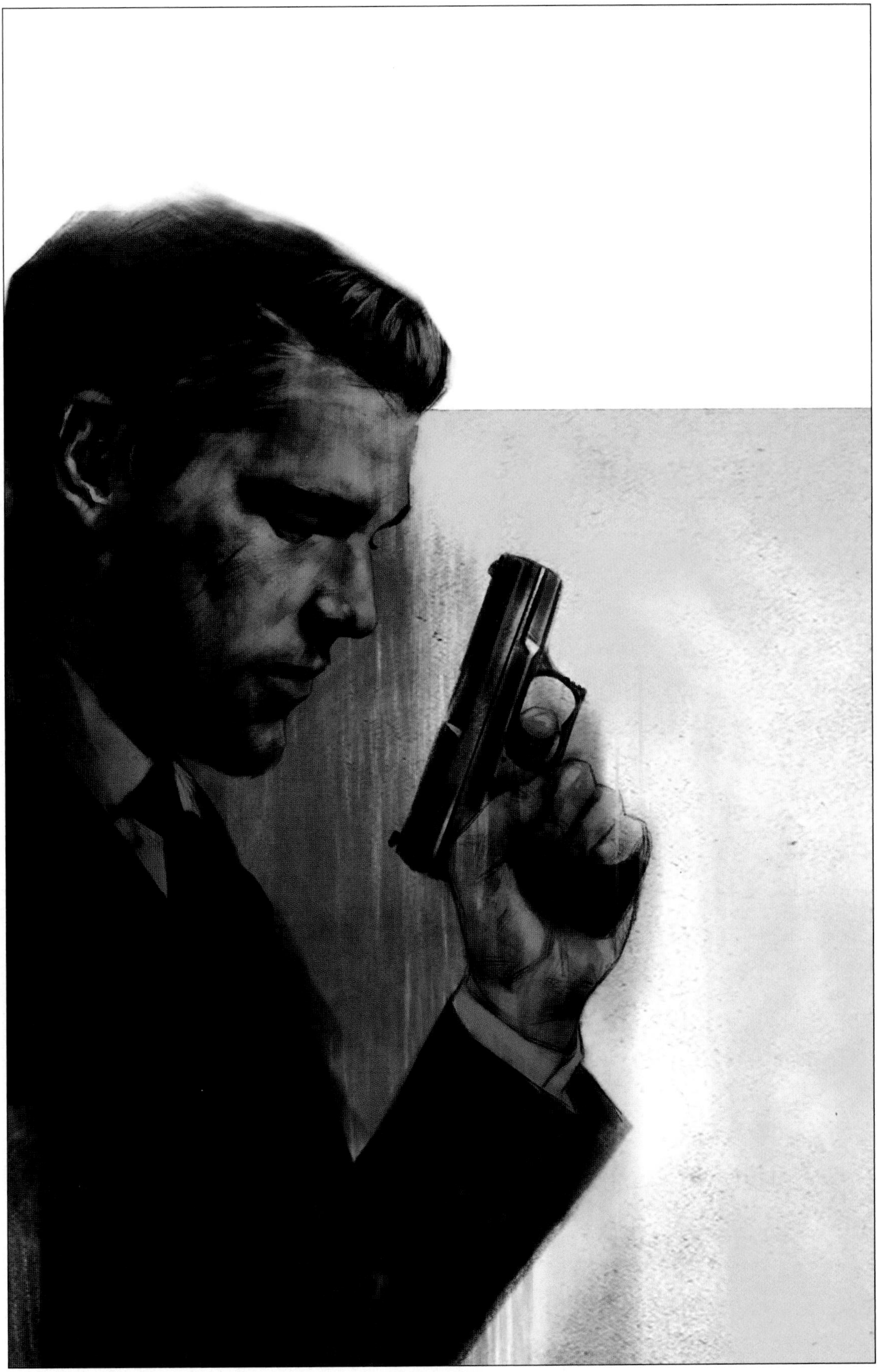

issue #1 Ssalefish Comics exclusivecover by **DENNIS CALERO**

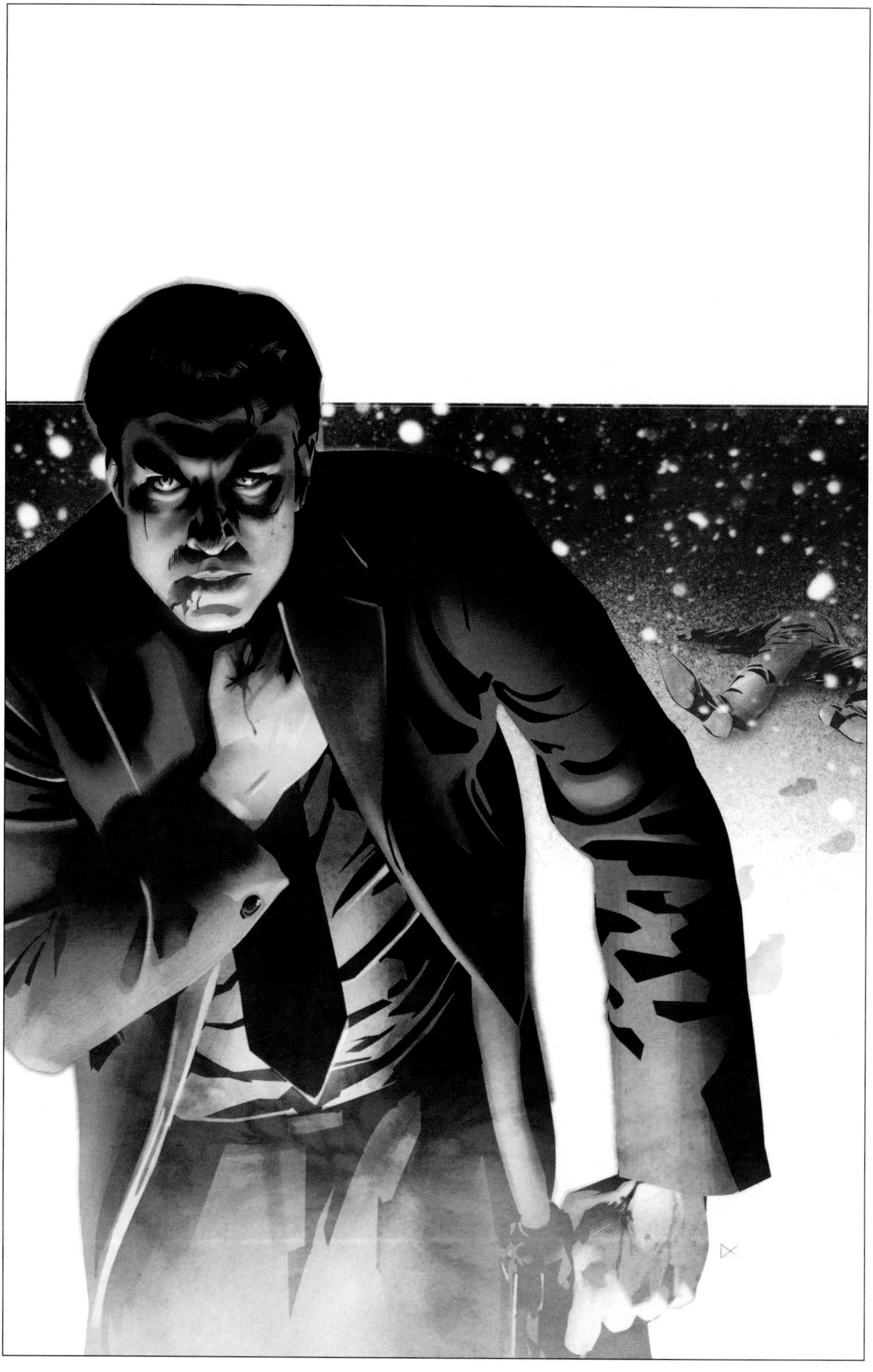

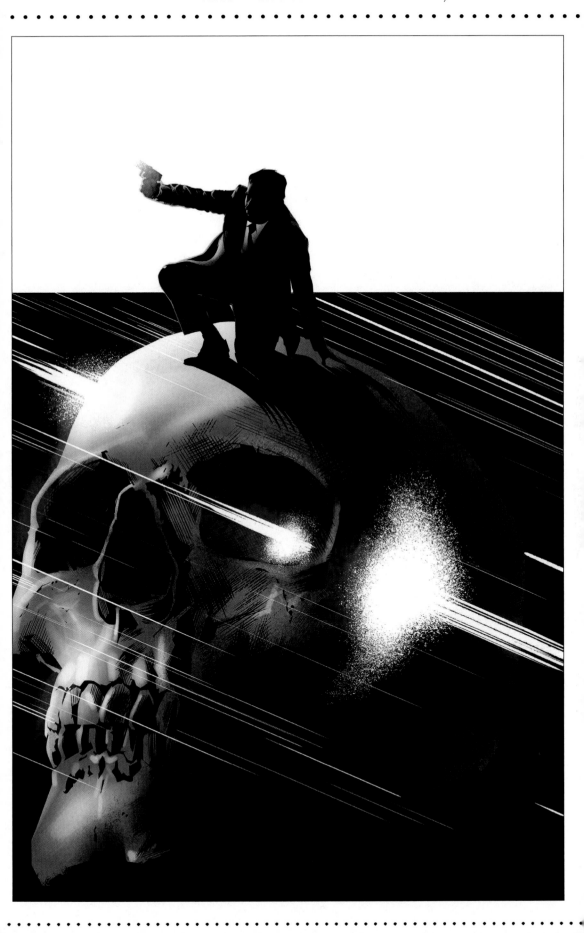

issue #2 alternate cover by **FRANCESCO FRANCAVILLA**

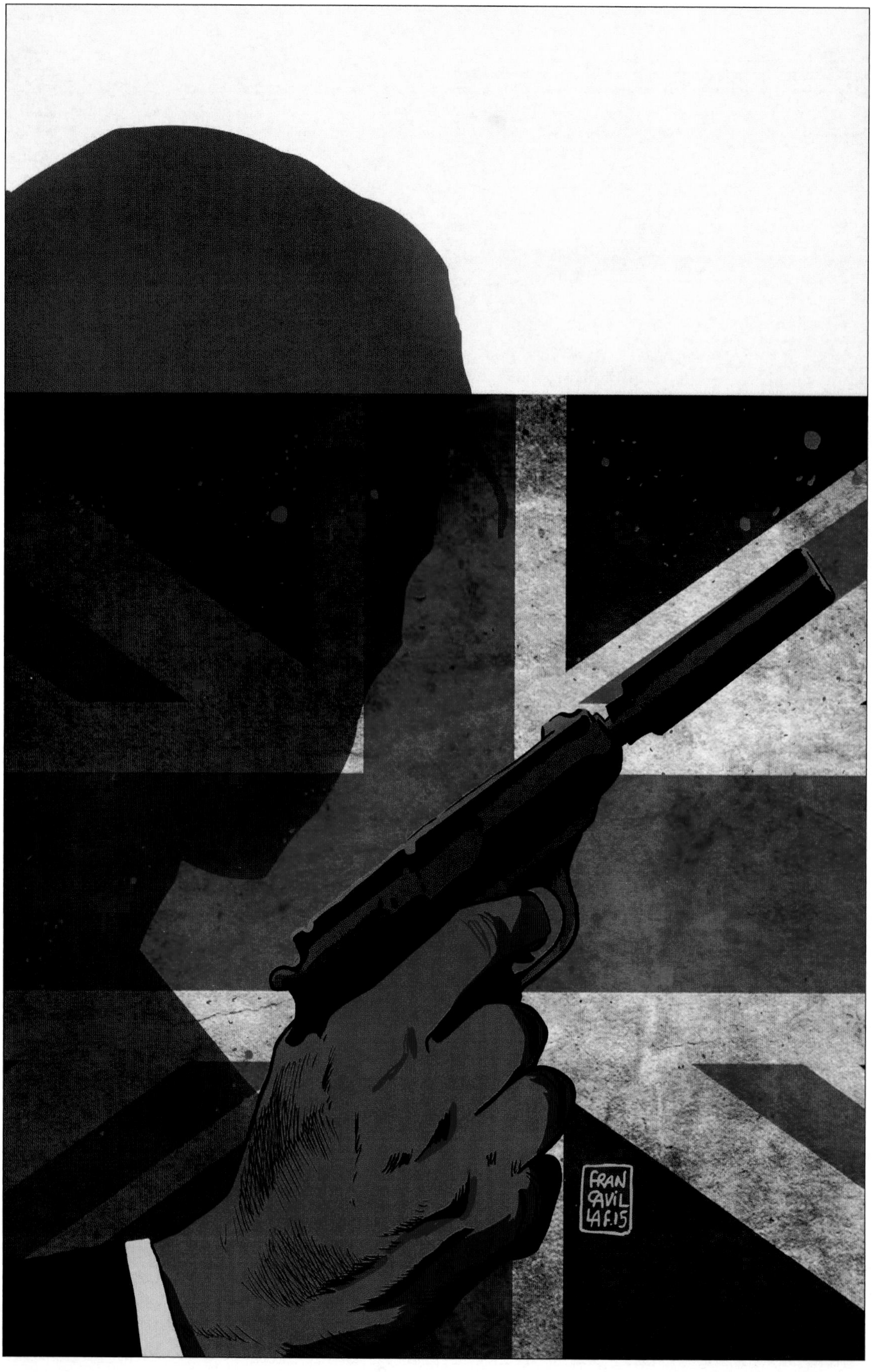
FRAN
CAVIL
LA F.15

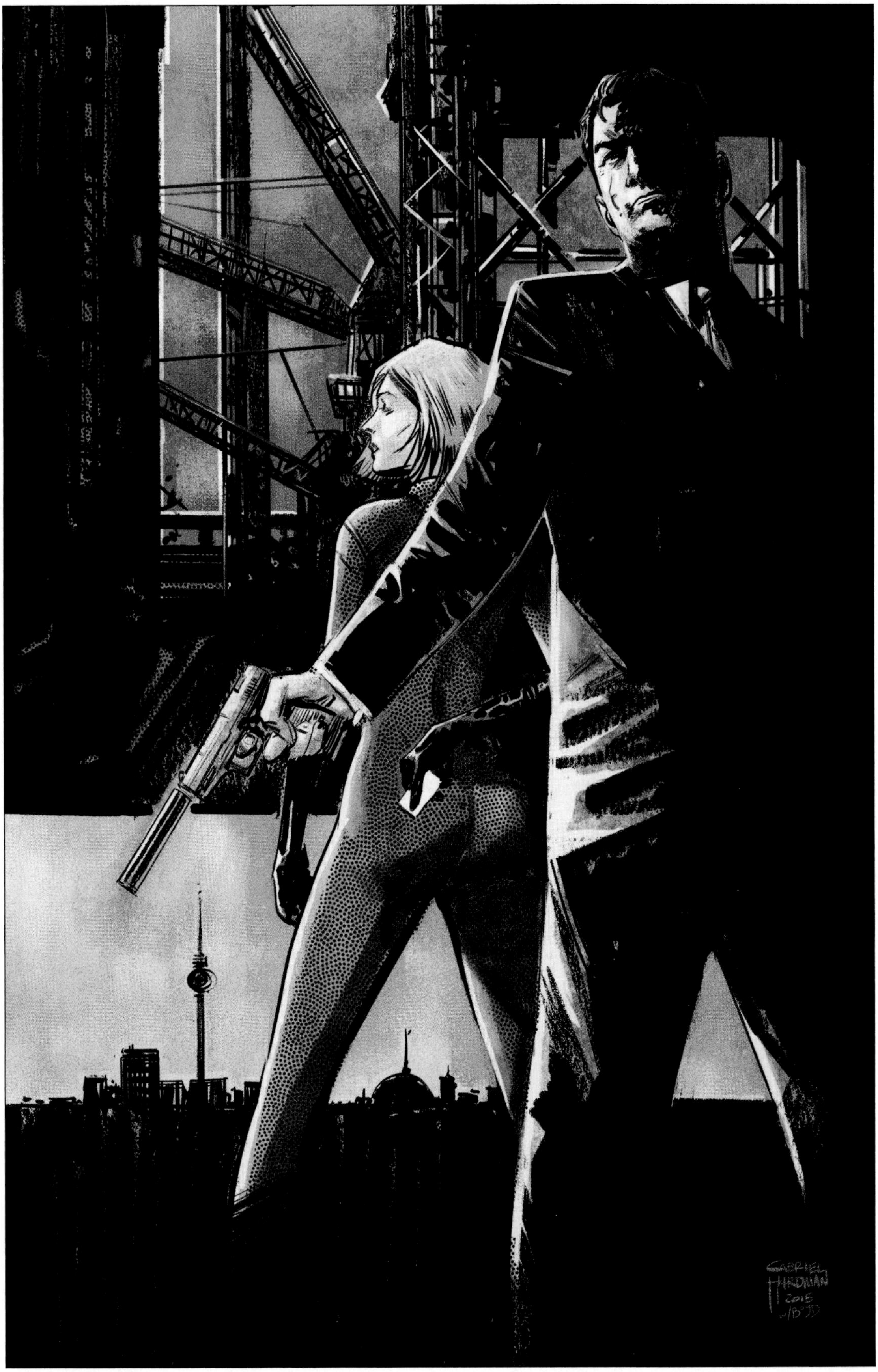
GABRIEL
HARDMAN
2015

issue #2 alternate cover by **DAN PANOSIAN**

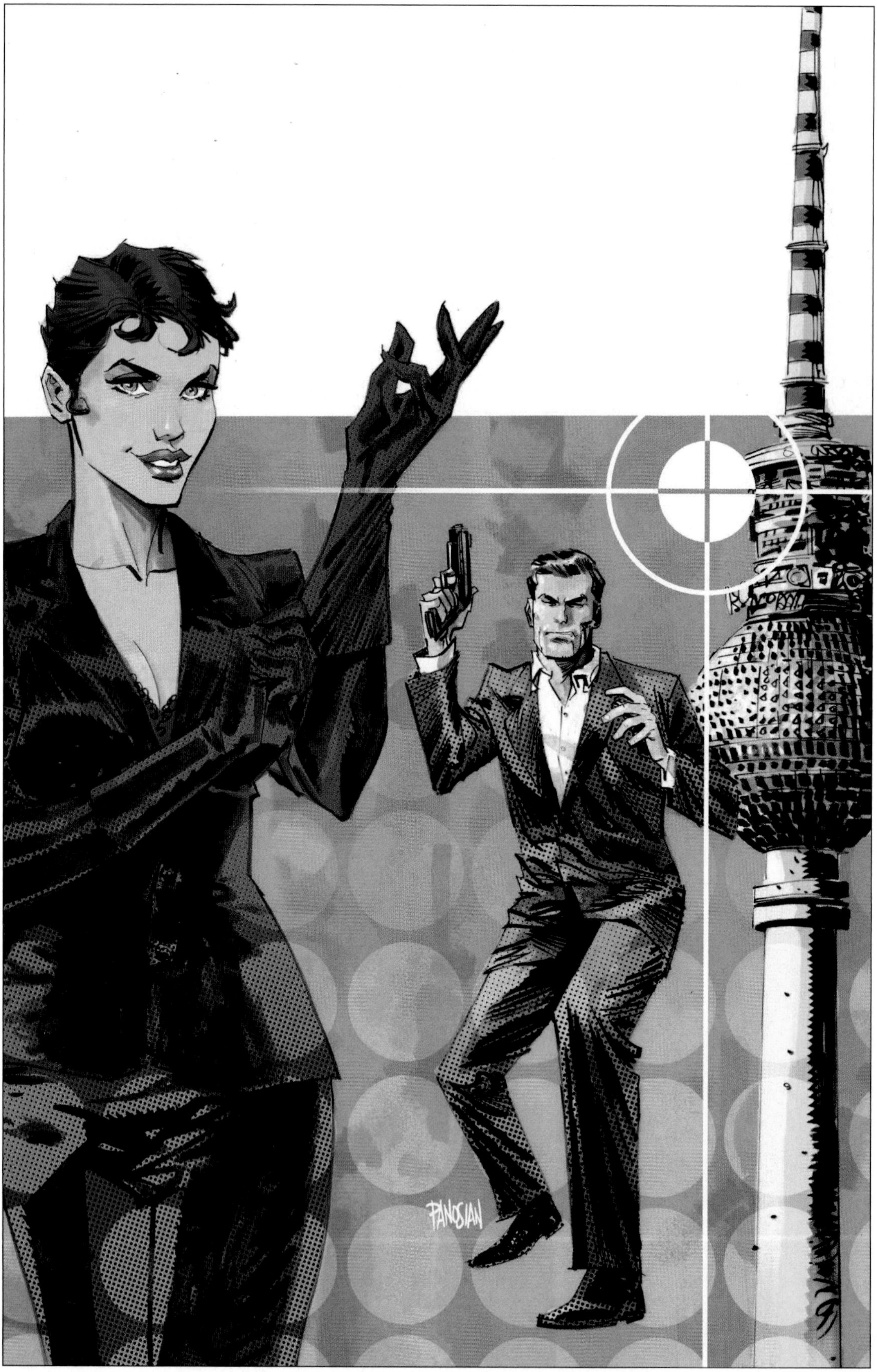
PANOSIAN

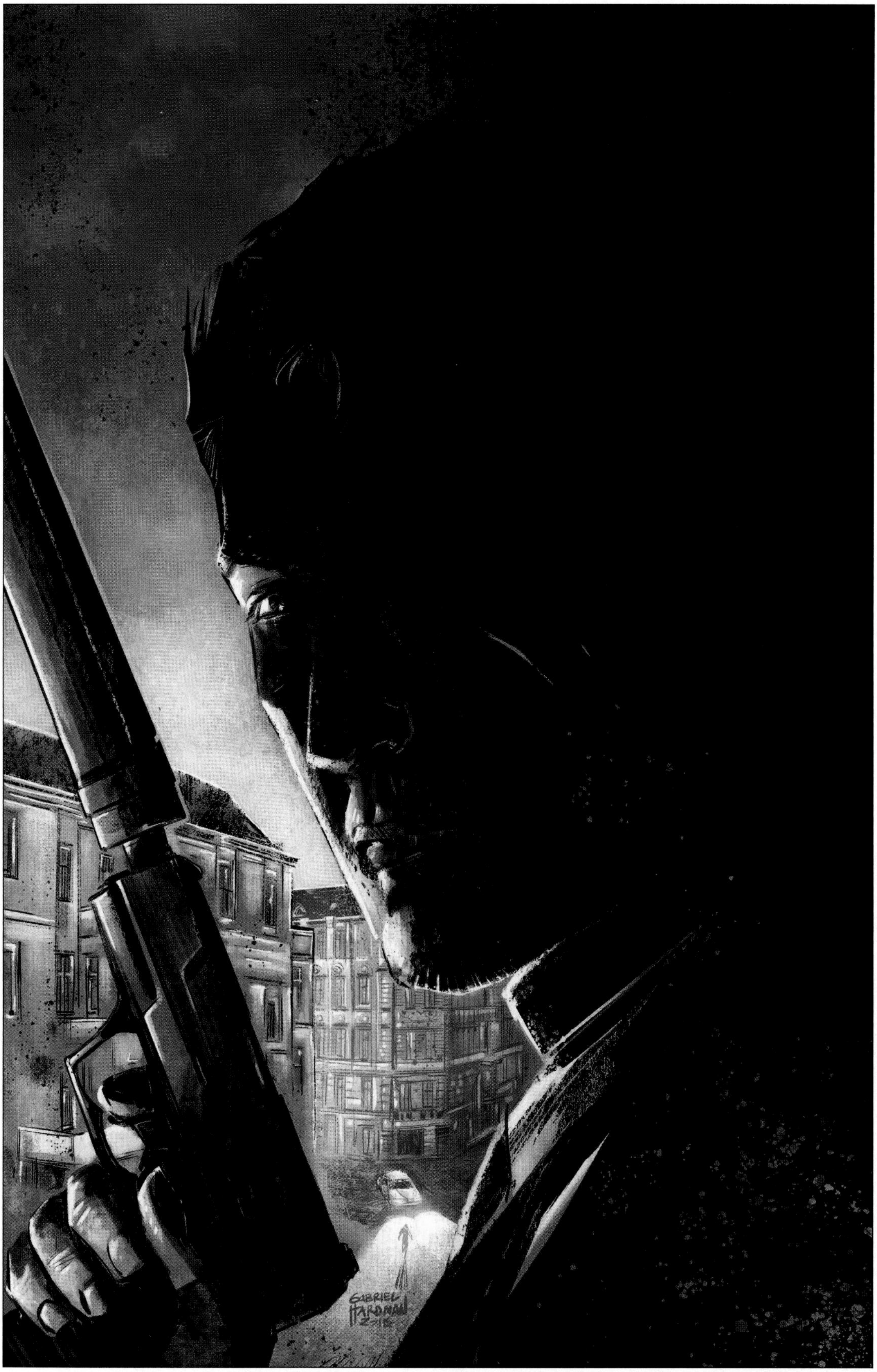
GABRIEL
HARDMAN

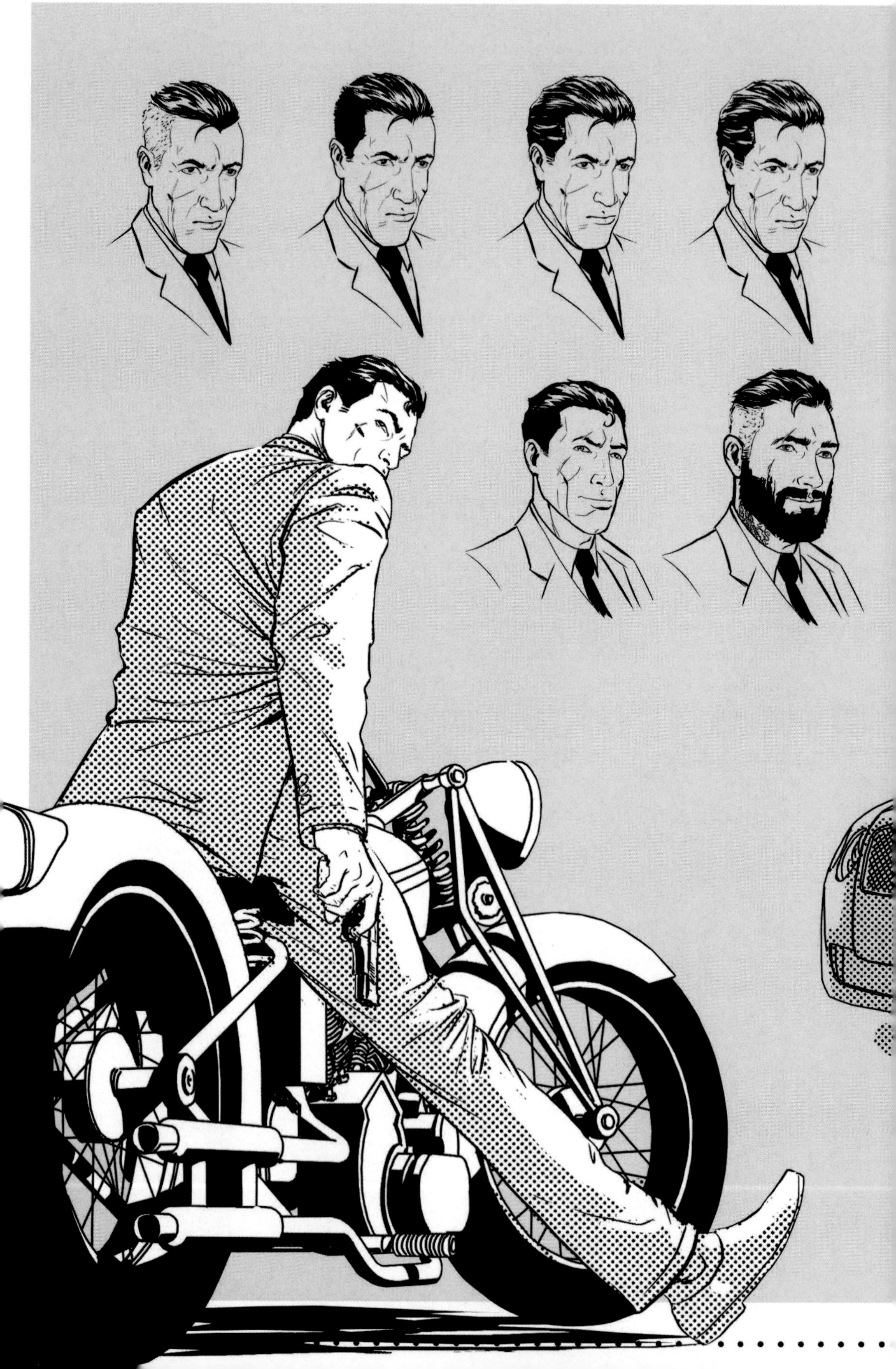

CONCEPT ART
by JASON MASTERS

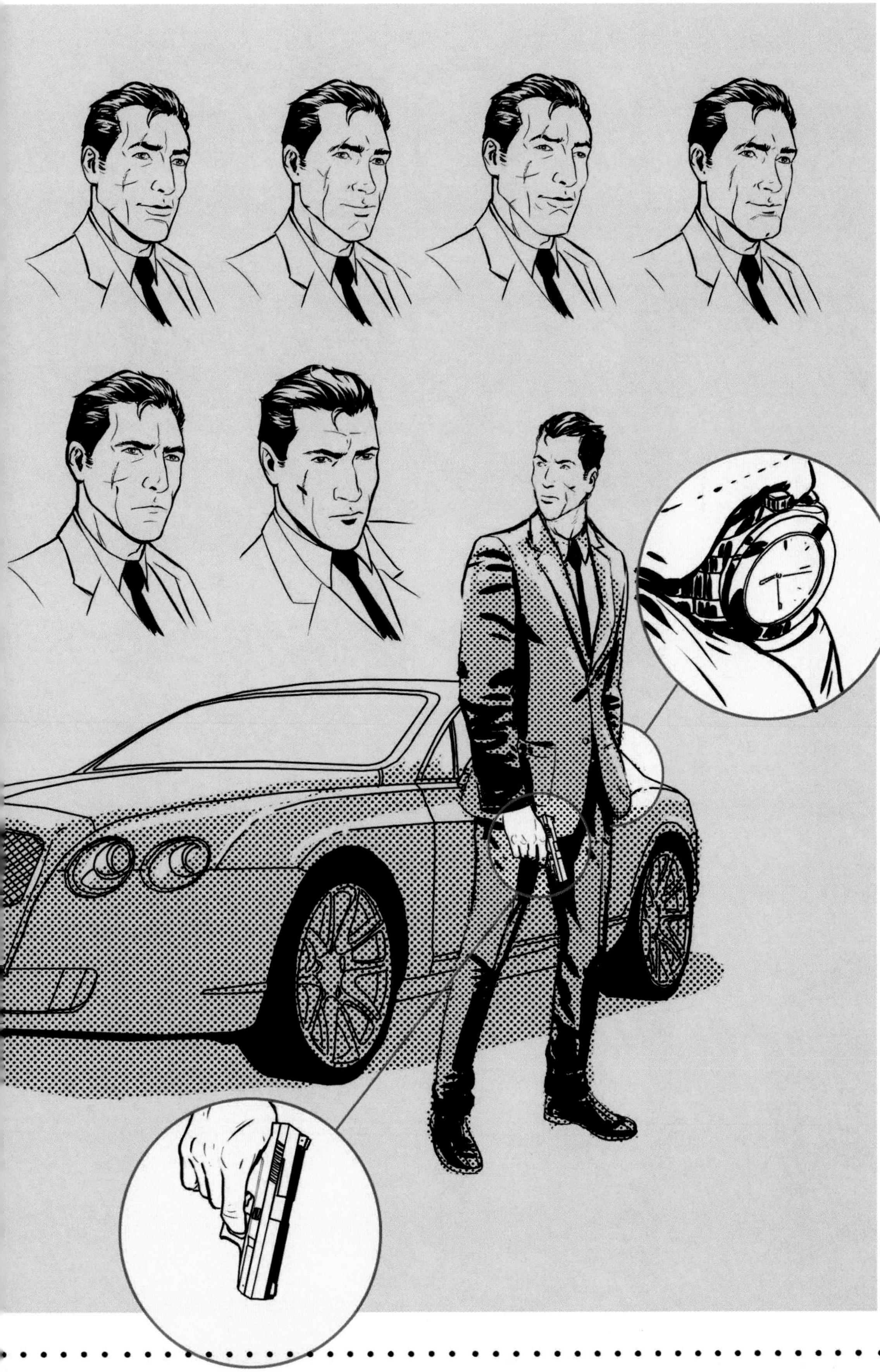

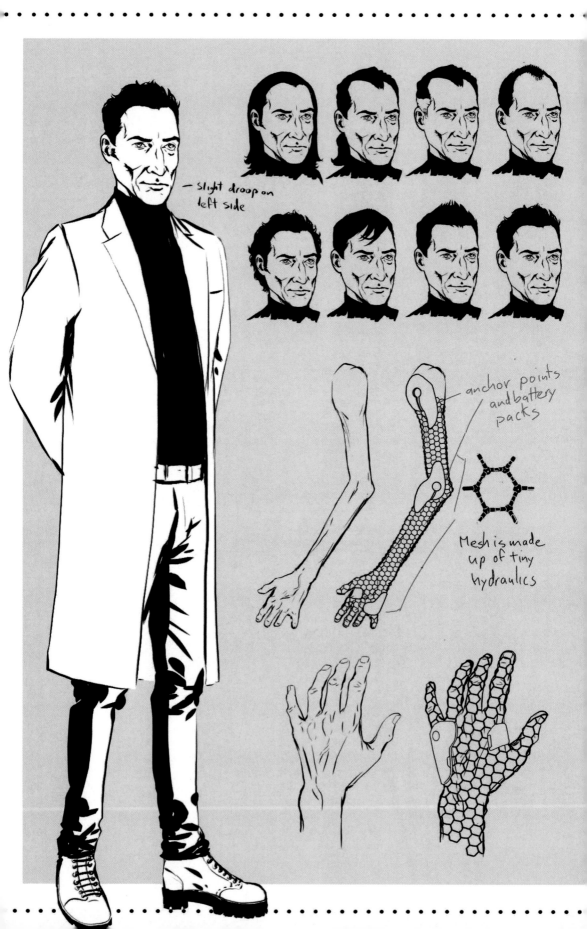

— Slight droop on left side

anchor points and battery packs

Mesh is made up of tiny hydraulics

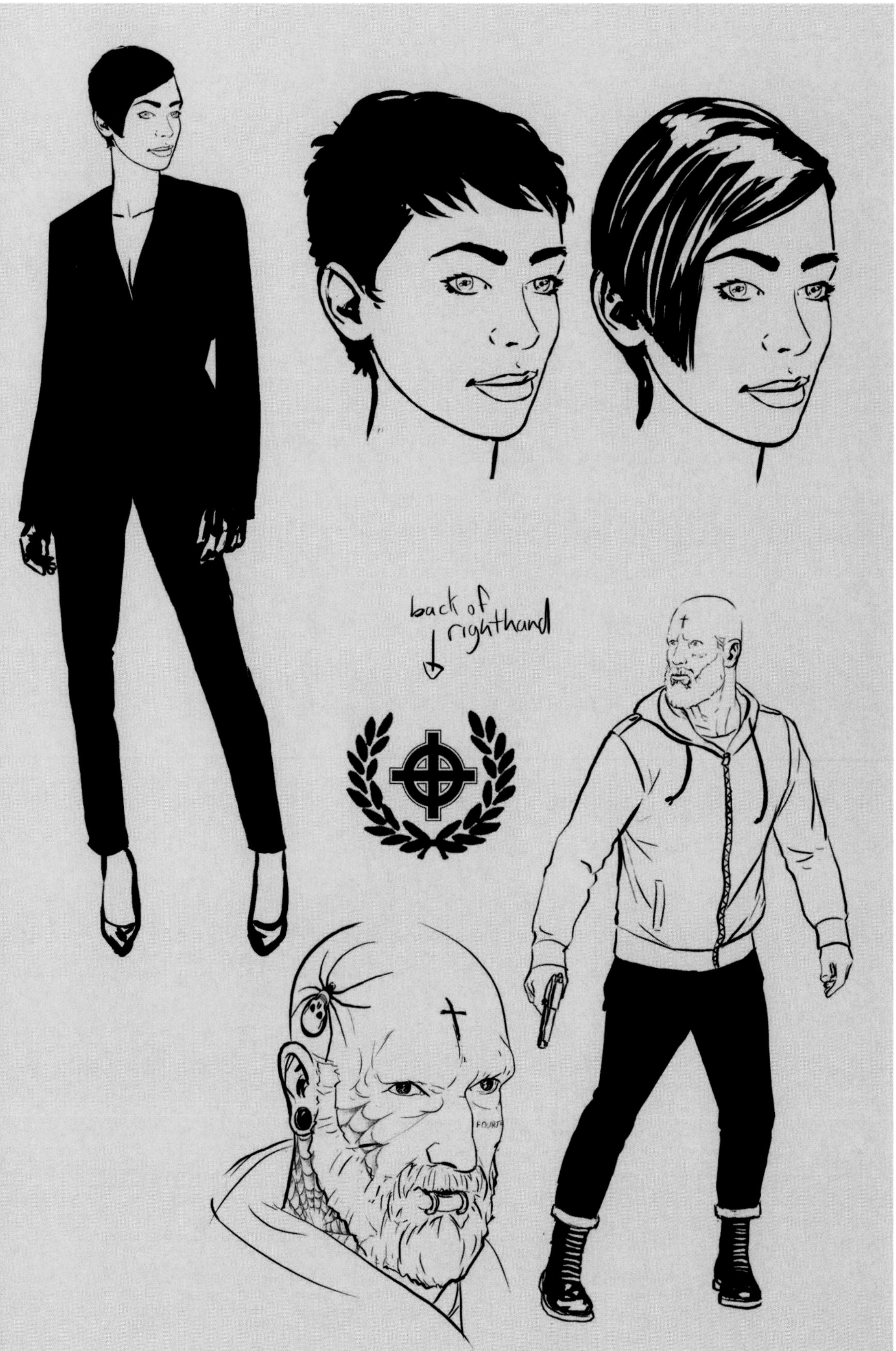
back of righthand

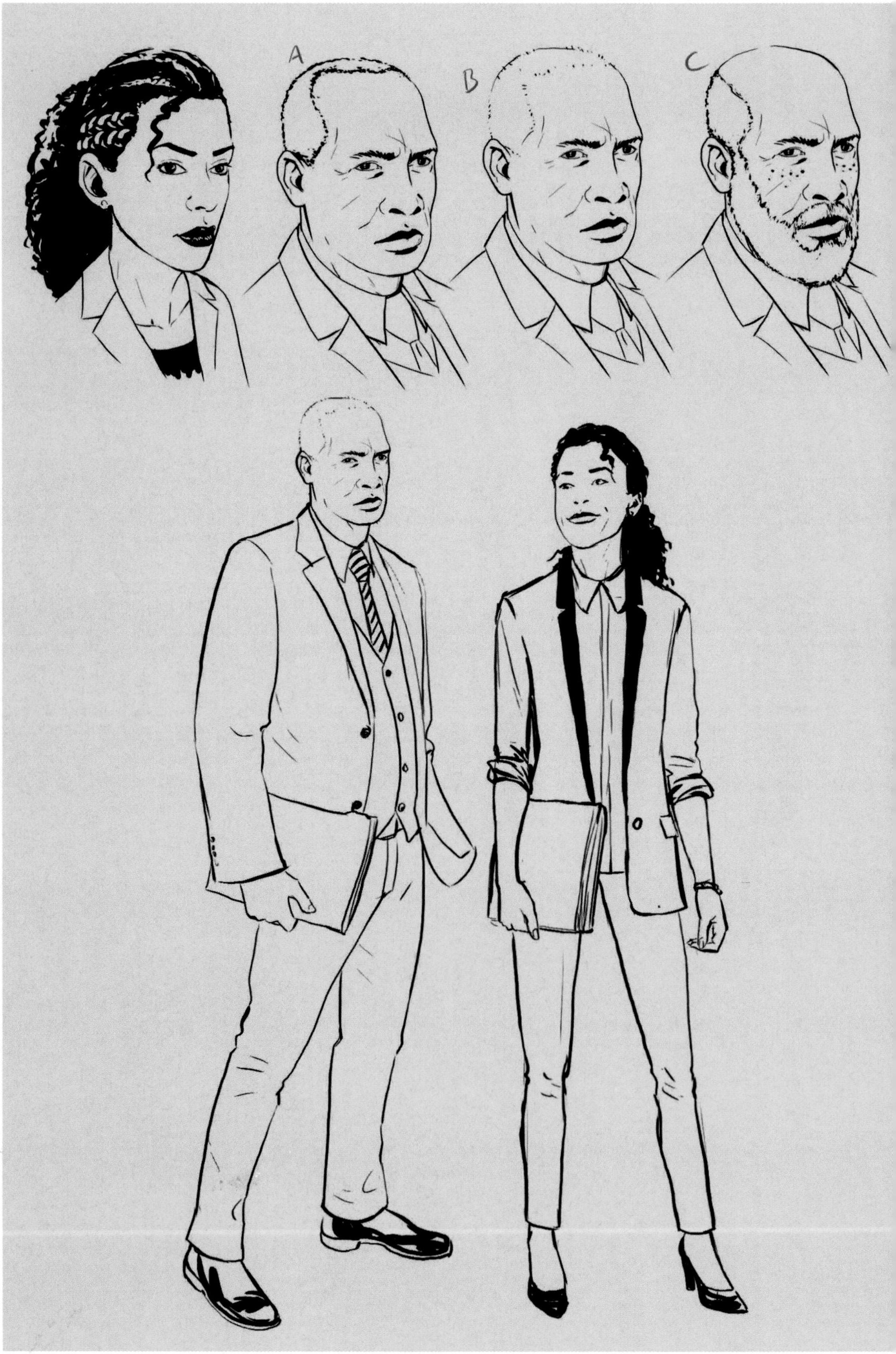
A
B
C